OLD YUKON

University of Mary Washington
Center for Historic Preservation

BOOK PRIZE
2010

1301 College Avenue
Fredericksburg, Virginia 22401-5300

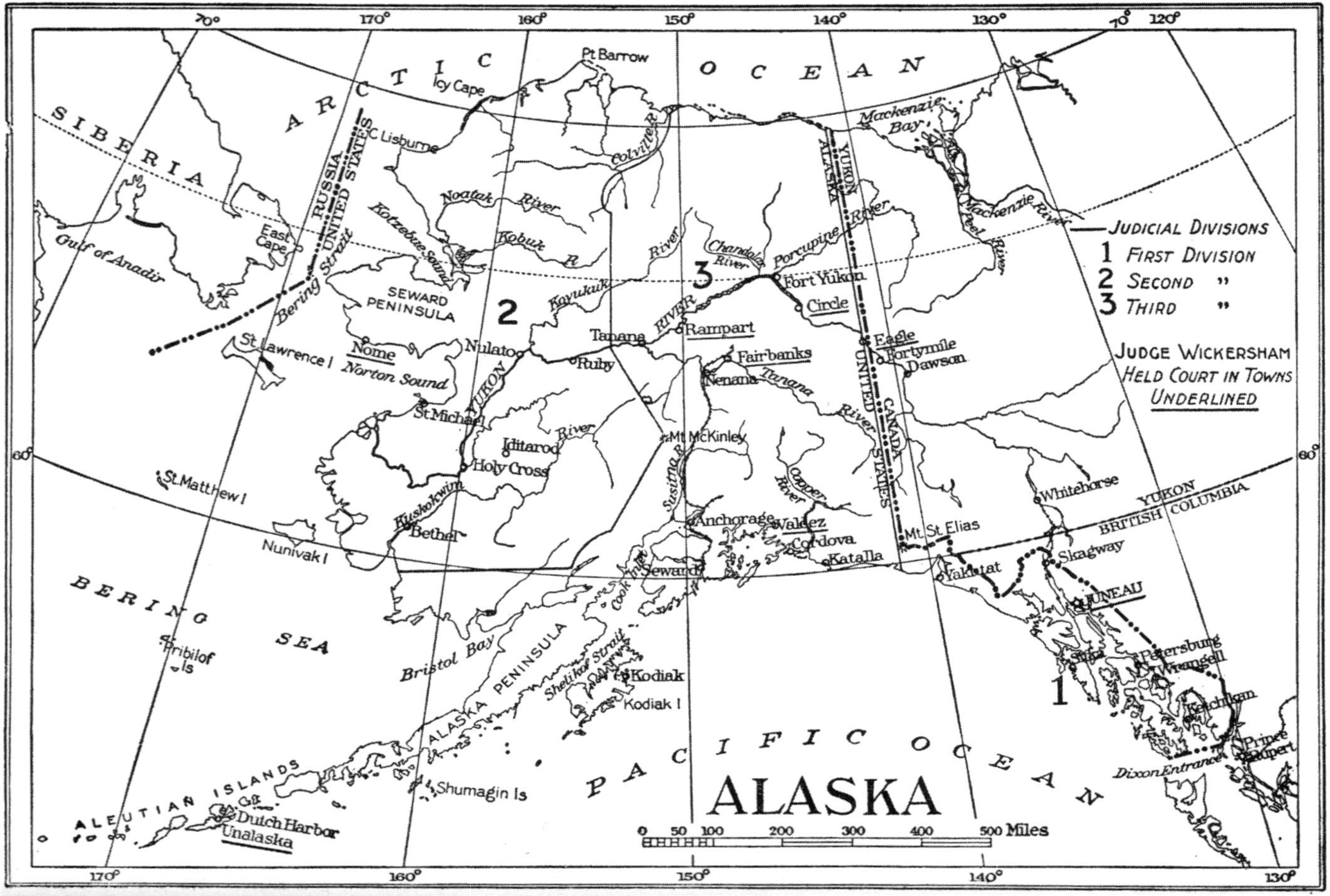

ALASKA
JUDICIAL DIVISIONS
1 FIRST DIVISION
2 SECOND "
3 THIRD "
JUDGE WICKERSHAM HELD COURT IN TOWNS UNDERLINED
ARCTIC OCEAN
PACIFIC OCEAN
BERING SEA
SIBERIA
RUSSIA
UNITED STATES
YUKON
ALASKA
CANADA
BRITISH COLUMBIA
SEWARD PENINSULA
ALASKA PENINSULA
ALEUTIAN ISLANDS
Pt Barrow
Icy Cape
C Lisburne
East Cape
Gulf of Anadir
Bering Strait
Kotzebue Sound
Noatak River
Kobuk R
Colville R
Kayukuk River
Chandalar River
Porcupine River
Mackenzie Bay
Mackenzie River
Peel River
Fort Yukon
Circle
Eagle
Fortymile
Dawson
Rampart
Tanana
Fairbanks
Nenana
Tanana River
Ruby
Nulato
Nome
St Lawrence I
Norton Sound
St Michael
Yukon River
Iditarod River
Holy Cross
Kuskokwim
Bethel
Mt McKinley
Susitna R
Copper River
Anchorage
Valdez
Cordova
Katalla
Mt St Elias
Yakutat
Whitehorse
Skagway
JUNEAU
Sitka
Petersburg
Wrangell
Ketchikan
Prince Rupert
Dixon Entrance
Seward
Cook Inlet
Shelikof Strait
Kodiak
Kodiak I
Bristol Bay
Shumagin Is
Dutch Harbor
Unalaska
Pribilof Is
St Matthew I
Nunivak I
0 50 100 200 300 400 500 Miles
70° 170° 160° 150° 140° 130° 120° 60°

OLD YUKON

TALES, TRAILS, AND TRIALS

by Hon. James Wickersham

Edited and Abridged by Terrence Cole

University of Alaska Press
Fairbanks, Alaska

University of Alaska Press
P.O. Box 756240
Fairbanks, AK 99775-6240

ISBN 978-1-60223-051-4

Library of Congress Cataloging-in-Publication Data

Wickersham, James, 1857–1939.
Old Yukon : tales—trails—and trials / by James Wickersham ; edited and abridged by Terrence Cole.
p. cm. — (Classic reprint series)
Includes bibliographical references and index.
ISBN 978-1-60223-051-4 (pbk. : alk. paper)
1. Alaska—History—Anecdotes. 2. Yukon River Valley (Yukon and Alaska)—History—Anecdotes. 3. Frontier and pioneer life—Alaska—Anecdotes. 4. Alaska—Trials, litigation, etc.—Anecdotes. 5. Courts—Alaska—Anecdotes. I. Cole, Terrence, 1953– II. Title.
F904.W66 2009
979.8--dc22

2008053232

Cover design by Dixon Jones, Rasmuson Library Graphics
Front cover: Discovery City, Otter Creek, Alaska. (Alaska State Library, Wickersham State Historic Site, ASL-P277-012-045). Back cover image of Wickersham from 1899 Washington State Legislature Class Photographs (Collections of the Washington State Archives).

This publication was printed on acid-free paper that meets the minimum requirements for ANSI/NISO Z39.48-1992 (R2002) (Permanence of Paper for Printed Library Materials).

TO THE PIONEERS OF THE YUKON!

Who first explored the Kwikpak wide,
  Who floated down wild Pelly's tide,
Who built fur-posts for Indian trade,
  And brought the Book to the Yukon glade;
Who blazed the trail o'er Dyea divide,
  Who built their boats on Lindeman's side,
Who worked the Stewart's bars awhile,
  And found the paystreak on the Forty Mile
Who mined at Circle, and Klondike creeks,
  Who camped at Nome, 'neath Anvil's peaks,
Who founded Fairbanks, opened its mines,
  And prospected where the Iditarod twines;
Who built its towns, its roads and trails,
  Who planned its railroads, and laid the rails,
Who guide in council, in creating homes,
  And in laying a State's foundation stones.

—James Wickersham

Classic Reprint Series
Edited by Terrence Cole

The Classic Reprint Series of the University of Alaska Press
brings back into print classic works of
enduring value and historical significance.

No. 10
Old Yukon: Tales, Trails, and Trials
James Wickersham

No. 9
Two Women in the Klondike
Mary E. Hitchcock

No. 8
Abandoned: The Story of the Greely Arctic Expedition, 1881–1884
Alden Todd

No. 7
Noel Wien: Alaska Pioneer Bush Pilot
Ira Harkey

No. 6
Across Arctic America: Narrative of the Fifth Thule Expedition
Knud Rasmussen

No. 5
Two Years in the Klondike and Alaskan Gold-Fields, 1896–1898
William B. Haskell

No. 4
The Thousand-Mile War: World War II in Alaska and the Aleutians
Brian Garfield

No. 3
Fifty Years Below Zero: A Lifetime of Adventure in the Far North
Charles D. Brower

No. 2
Exploration of Alaska, 1865–1900
Morgan Sherwood

No. 1
Arctic Village: A 1930s Portrait of Wiseman, Alaska
Robert Marshall

CONTENTS

James Wickersham.

(Alaska State Library, Wickersham State Historic Sites Photograph Collection, ASL-PCA-277-019-031)

INTRODUCTION

by Terrence Cole

BETWEEN THE KLONDIKE GOLD RUSH and the Second World War, no name came to be more synonymous with the Territory of Alaska than that of Judge James Wickersham, and no individual would be more loved, hated, respected, or despised than the man who would always be "The Judge." As one writer claimed in the 1940s, "True, there are many judges in Alaska today, but any sourdough speaking of 'The Judge,' regardless of where he might be, refers only to Judge Wickersham."[1]

Old Yukon: Tales, Trails, and Trials is one of the great books by one of the great men of Alaska history. James Wickersham's 1938 memoir describes his seven and a half years as the first and only federal judge in Interior Alaska during the gold rush era, dealing justice by dog team at fifty below zero to murderers, thieves, con men, and scoundrels. "Every mile of trail," he wrote, "had its own stories of hardship and adventure."[2] Driving down the Yukon, he encountered the worst of nature and human nature, weathering corruption charges, blackmail, death threats, and a constant campaign of harassment and political intimidation. Yet this would be only the first chapter of his remarkable life in the north, a long and productive career that changed Alaska forever.

BORN ON AUGUST 24, 1857, on a small farm in Illinois, James Wickersham lived his life in the shadow of the Civil War. Even eighty years later the traumatic memories of those early days never faded. On September 1, 1939, as the Judge listened in Juneau to radio reports of the Nazi blitzkrieg against Poland, the news instantly brought back the tragic events of 1865. "I remember very well the black funeral cloth that my father draped over the house at the time of the assassination of Abraham Lincoln," he wrote in his diary after hearing Hitler's speech to the Reichstag. "I also remember the way we felt at the surrender . . . of Vicksburg and the opening of the Mississippi River to the sea."[3]

According to the Judge, members of the Wickersham clan from the Land of Lincoln generally had dark eyes, dark brown hair, and a healthy skepticism in matters of faith, except that they religiously "voted the Republican ticket as soon as they were born!"[4] The family had its share of courageous characters. One of his father's uncles was Daniel Boone Wickersham, who at age seventy-five in Arkansas in 1863 stood up against a gang of robbing bushwhackers. The bandits shot and killed the old man—after first botching an attempt to lynch him—as he tried to protect his family.[5] On his mother's side of the family—which hailed from Tennessee—two uncles had fought for the Confederacy, but the Illinois Wickershams were staunch Union men. According to family lore, Alexander Wickersham, the father of the Judge, was sometimes called "Abe Lincoln Wickersham" due to his striking resemblance to the Great Emancipator, and years later the Judge's younger brother Frank was supposedly so Lincoln-like "even to the mole on his chin" that he played Lincoln in several movies and "did not need any make-up."[6]

Unusual though it may have been for a Republican *not* to look like Lincoln—GOP partisans swore they could see the image of the Rail Splitter even in 332-pound "Big Bill" Taft—no one ever accused Judge Wickersham of being as homely as Honest Abe. But any self-taught Illinois farm boy—Wickersham's formal schooling apparently ended with grammar school—who read law in Springfield and who loved history, literature, and politics could hardly ignore the echoes of Lincoln's life in his own.[7]

Wickersham's legal apprenticeship started at about age twenty in the Springfield office of former Union Army General and Illinois Governor John M. Palmer, a longtime ally and friend of Lincoln. (The Judge would name his first son Darrell Palmer Wickersham.)[8] Wickersham taught school in a small town outside of Springfield on the side, but his real ambition was the law. As Governor Palmer's assistant for some two years, Wickersham earned about five dollars a month; in addition to poring through the law books, he "swept the floors, kindled the fires and washed the windows," sleeping occasionally at night in the back room in a homemade bed.[9] In the fall of 1880, less than a year after being admitted to the Illinois bar, he married a recent Springfield high school graduate, eighteen-year-old Deborah Bell; almost thirty years later the Judge would

Young Wickersham, 1880.
(Alaska State Library, Wickersham State Historic Sites Photograph Collection, ASL-277-019-18)

James Wickersham with his son Darrell.
(Alaska State Library, Wickersham State Historic Sites Photograph Collection, ASL-PCA-277-019-15)

name one of the giant peaks in the Alaska Range in her honor as Mount Deborah.*

IN SEARCH OF OPPORTUNITY, the young lawyer and his family went west in 1883. They settled near Tacoma, Washington, the "City of Destiny" on the southern end of Puget Sound, where the Judge rapidly made a name for himself as an energetic and independent-minded attorney and rising political star; after only a year in Tacoma he won the first of two terms as Pierce County probate judge (1884–1888) and later served as Tacoma city attorney (1894–1896), winning a famous million-dollar lawsuit against a utility that defrauded the city and local taxpayers.[10] In 1898, as the Klondike Gold Rush swept through Seattle, Wickersham won election to the Washington State Legislature, and that would prove to be his stepping-stone to Alaska. In February 1899, Representative Wickersham helped engineer the election of a fellow Tacoma man, Addison G. Foster, to the U.S. Senate. (Until the passage of the seventeenth amendment in 1913, U.S. senators were still chosen by state legislatures.) The freshly minted U.S. senator repaid the favor by promising Wickersham a federal appointment. One of the two possibilities under consideration was the post of U.S. consul general in Yokohama, and the other a newly established district court judgeship in Alaska.

---

* During Wickersham's failed 1903 attempt to climb Mount McKinley, he spotted in the west what he thought was a previously undiscovered "new giant," a "beautiful peak" below Denali and "joined to it by a tremendous ridge of stone." In comparison with the massive bulk of Mount McKinley, he thought this new mountain was "feminine in appearance" due to its "lesser height."

"This splendid peak," he wrote in his diary on May 28, 1903, "we named Mt. Deborah in honor of my good wife, whose pure clean mind and heart are as fairly typified by the white snow as ever resting upon its 16,000 feet in altitude." A short while later Wickersham realized he was mistaken and that the ladylike summit of wind-blown snow below McKinley already had an official name. "We soon discovered this to be Mt. Foraker," Wickersham wrote across the page of his expedition diary, "a fact which I really regretted since I so wished to fix my wife's name to the beautiful Peak" (see Chapter 16). The Judge remedied the error about four years later when he named a 12,339-foot peak in the central Alaska Range (about 125 miles northeast of McKinley) as the new "Mount Deborah."

Seven places in Alaska are named for Judge Wickersham, including three creeks, two domes, one mountain, and one cliff (Wickersham Wall on the west face of McKinley in honor of the route he tried to take in 1903). Other prominent names on the map left by Wickersham include the city of Fairbanks (Sen. Charles W. Fairbanks), the town of Dillingham (Sen. William P. Dillingham), and Isabelle Pass (Isabelle Cleary Barnette), where the Richardson Highway and the Trans-Alaska Pipeline cross through the Alaska Range.

Judge James Wickersham of the Third Judicial Division of Alaska, headquartered at Eagle City on the Yukon River.
(Alaska State Library, Wickersham State Historic Sites Photograph Collection, ASL-PCA-277-007-107)

James Wickersham was in the 1899 state legislature in Washington (bottom row, center).

(Washington State Archives, 1899 Washington State Legislature Class Photographs)

PERHAPS BECAUSE HE ENDED up spending the last half of his eighty-two years in Alaska, in his old age the Judge preferred to recall that Alaska had been his first choice. As he tells the story in *Old Yukon*, the notion of becoming the American consul in Japan "tickled my vanity" but "it was not otherwise satisfactory to me." He claimed the job in Japan was akin to "hitching a very small wagon to a very distant star, and the proposal was declined."[11] In his memory at least, he said he yearned for the Yukon, not Yokohama, because for two hundred years, ever since his first Quaker ancestors had moved into the dark woods of Pennsylvania, his family had been freethinking pioneers and rebels, backwoodsmen only at home on the frontier.

In fact Wickersham's private diary reveals that if he had had his way, he would have never set foot in Alaska, and that at age forty-two it was the Rising Sun he yearned to see, not the Midnight Sun. In the spring of 1900 he confessed that he desired the job in Japan "very much," and at one point he telegraphed Senator Foster: "Much prefer Japan, but leave everything with you."[12] Though deeply disappointed when another man was given the position in Yokohama, he then focused his hopes on Alaska, and after anxious weeks (one not-so-reassuring telegram from Senator Foster read: "I called on President and Attorney General this morning—your case is not dead yet by any means") he finally learned in early June 1900 that he had been nominated by President William McKinley and unanimously confirmed by the Senate for one of two newly established judgeships in Alaska, the Third Judicial Division, headquartered at Eagle City on the Yukon River.[13]

If there had been a last-place consolation prize in the U.S. Justice Department for ambitious office seekers, it was the lonely seat of the Third District Court of Alaska. According to Wickersham, he was "the lowest judge on the bottom rung of the American court system." All along Wickersham had anticipated he would be dispatched to the booming gold rush city of Nome, the site of the Second District Court (the First District Court was located in the designated capital city of Juneau). In comparison Eagle was a modest assignment in an isolated backwater with few demands and sparse opportunities. Trying to put the best face on it, Senator Foster broke the news to Wickersham this way: "Indications you will be assigned to Eagle City.... Eagle City District will be [by] far easiest."[14]

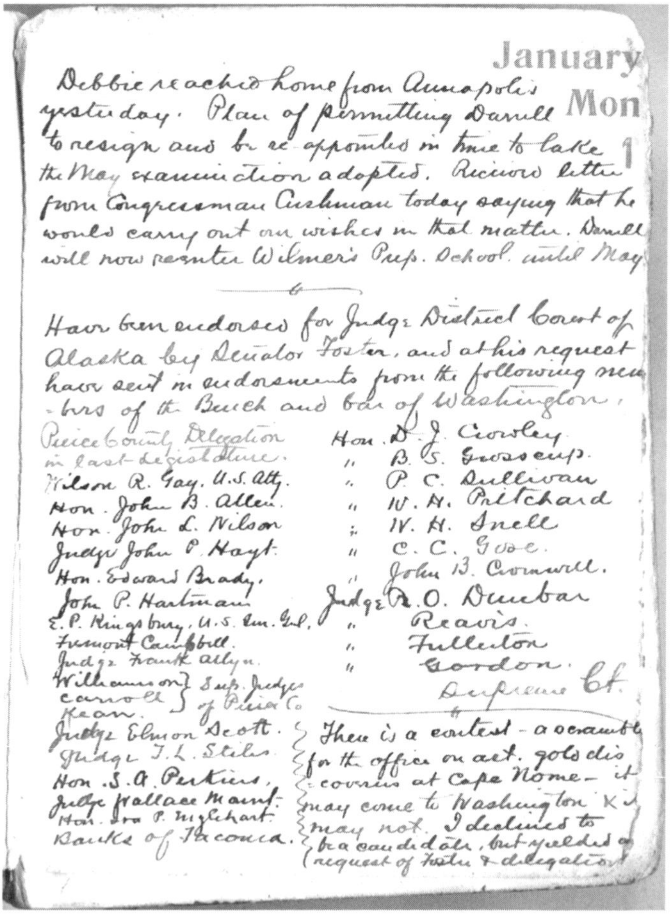
January
Mon
1
Debbie reached home from Annapolis yesterday. Plan of permitting Darrell to resign and be re-appointed in time to take the May examination adopted. Received letter from Congressman Cushman today saying that he would carry out our wishes in that matter. Darrell will now reenter Wilmer's Prep. School until May.

Have been endorsed for Judge District Court of Alaska by Senator Foster, and at his request have sent in endorsements from the following members of the Bench and bar of Washington.

Pierce County Delegation in last Legislature.
Wilson R. Gay. U.S. Atty.
Hon. John B. Allen.
Hon. John L. Wilson
Judge John P. Hoyt.
Hon. Edward Brady.
John P. Hartman
E. P. Kingsbury, U.S. Com. Gel.
Fremont Campbell.
Judge Frank Allyn.
Williamson, Carroll, Kean } Sup. Judges of Pierce Co.
Judge Elmon Scott.
Judge T. L. Stiles.
Hon. S. A. Perkins.
Judge Wallace Mount.
Hon. Ira P. Englehart.
Banks of Tacoma.

Hon. D. J. Crowley.
" B. S. Grosscup.
" P. C. Sullivan
" W. H. Pritchard.
" W. H. Snell
" C. C. Gose.
" John B. Cornwell.
Judge R. O. Dunbar
" Reavis.
" Fullerton
" Gordon. Supreme Ct.

There is a contest - a scramble for the office on act. gold discoveries at Cape Nome - it may come to Washington & it may not. I declined to be a candidate, but yielded at request of Foster & delegation.

The first page of one of the great treasures of Alaska's historical literature, James Wickersham's daily diary, which he kept without fail for some 14,540 days from January 1, 1900, to his death in October 1939.

(Alaska State Library, Wickersham State Historic Site Collection)

Having little responsibility was hardly a recommendation to a man of Wickersham's restless energy and ambition, and he could not help but feel he had been "shunted to an obscure place in the Yukon wilderness."[15] But low expectations aside, he was not about to let his supposed exile to Eagle dampen his enthusiasm or limit the scope of his ventures, and Alaska's third-string judge would soon enough find himself at the center of the action.

DURING THE FORTY YEARS Judge James Wickersham would spend in the Alaska wilderness from his appointment at Eagle in the summer of 1900 until his death in Juneau in the fall of 1939, he transformed the territory, leaving behind, one tribute noted, "more of lasting value" than any other person in its entire history.[16] Driven by the need to challenge himself at every opportunity, "Wick" crammed nine lives' worth of adventure into his four decades in Alaska. The federal judge, frontier lawyer, congressional delegate, political power broker, legal scholar, mountain climber, self-taught ethnologist, linguist, historian, and book collector shaped the literature, law, history, education, commerce, and politics of Alaska.

The enormous range of his interests was matched only by his phenomenal discipline and relentless work ethic—when he gave the commencement address at Fairbanks High School in the spring of 1915 his theme was "Work, Work!"—and he knew few pleasures in life as sweet as the satisfaction of a job well done.[17] His disciplined approach to life shines through in the pages of his daily diary, an invaluable and exhaustive record of his trials and tribulations that he kept for forty years and that would provide the raw material for *Old Yukon*. When the calendar turned over from December 31, 1899, to January 1, 1900, Wickersham apparently resolved to record his life story in the 1900s day by day. (If he kept a diary in the 1800s it has never come to light.) For the next 14,540 days he seldom neglected his journal, even if the day's entry might only be "Same as yesterday." In all he filled forty-seven notebooks, an unrivaled personal chronicle of Alaska history and his part in it.*

* Thanks to the dedicated staff of Alaska State Library in Juneau, the many thousands of pages of the diary have been painstakingly transcribed and are available online at the Alaska Digital Archives. Entries from the Judge's diary have been added as explanatory footnotes throughout this volume.

FAIRBANKS, ALASKA, OCTOBER 26, 1913.

WICKERSHAM WILL ASK FOR COLLEGE

Alaska's Delegate to Congress Tells People of Seattle That He Intends to Ask Congress to Provide North With University, Mining College and Agricultural School. All Three Institutions Are to Be Erected at Fairbanks if Bill Is Passed.

SEATTLE, Oct. 25.—If Delegate Wickersham is successful in carrying out his latest plan for the betterment of conditions in Alaska, Fairbanks can soon claim distinctoin as an educational center of no mean proportions.

The delegate has announced that it is his intention, upon his return to Washington, to introduce a bill providing for the establishment at Fairbanks of three educational institutions which will compare favorably, in the matter of training, with similar institutions on the Outside. One will be a regulation college, to be known as the University of Alaska; another will be a school of mines, and the third an agricultural college.

The delegate is hopeful of securing a large grant of land upon which to erect the several buildings that will be required and to carry on the outdoor work in connection with the other branches of study.

The Fairbanks Daily News-Miner *1913 report of Wickersham's campaign to create a land grant college in Alaska. The legislation granting the land for the Alaska Agricultural College and School of Mines passed two years later in 1915.*

(Fisher Collection)

James Wickersham can rightfully be called the father of Alaska's most vital and enduring public institutions and the champion of territorial self-government and statehood, which came in 1959, two decades after his death. Forty-nine years before Alaska became the forty-ninth state, he was laying the foundation for its ultimate creation. "Nothing less than the dissolution of the nation," he predicted in 1910, "will prevent the organization of the State of Alaska."[18] An editor in Butte, Montana, claimed in 1911, "When Alaska finally does get into the Union, Wickersham will be entitled to much credit for bringing the union about."[19] Although it was merely a symbolic gesture, on March 30, 1916, the forty-ninth anniversary of Seward's 1867 purchase, Wickersham introduced the first statehood bill providing for Alaska to become the forty-ninth state.

Although modern readers cannot help but be struck by Wickersham's generally patronizing and sometimes contemptuous references to Alaska Native peoples, he was one of the few serious students of Native language and culture among the non-Natives living in Alaska, and he was in the forefront of the land claims movement. As a private citizen in the 1930s, he devised the landmark strategy of suing the federal government for compensation for the Tlingit-Haida peoples, whose land had been taken without payment in the creation of the Tongass National Forest.

During the seven terms Wickersham served as Alaska's lone delegate to Congress (1909–1921; 1931–1933)* he crafted four pillars of territorial existence; even though as a delegate he never had a vote, he wrote legislation that created the Alaska Territorial Legislature, the Alaska Railroad, the Alaska public school system, and the University

* Wickersham's legislative accomplishments are all the more remarkable because the Judge's tenure as a seven-term delegate requires a bold asterisk behind it. While technically true that he served six terms in the House between March 1909 and March 1921, he was only officially seated for eight of the twelve years. This was because the partisan courts in Alaska initially ruled that Wickersham had lost the 1916 election. Due to charges of electioneering fraud and other irregularities, the U.S. House of Representatives later declared Wickersham the winner, but by that time only two months were left in the term. A nearly identical scenario played out once again after the 1918 election, with the Alaska courts declaring Wickersham the loser and the U.S. House ultimately overturning the decision. However, the House vote to seat Wickersham came as the session was nearly set to expire, on the eve of adjournment in March 1921. As a result Wickersham's sixth term in Congress was actually only two days long, from March 1 to March 3, 1921.

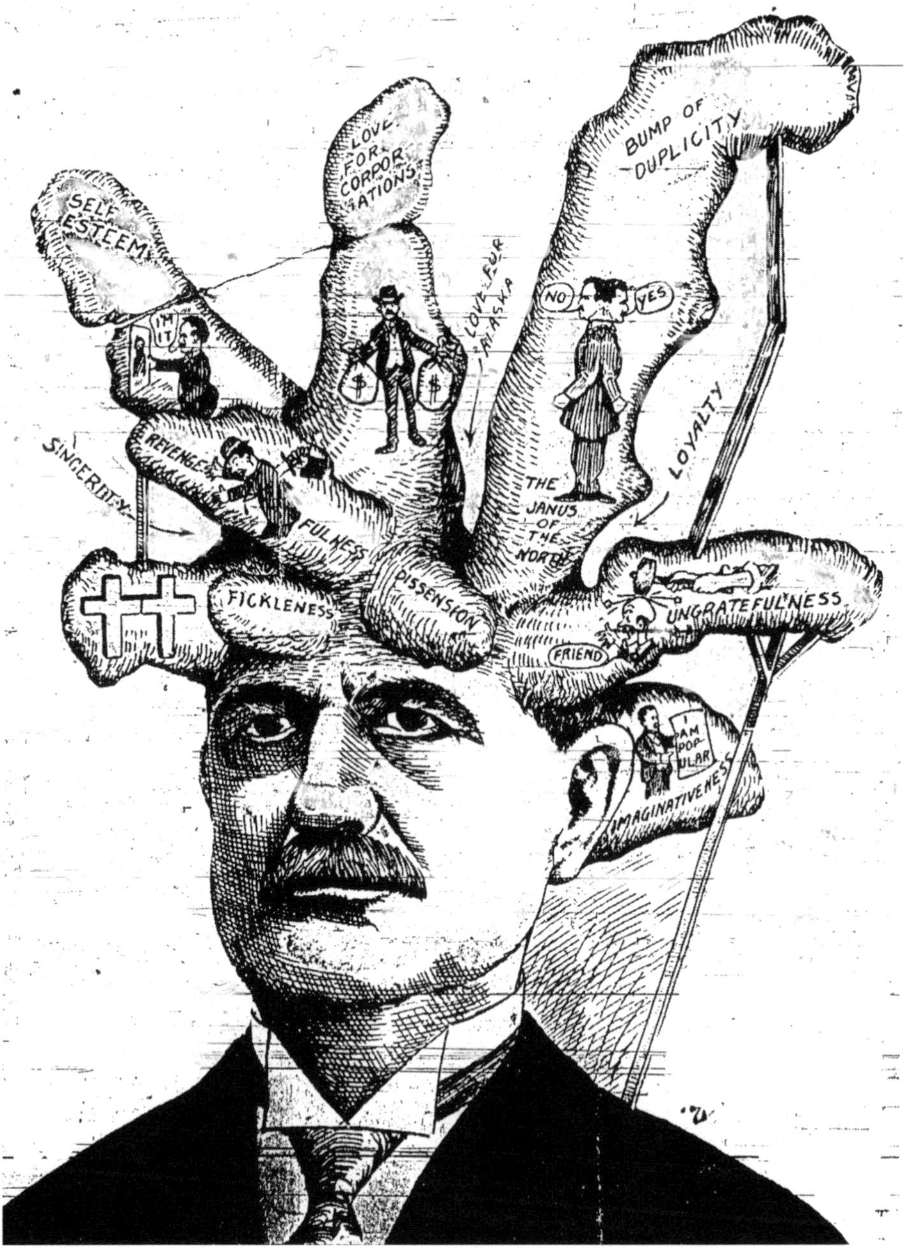

To his enemies, Wickersham was a self-serving, rabble-rousing demagogue. During his run for delegate in 1908 this newspaper cartoon purportedly showed the "phrenlogical" bumps on his head: giant growths for "Duplicity," "Ungratefulness," and "Revengefulness," and none for "Loyalty," "Love for Alaska," or "Sincerity."

(Fisher Collection)

of Alaska. He also authored the legislation that established Mount McKinley National Park.

Invariably he achieved these congressional victories against entrenched opposition from corporate interests that viewed Wickersham as a rabble-rousing demagogue building a self-serving political machine, shamelessly promoting costly public institutions the territory could not afford. One opponent claimed Wickersham was constantly "humbugging" and "more anxious to create an issue of some kind for campaign purposes than to secure legislation of real benefit to the Territory."[20] Critics accused him of attacking anyone who stood in the way of his insatiable quest for power, but the Judge's faithful army cheered his fight against the Morgan-Guggenheim "Alaska Syndicate," the shadowy partnership of eastern financiers bankrolling the gold mines, copper mines, salmon canneries, steamships, and railways in the territory.

A WICKERSHAM RIVAL FAMOUSLY charged that the support for Alaska self-government came predominantly from "saloon bums," gamblers, and crooks, and that responsible businessmen knew it was out of the question for transient mining camps to pay the tax burden local government required.[21] President Taft himself was a believer in the saloon bum theory; rather than an elected legislature, he wanted Alaska to be governed by an appointed commission, similar to that which operated in the Philippines. After a three-year struggle the delegate from Alaska, not the president of the United States, prevailed. Fittingly, it was on Wickersham's fifty-fifth birthday, August 24, 1912, that a reluctant President Taft signed the bill creating the Alaska Territorial Legislature. It was the finest birthday gift Wickersham ever received.

"This victory shows that when you are right & fight," Wickersham wrote privately, "you can sometimes win victory even though President Taft & his cohorts oppose you. I have won this victory by a single handed fight against all odds—simply by standing at my station and never ceasing the effort." But he knew the price he had paid: "Taft and his 'Big Business' allies have destroyed me politically for it."[22]

As much as Wickersham's enemies may have hated his legislative proposals, they had even greater contempt for the Judge himself. So thoroughly did the Judge's mercurial personality rule the political landscape of Alaska for so many years that every election was ultimately a referendum on Wickersham himself. No political party, ideology, or faction could contain him; the Judge was variously a Republican, an Independent, a Roosevelt-Insurgent Republican, a Bull Moose Reformer, and a Woodrow Wilson Progressive. His obituary rightly said that despite whatever partisan label he might have been using at the moment, "more than anything else he was a whole party by himself."[23]

During his tenure as judge he endured three official inquiries into his judicial conduct—sore losers and corrupt politicians invariably charged the court with corruption—and a disgruntled jury fixer gave the Judge the ultimate crooked compliment: He claimed Wickersham "was a damn bad man but a good judge," in contrast with another, more pliant Alaska jurist whom he called a "damn good man but a bad judge." (The Judge's response was that the jury fixers and those who made these allegations were so "'damn bad' themselves, their evidence as to my wickedness does not seem to have had much weight.")[24] After the Judge's first election as delegate in 1908, the defiant editor of the *Fairbanks Times* acknowledged the victory of "our enemy" with little grace. "With Wickersham the legislator we are at peace," the *Times* claimed. "As to Wickersham the politician, we shall bury the hatchet only in his vitals."[25] The editor accused Wickersham of "a penchant—almost a mania—for stabbing his best friends to the heart" whenever "the idol of popularity demands such sacrifices," and that was why the Judge had such "a large number of bitter enemies, who will go to almost any length to accomplish his defeat in anything he might undertake."[26]

THE GREAT SKELETON IN Wickersham's closet that his enemies resurrected to smear his character at every opportunity was his arrest and conviction for the crime of seduction of a teenaged woman named Sadie Brantner in Tacoma in 1889.* Though the Judge always maintained that the seduction case was nothing but political blackmail, and that

* Wickersham's private diary discreetly proves he was no stranger to secret romantic interludes. On board the S.S. *Yukon* on March 25, 1929, traveling between Ketchikan and Juneau, he saw several old acquaintances, including "my Fairbanks friend Mrs. 'Jennie O'Brien'—with whom I passed some interesting hours some ten years ago. She ran when she saw me & has kept in her room. Verily conscience makes cowards of us all. Of course she married after our Fairbanks acquaintance—but she ought to know I never forget to be a discreet gentleman—even to my diary."

he "was more sinned against than sinning," the record is clear that he did have an affair with the nineteen-year-old Brantner that lasted for at least several months. According to her testimony, when she became pregnant, the Judge arranged for her to have a "criminal operation" that aborted the pregnancy.[27] Neither the crimes of illegal cohabitation nor abortion were pertinent issues in the case, because he was only charged on the narrow grounds of seducing an unmarried virgin. As the presiding judge explained when the case went to the jury, the crime of seduction "can only be committed upon an unmarried woman of previously chaste character." Hence the case came down to the chastity of Sadie Brantner, with the prosecution painting her as "modest, pure and chaste," an innocent teenaged girl whose virtue had been soiled by Wickersham, while the defense said she had committed "acts of the grossest lewdness and immorality and of carnal intercourse" and that she was the one who had seduced him.[28]

The jury took seven hours to find Wickersham guilty. Immediately the police arrested him on further charges of subornation of perjury. But further twists were yet to come. A few months later Brantner recanted her testimony, swearing her false accusations had been made "so that Wickersham would be accused of crime and destroy his influence, honor and credit." Despite allegations spread by enemies that Wickersham had coerced Brantner into retracting her story, the court dismissed all the charges.[29]

For the rest of his life the Judge carried the shame of the Brantner blackmail affair; his biographer reports that he mentions it in his diary on at least twenty-three occasions.[30] Every time questions about his character or his professional conduct arose, and in every election and official inquiry, he was forced to explain it all again in order to save himself from further blackmail. For example, during one of the Department of Justice official investigations into his conduct, the 1889 seduction conviction in Tacoma was the principal charge brought against him by those who mistakenly believed he had not previously divulged the information. "I am simply disgusted," he wrote, "at the 'small talk' which disappointed litigants and narrow minded enemies imagine are worthy of consideration by the Dept. of Justice."[31]

In 1915, Senator J. Ham Lewis of Illinois, the flamboyant attorney who a quarter-century before had been Wickersham's defense counsel in the seduction case, stopped the Judge in the corridor of the House of Representatives to inform him that he had recently seen Brantner again. According to Lewis, as the Judge bitterly recorded in his diary, Sadie had "married an Army officer who died—she is now a widow & resides here in Washington...she is frequently in the galleries & expressed real regret at her action toward me. He did not give me her name or residence. I have not heard from or about her for 25 years—not since her last affidavit in the case wherein she fully exonerated me from wrong toward her."[32]

BEHIND THE BENCH OR on the stump, James Wickersham was an imposing figure. At 183 pounds in his prime, he kept in shape with a punching bag in the back of his office. When the Judge took off his jacket and rose to speak, like a bare-knuckle brawler entering the ring, the audience knew they were going to see a spectacle.[33] "Mr. Wickersham," an admiring journalist once wrote, "is a perfect blunderbuss of argument and fact about Alaska."[34] With a superb command of the English language, an encyclopedic knowledge of the facts, and a blistering combination of sarcasm, hyperbole, and ridicule, he "roasted"—the Judge's favorite verb to describe his debating style—anyone foolish enough to challenge him; more often than not the Judge was the last man standing. "Well if they do defeat me," he once wrote in his diary, "they will have some scars to remember the conflict by."[35]

The Judge's physical endurance was legendary, as befitted a man not afraid to walk twenty-five miles a day at forty degrees below zero. When Wickersham volunteered to hold court along the Yukon River during a bitter cold snap in the winter of 1901, he was the only official to make the trip because none of the other court staff would go with him. The Judge estimated that in thirty-nine days of traveling he and a lone companion covered more than one thousand miles, mostly on foot, averaging on the high end thirty-four miles a day (see Chapter 6).

On a bad trail with a heavy load even he had limits. On February 12, 1901, he held up at the gold rush camp of Nation City on the upper Yukon. "Thermometer was 56 degrees below zero," he wrote that night in his diary, "and we remained in camp today—tonight it is up to 35 degrees below and we hope for warmer weather by morning." The next day he pushed ahead, though conditions were anything but tropical. "It was 45 degrees below zero when we left Nation this morning, but within an hour it had gone down to 50

"Fighting Jim" Wickersham on the left would take on any comers when it came to politics. He kept in shape with a punching bag in his office.

(Fisher Collection)

degrees; it was 35 degrees at noon and 40 degrees below when we went in for the night."[36]

Even though fifty below zero would make any warm bed on a rough board welcome, conditions in the roadhouses were none too luxurious. One of the Judge's favorite stories was his first encounter in 1901 with "Old Man Webber," the proprietor of a dingy roadhouse with a mud floor about forty miles down the Yukon below Circle City. Even among other Yukon River notables the Judge had met, including "Pete the Pig," "Mag the Rag," and "Windy Jim," Webber was unforgettable.[37]

"Mr. Webber, I am the United States district judge from Eagle City," Wickersham introduced himself when the dogs came to a halt near the roadhouse.

"Oh, the hell you are," Webber said. "Well, this *was* a good country before the shyster lawyers and grafting deputy marshals began to come through it with their damned law books and commissioners' warrants, but it's going to hell now as fast as it can go."[38]

AFTER WICKERSHAM HAD FINISHED setting up the court system in Fairbanks in 1903, he said he took the "time to look round and consider what to do next." The Judge quickly decided the "most interesting object on the horizon" was about four miles high and that he would be the first man in the world to climb it. Though his Mount McKinley expedition only reached halfway up the side of the mountain, he always thought the climb was one of the peak experiences of his life, and the story of that two-month-long trek in 1903 to ten thousand feet, which takes up nearly one-fourth of this book, showed the mettle of the man.

Geologist Alfred H. Brooks, the highly respected U.S. Geological Survey (USGS) scientist (the Brooks Range was named in his honor) and no mean traveler himself, explained that anyone who thought it surprising for a sitting judge to be physically fit enough to mount such an adventure must realize the "life of a judge in this frontier region is by no means comparable to that of his colleague in a more civilized community. Every year Judge Wickersham travels thousands of miles—by steamer and horse in summer, by dog team and sleigh in winter. His position . . . requires not only legal training but also power of endurance."[39]

His stamina as a public speaker in those years before microphones and amplifiers equaled his prowess on the trail. Whether in front of a raucous crowd of miners or the members of the U.S. House of Representatives, his booming voice could echo off the walls for hour after hour. During the heated congressional debate in January 1914 over the authorization of the construction of the Alaska Railroad, he gave what he considered his greatest speech, a marathon lecture defending government funding for a nationally owned and operated railroad in Alaska. It was a radical proposal; never before in the history of the American West had the federal government stepped in to construct and operate a railroad itself rather than let private enterprise do the job. Wickersham modeled the Alaska Railroad Bill after the law authorizing the construction of the Panama Canal, and he meticulously made the case why conditions in Alaska demanded this seemingly un-American approach to railroad building.

Wickersham won the battle against the charges of socialism with a virtuoso performance, giving before the packed galleries on January 14, 1914, one of the longest speeches in the history of the U.S. Congress. As he wrote that evening in his diary: "It was truly a great physical effort, whatever it may have been intellectually—for I talked for five-and-a-half hours."[40] When he awoke the following morning, his raw throat was a reminder that he had spoken his piece. "My voice lasted fine—did not weaken the whole day—but am sore & worn out today." A colleague from Mississippi asked how he felt, and the Judge said: "Like a woman who has had a baby—very proud but damned sore!"[41]

After dueling with Wickersham for nearly six hours, his opponents were likewise bruised and exhausted. "There was not a dull moment during the delivery of the speech," one newspaper said, as critics harassed him continually. "The questions fired at the judge were from every conceivable angle and were barbed with unmistakable hostility," but the reporter believed the record would show that "the myriad enemies of Alaska" and not Delegate Wickersham bore "the most scars" at the end of the battle.[42]

IT WAS HARDLY INTELLECTUAL and physical firepower alone that enabled Wickersham to win more than he lost. The word *stubborn* does not do justice to his tenacity in the face of adversity.

Wickersham's rivals claimed he was an opportunistic glory-hound who shifted his principles with every fresh breeze, hence the name "Flickering Wick."

(Fisher Collection)

"Mr. Wickersham's career," the *Washington Times* noted in 1914, "has been one of fighting . . . for Alaska."[43] A rival once admitted that the Judge was a man of "pronounced individuality" due to his "absurd pigheadedness."[44] In his heart the Judge possessed the righteous certainty and conviction of a dragon slayer, a lone crusader battling against the odds and the "big interests," fighting corruption and injustice in whatever guise it might appear, and his elemental message resonated with voters about the simple struggle of good against evil, Wickersham against Wall Street, St. James against the Guggenheims.[45]

Strange marriages of convenience, however, are as common in law as politics. After his resignation from the judgeship, but before he became delegate, Wickersham applied to become general counsel for the same Alaska Syndicate upon which he would heap so much scorn in public.[46] For whatever reason the syndicate, which had repeatedly urged Wickersham to join them, refused his application, and so rather than working for the Guggenheims, Wickersham instead went to Congress to crusade against the Guggenheims.[47]

The revelation that the Judge had tried to represent the very interests that he publicly professed to despise, that St. James himself had been tempted to become the Devil's advocate, proved a stinging embarrassment. While Wickersham's flirtation with the Guggs might be seen as proof of the fickle nature of the opportunistic glory hound derided as "Flickering Wick"—enemies claimed he shifted his principles with every fresh breeze—it also demonstrated that the economic reality of Alaska was far more complicated than the black-and-white morality tale that appealed to voters. Nevertheless, the rhetoric shaped reality, not the other way around, and in Wickerham's never-ending war against Washington and the Morgans and the Guggenheims, the Judge was the man who fueled the fire, riding the crest of popular suspicion of monopolies and large corporations with the trust-busting gusto of his hero Teddy Roosevelt, charging the New York robber barons with stealing the riches of Alaska's resources and leaving nothing of value behind.[48]

FEW WITNESSES EVER ACCUSED James Wickersham of possessing a judicial temperament. His friend and sometime spiritual advisor Presbyterian missionary Rev. S. Hall Young, the "Mushing Parson," admitted that as a general rule Wickersham was "much more inclined to present the other fist than the other cheek."[49] With his tightly coiled temper, he wielded his barbed opinions with little concern for those on the receiving end. Critics claimed he was "guided by his antipathies and predilections rather than by judgment and reason."[50] One victim of Wickersham's wrath swore the Judge had a tendency to see criminal conspiracies behind any opposition and was "absolutely overmastered by the presumption of guilt" on the part of anyone with whom he disagreed.[51]

Wickersham's hanging judge mentality had surfaced when as a young man during the anti-Chinese riots in Tacoma in 1885, he was one of the leaders of the so-called "Committee of Fifteen," a vigilante group that conspired to drive about one thousand Chinese workers out of the community and spawned a wave of mob actions throughout the Northwest. During the course of the riots Wickersham swore that he did "absolutely nothing except to protect the Chinamen from violence." According to Wickersham the rights of the "Chinamen" were not the issue, and he maintained for the rest of his life that this vigilante action was the right thing to do. "I always felt that we did a great and good work for the Pacific coast that day," he said more than thirty years later.[52]

Even Judge Wickersham's closest friends admitted that he had a big temper and a short fuse. As a highly favorable *Seattle Post-Intelligencer* editorial praising him in 1906 admitted, Wickersham seemed all too expert at "the gentle art of making enemies" and apparently lacked that "graceful combination of tact and personal magnetism which in a woman is called charm."[53] A skeptical congressional colleague supporting Wickersham in 1921 explained his ambivalence this way: "I did not enter this case with any prejudice in favor of Mr. Wickersham. I will say frankly that I think frequently he rubs the fur the wrong way."[54]

WRONG-WAY WICKERSHAM WAS NEVER more plainly on public display than on February 23, 1911, when the Judge was speaking against a coal leasing bill for Alaska on the floor of the U.S. House of Representatives. Rep. Frank Mondell of Wyoming, the author of the leasing bill, was seated about ten feet away from where Wickersham was standing. As Wickersham continued to blast the proposed legislation, Mondell turned to his neighbor and none too quietly called Wickersham a liar.

The "Committee of Fifteen," the vigilante group that masterminded the expulsion of the Chinese from Tacoma in 1885 posed proudly for this photograph. James Wickersham (labeled as 7) stands in the center.
(Alaska State Library, Jack Allman Manuscript Collection, ASL-MS-220-01-04-01)

"You are the liar if you say that," Wickersham yelled. In an instant the Judge jumped across the aisle; blind with rage, he took two wild swings with his right arm trying to punch Mondell in the face and ended up with his hands around the throat of the honorable gentleman from Wyoming.[55] As the *Washington Post* reported the affair: "Mr. Wickersham, his fingers around Mr. Mondell's neck, was seized in similar fashion by Representative Foster, of Vermont. And all the time the Wyoming representative was wriggling to get himself free, and making futile efforts to use the chair from which he had risen . . . as a weapon against his assailant." A tag team of other congressmen rushed to prevent Mondell from "breaking the house furniture over the cranium of the delegate from Alaska," and Wickersham's rage increased as his colleagues tried to restrain him. According to the reporter from the *Post*, in spite of Representative Foster's stranglehold on Wickersham's throat, the delegate from Alaska "was still able to express his sentiments in vigorous, if not parliamentary language."[56]

When the tumult and the shouting ceased, Wickersham justified his attack on Mondell as a matter of honor. "I want the record to show," the Judge told his colleagues when order was restored, "that I apologize to the house, but"—a newspaper account said at this point his "voice rose to a shout"—"I also want it to show that I was called a liar."[57] Though chagrined that he had lost his temper, the Judge privately maintained that it would henceforth "warn all that when they begin to try their patent nostrums on Alaska they must reckon with the Delegate & . . . they will be more polite, anyway." No matter what the cost, he would be heard. "I will not be snubbed anymore."[58]

"This has been a day of battle," the Judge wrote that night in his diary. "I attempted to strike him but was prevented. The row was unseemly and I am very sorry that it occurred—but when a man calls another a liar, without smiling, it means a blow."[59]

As territorial judge, Wickersham heard more than his share of fighting words. *Old Yukon*—which might just as well have been entitled *Fighting Words*—illustrates clearly that harassment of territorial judges came with the territory. Unlike other federal judges who derive their power and independence, including de facto life tenure pending "good behaviour" from Article III of the U.S. Constitution, Wickersham and the other 607 territorial

"LIAR" IN THE HOUSE NEARLY BRINGS FIGHT

Mondell Denounces Wickersham, Who Rushes Over to Strike Him.

MEMBERS KEEP THEM APART

Apology to the House for Disturbance Brought on by Alaskan Coal Land Bill.

Special to The New York Times.

WASHINGTON, Feb. 23.—The lie direct was passed on the floor of the House today, and a fist fight was only prevented by the timely interposition of members. The trouble was between Representative Mondell of Wyoming, in charge of the Administration Alaska Coal Land Leasing bill and Delegate Wickersham of Alaska. The incident closed with mutual apologies to each other and to the House, while the bill itself was defeated. The debate was at its height, after a hard day's work when Mr. Mondell shouted the word "liar" to the Alaskan and Mr. Wickersham, returning the epithet, hurled himself at Mr. Mondell. Mr. Wickersham's arms were swung wide and in a moment Mr. Mondell was endeavoring to get out of his chair.

A score of members jumped to their feet. The chamber roared with the noise of excited voices, and within half a minute, Wickersham was struggling vainly to free himself from the clasp of Representative Foster of Vermont, and Representative Dwight of New York, while Mr. Mondell was effectually subdued by Representative Longworth of Ohio.

"Let me at him. Don't hold me back," cried Wickersham, endeavoring to evade his captors.

The New York Times *1911 front-page story of Wickerham's slugfest on the floor of the House of Representatives with Rep. Frank Mondell of Wyoming, and a cartoonist's version of the "debate."*

(Alaska State Library)

judges who served in the United States between 1789 and 1959 were a peculiarly weakened hybrid, low-paid, term appointees—typically only for four years, or one presidential term—with neither the constitutional protection nor the political autonomy of their Article III brethren.* Territorial courts comprised a dependent judiciary, a constitutional aberration at the mercy of Congress and the executive branch. These so called "quasi-judges" have often been branded as greedy carpetbaggers, political hacks, or incompetents, inordinately vulnerable to the influence of political machination, influence peddling, and character assassination.[60] This low opinion of the average territorial judge was as true in Alaska as everywhere else. No less an authority than General A. W. Greely, the head of the U.S. Army Signal Corps and the U.S. military's reigning expert on arctic affairs, quipped in 1907 that the judges in Alaska were so derelict in their duties they deserved to be hung.[61] The average career of a territorial judge was contentious, brutal, and short; sixty percent of territorial judges in the late nineteenth century never lasted more than two years on the job.[62]

By all rights Wickersham should also have been a short-lived statistic, because within two years of his appointment he had received enough hate mail to last a lifetime. "It's a great chance to accumulate enemies—is the judgeship," he jotted in his diary after one particularly bad day at the office.[63] He looked forward to the day he could retire "for it is hell in Alaska."[64]

Because Alaska had a mere figurehead for a governor, and before 1913 no legislature, its territorial judges labored under particularly stressful conditions. In effect Wickersham and the two other federal judges who served with him shouldered responsibility for all three branches of the U.S. government in their respective judicial divisions, an un-American imbalance of power. "The judges in Alaska have all the power," Wickersham complained in a 1907 speech. "It is a wrong system and never should have been allowed."[65] Since disgruntled citizens had no one else they could readily blame for real and imagined problems, the judges bore the brunt of all the outrage.

* As one early opinion from the U.S. attorney general concluded in 1838: "Territorial judges are not judges under the Constitution, but are mere creatures of legislation." See William W. Blume and Elizabeth G. Brown, "Territorial Courts and Law: Unifying Factors in the Development of American Legal Institutions," *Michigan Law Review* 61(1) (Nov. 1962):81.

Far from the corridors of influence in Washington, D.C., where critics prowled trying to have them removed on any pretext, the Alaska judges were sitting targets for anonymous attacks. "There was never a closed season for protection of the district judges in Alaska," Wickersham wrote in *Old Yukon*, "as there was for brown bears and other varmints." They were marked men from the moment they raised their right hands to solemnly swear. "Most of our early Alaska judges were removed from office upon secret charges without notice or a hearing; all of them were maliciously assailed and . . . intimidated in the performance of their judicial duty . . . from the secret malice of disappointed litigants."[66]

NATURALLY ANY DECISION BY a judge had the potential to make at least one party desperately unhappy, but the cases that proved most troubling to Wickersham originated with a scandal in the Alaska court system itself. In 1901–1902, he tackled rampant corruption in the Second Judicial Division in Nome, where his colleague Judge Arthur H. Noyes and co-conspirator Alexander McKenzie had masterminded an audacious scheme to loot the gold mines. In the course of his efforts to clean up the Noyes-McKenzie gold conspiracy—famously chronicled in the Rex Beach novel *The Spoilers*—Wickersham faced an epidemic of bribery, jury tampering, and perjury, described in *Old Yukon* in Chapter 10, "Liars and Thieves." He always believed it was his uncompromising stance against official corruption that earned him the enmity of powerful politicians in Congress, such as Sen. Knute Nelson of Minnesota, who became an implacable foe for as long as he lived. "I went to see Senator Nelson today," Wickersham wrote some years later, "and he was friendly toward me—that is he did not throw me out of the office."[67]

Largely due to Nelson and several other influential senators, the Senate refused to confirm Wickersham's renomination as judge following the expiration of his first term in 1904. Hounded by men he thought were a pack of "liars" and "wolves," Wickersham often thought of simply resigning and going into private practice. "If I can make arrangements for money will abandon the judgeship," he wrote at one dark moment in early 1904. "Have not made $1,500 per year out of it—nothing but honor & worry!!"[68] But the Judge refused to leave office under a cloud; an admirer said there was "too much fight in his nature for him to retire . . . in a way that would permit his enemies to claim a victory," and so year after year he persevered, as did Wickersham's most important supporter, President Theodore Roosevelt.[69]

Wickersham first met Teddy Roosevelt in a private meeting at the White House in February 1904. His initial impression was that the youthful chief executive was not "as ugly as the pictorial papers and his photographs make him appear."

"The president is a strenuous and rapid talker," Wickersham wrote, "and began at once to ask questions and answer them. He was much interested in the big Kodiak bear." Roosevelt claimed "every Alaskan official had been accused of every crime imaginable," and thus was readily convinced that the barrage of charges against Wickersham were groundless and the Senate's refusal to confirm his nomination a gross injustice.[70]

The president promised that despite the obstructionists in the Senate, Wickersham could stay on the Alaska bench by recess appointment as long as Roosevelt stayed in the White House.[71] True to his word Roosevelt reappointed Wickersham eight times between 1904 and 1907.* The Judge thought Roosevelt's unwavering support "in face of the most extraordinary fight ever made against a presidential appointment . . . gives me great satisfaction. . . . My enemies will thrust greatness upon me if they do not quit!"[72]

Wickersham finally decided to retire as judge on December 31, 1907, and as he prepared to adjourn for the final time he could look back on his seven and a half years of service with a keen sense of accomplishment. "When I went to the North there was no courthouse; there were no records, no jails, nothing. There was merely a broad expanse of territory and the only thing between Alaska and Siberia that looked like a semblance of government was the commission I bore signed by President McKinley. I began up there with only the assurance of the government at Washington that they would support every good thing I did."[73]

Governing a territory the size of Texas between Sitka and Nome, he made many good decisions, and Wickersham's sustained performance as a judge, especially in light of all the obstacles, was nothing

* The eight recess appointments occurred on November 16, 1904; December 24, 1904; March 6, 1905; March 21, 1905; December 5, 1905; March 21, 1906; June 30, 1906; and March 4, 1907. See Evangeline Atwood, *Frontier Politics: Alaska's James Wickersham* (Portland: Binford and Mort, 1979), p. 405.

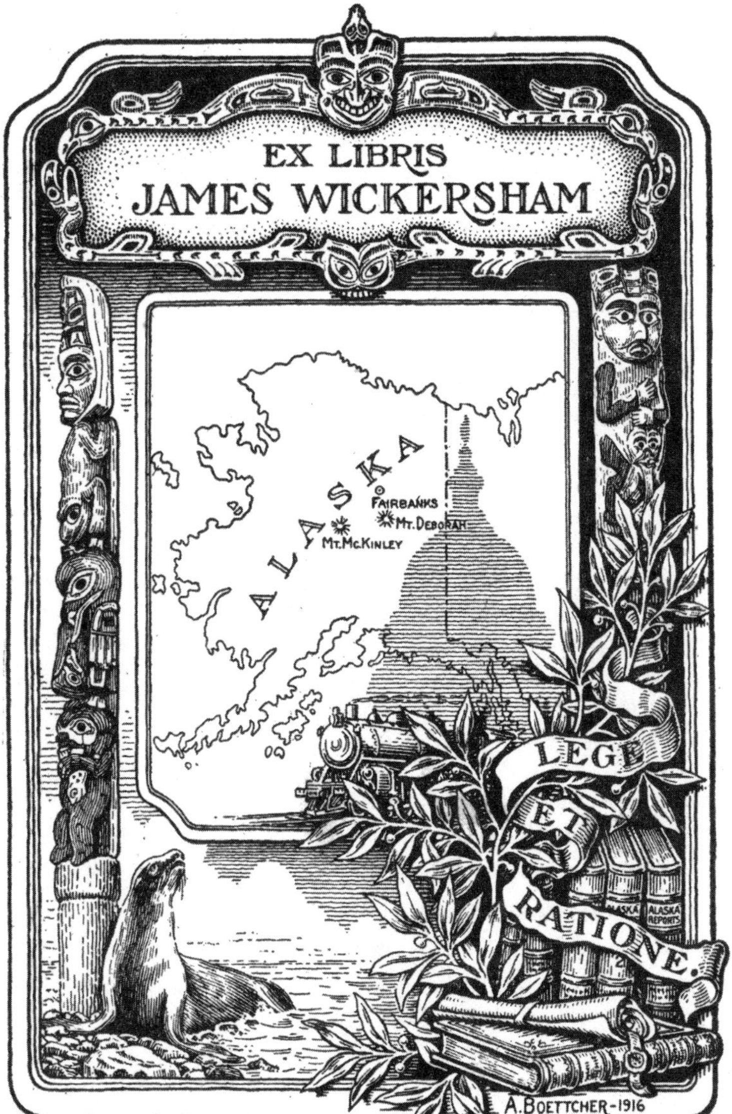

Wickersham's specially designed book plate highlighting moments of his career: the shadow of the capital for his long service in Congress; a locomotive for his bill authorizing the construction of the Alaska Railroad; Mount McKinley for his 1903 expedition; his hometown of Fairbanks that he had named; and Mount Deborah, which he had named for his wife.

(Alaska State Library, Schieffelin Brothers Yukon River prospecting trip collection, 1882–1883) less than exemplary. He left office as he entered it, a man of modest means: proof enough, supporters claimed, that he was honest to the core.[74] Sitting on the Alaska bench for close to eight years, by far the longest reigning judge in Alaska up to that time, he had ruled on 1,726 cases, of which only thirty-three had been appealed, and of those only ten had been reversed.[75] One kindly editor thought those statistics should put to rest any complaints about the Judge. "The very figures of cases tried, appealed, sustained and reversed speak in more eloquent terms of his ability, keen judgment, knowledge of law, fearlessness and honesty than a volume of praise."[76]

AS MUCH AS THE Judge enjoyed the rough-and-tumble combat of the courtroom and the campaign trail, looking back his most lasting satisfaction came from his work as a scholar and literary man. When the Judge had first arrived in Alaska in 1900, he had brought with him a small reference library of law books and an unbound copy of the recently passed Alaska Civil Code. In those days the prevailing legal procedures found in most parts of Alaska were a peculiar mix of rather uncommon law. For example, in the fall of 1899 the authorities in Nome "shipped out" a man named John Ginivan for the supposed crime of "worthlessness and general cussedness." For his part Ginivan claimed he had been framed and promised to "sue the government for heavy damages."[77]

To systematize Alaska's legal precedents and create a solid foundation for all future case law, the Judge decided in late 1902 that on his own time and at his own expense he would write the law books for Alaska himself, creating a series that would be known as *Wickersham's Alaska Reports*, in which he compiled, digested, and outlined "all prior and published decisions," including appeals, that embraced "the entire field of decided law from Alaska since 1868."[78] As in so many of his endeavors, this monumental effort to record Alaska's case law—which would engage his energies for more than three decades—testified to his dogged determination and capacity for work. "Truly there is no excellence without great labor," he wrote while at work on volume one, "for I have been obliged to turn every page of 115 volumes of the *Federal Reporter*, examine every case from Oregon, Washington and California in 30 vols. of Federal Cases, and turn every page of the [U.S. Supreme Court] reports...from 1867 to date."[79] By 1907 he had completed the first two volumes of *Alaska Reports* (eventually he would edit eight volumes totaling nearly seven thousand pages of legal decisions from 1868 to 1935).

Compiling the decisions he authored personally during his years on the bench brought a true sense of accomplishment. When he received his first copy of volume two in February 1907 he said he felt like a proud parent who had borne all the "insult and degradation" that the Department of Justice could deliver, in order to see those two volumes sitting safely on the shelf for all time.[80] "It is immaterial how hard my enemies may damn me," Wickersham wrote, "they can't take away the success of my work in Alaska as it is embalmed in the 1st or 2nd *Alaska Reports*!"[81] Though weary from the endless fight for reconfirmation by the Senate, he always bristled when well-meaning friends repeatedly suggested he quietly resign and go into a more lucrative private practice. "Everyone says that to me, as if money were the one great object of life! I would rather leave the 1st and 2nd *Alaska Reports* as a monument of my work in Alaska—than to have money!"[82]

MUCH OF THE FINANCIAL wealth that the Judge did accumulate, he spent on amassing a huge private library. Starting with his election as congressional delegate in 1908, Wickersham vowed to get a copy of everything that had been published in Alaska or about Alaska, including newspapers, books, magazine articles, and government documents. With the assistance of the Library of Congress, he tracked down more than three thousand government documents concerning Alaska, and scavenging through bookshops and dealing with collectors around the world, he purchased thousands of volumes, creating the largest private library in Alaska and the finest collection of Alaskana in existence.

Nearly twenty years of book collecting and bibliographic work culminated with the publication in 1927 of Wickersham's *Bibliography of Alaskan Literature 1724–1924*, in which the Judge identified and categorized all of the known publications about Alaska that had appeared during the previous two hundred years, totaling 10,380 items, many of which were in Wickersham's personal collection.* Appropriately enough, the Wickersham bibliography was the first book

* The Wickersham Library today forms the core of the Alaska State Library's Historical Collections in Juneau.

published by the fledgling Alaska Agricultural College and School of Mines (now the University of Alaska), the institution that Wickersham had founded. Scholars and librarians immediately recognized that his "monumental" bibliography was probably the most valuable single book ever written about Alaska. "The importance of this new publication is much greater . . . than that of an ordinary book," said Charles W. Smith of the University of Washington, "since it will multiply the usefulness of all existing books relating to Alaska."[83]

OF ALL THE BOOKS in the world, the single volume that Wickersham devoted most of his energies to during the last two decades of his life, the one book he longed most to see in print before his death, is the book you hold in your hands, *Old Yukon*. Based largely on his voluminous diaries, he thought this book would be the most truthful firsthand portrait ever published of life in Alaska in the early 1900s. Admittedly he was not a professional writer, and given his wide stubborn streak, he did not readily accept editorial suggestions. Often afflicted with the legal disease of using too many words to say too little, he also readily acknowledged that he "sometimes wandered from the rules of grammar." But he hoped his honest and unvarnished account, as rough as it might be, would strike a chord with those who loved the territory.[84]

Originally entitled "Pioneering Around Mount McKinley," the book had its origins in 1917 after the passage of Wickersham's bill creating Mount McKinley National Park, when the Boone and Crockett Club sent a congratulatory telegram urging the delegate to someday "publish in detail the record of his arduous trip to the mountain in the summer of 1903." He finished a first version of the manuscript in May 1918, focused principally on the 1903 expedition. Charles Scribner's rejected the manuscript, and it was not until five years later in 1923, by which time he had left the office of delegate, that the Judge was motivated to rewrite the story.[85]

By July 1924 he felt the revised manuscript was in good shape. "I have again rewritten 'Pioneering Around Mount McKinley'—and think I will permit it to go now, without further ironing or polishing. Of course, if I had time. . . . "[86] He sent this "second edition" of the story to World Book and then to Century, but both publishers turned him down. Undaunted, he went back to his desk and hammered out a new version with expanded chapters on Native life, early traders,

James Wickersham at his house in Juneau.
(Alaska State Library, Wickersham State Historic Sites Photograph Collection, ASL-PCA-277-021-003)

exploration, and the history of the Yukon. The new title was "Old Yukon Trails."[87]

In 1927, Arthur H. Clark Company of Cleveland agreed to publish "Old Yukon Trails," but only if Wickersham would agree to pay half the cost. "Since the publication will cost about $6,000, I must decline to go into the publishing business," the Judge wrote in his diary. He hoped Clark would reconsider and undertake the venture without subsidy. "I shall write to him a good letter of explanation, for I think it will prove, not a best seller, but a long continued and steady seller, especially to tourists on the Mt. McKinley Railroad." Clark refused. The publisher assured Wickersham that he had "read every word of the manuscript" and had found it most interesting, but due to the limited market he could not make any money on the project.[88] Many more rejection slips and revisions followed in the years to come.

JUDGE WICKERSHAM WAS BACK in office in 1931 for his final term as delegate and still revising the seemingly unpublishable manuscript yet once again. On nights and weekends he stayed at his desk, gradually making the book as much a massive history of Alaska and the Yukon Valley as a personal memoir. Anyway, he thought the story was "so old now that it takes its place as History & a few years more or less will make no difference in its value—may even make it more interesting—& I have so much of the present day work to do for Alaska in this Congress that I feel justified in taking my time on the Ms."[89]

Wickersham's defeat in 1932 by Anthony J. "Tony" Dimond, and the arrival of Franklin D. Roosevelt and the New Deal, ended his active political career and gave him more time to plug away on his memoirs. "Busy in the office during the day & reworking over some of my chapters in Old Yukon Trails," he noted in Juneau on October 7, 1933. "I shall be lost for pleasant employment when that Ms. [ends], if I ever get to the end!"[90] He need not have worried. Like many a near-sighted scholar and amateur author, the Judge had a nearly impossible time in deciding when enough was enough, promising himself week after week, year after year, that he would swear off any more revisions, additions, or corrections. "That damned manuscript," he wrote in January 1934, "is now completed—again!"[91] In fact not until a year later was the manuscript ready to send out one more time, "like the dove from [the] Ark—to seek a publisher," but just as in earlier years the flood of rejection slips from commercial publishers continued.[92]

Finally in 1937, twenty years after he had started his memoirs, Wickersham thought as a last resort to try the West Publishing Company of St. Paul, Minnesota, the leading legal publisher in the United States and the same firm that had published *Wickersham's Alaska Reports* for three decades, arguing that it was "a biography of myself & my law reports" and therefore West should "print it for that reason!"[93] To his great relief, West Publishing took on the project with the initial stipulation that the book be titled *Judge Wickersham's Old Yukon*, believing rightly that the author himself was the book's primary selling point. The Judge was less than comfortable with having his name at the top. "It seems egotistic to me, [and though] it will be understood by my Alaska friends... what of the newcomers?"[94]

READERS GREETED THE PUBLICATION of *James Wickersham's Old Yukon* in the summer of 1938 with generous applause. The rich details of the Judge's life on the bench, taken from the pages of his diaries, gave *Old Yukon* a flavor and fullness not found in any other volume ever written about the early days of Alaska, and what the book may have lacked in literary style was far outweighed by the unmistakable voice of a genuine original.

Joseph Henry Jackson, the noted California historian and book critic, thought that despite any defects in craftsmanship—Wickersham himself remarked that the poor quality of his portrait in the frontispiece was probably a more accurate reflection of his weathered visage anyway—the book was richly deserving of recognition: "Like its honored author, this volume of reminiscences, made up from his diaries and notes over more than a quarter century, will remain a permanent part of that incredible Alaska he saw and knew. In spite of the fact that the book suffers a bit from lack of proper editing and is not too well printed, it will be a source volume for many years for all who want to study the epic story of Alaska, its minerals and its men."[95]

As Jackson's kindly review hinted, the original published version of *Old Yukon* was in places a rough read. As a legal publisher of handbooks, the West Publishing Company did not have the staff or the resources to revise the manuscript in any significant way, and after struggling with the story for two decades, the Judge had neither the energy nor the inclination to run it through his typewriter yet again.

As much as the Judge relished the rough-and-tumble combat of politics, his most lasting satisfaction came from his prodigious work as a scholar and a literary man. He kept reading and writing until almost his final days. The last words he wrote were in his diary on October 19, 1939: "Just a shadow—cannot see—blind."

(Alaska State Library, Wickersham State Historic Sites Photograph Collection, ASL-PCA-019-076)

In this new edition we have tried to prune and polish the Judge's work by eliminating extraneous material—such as lengthy descriptive and historical passages not relevant to his life and career—tightening up wordy paragraphs, and reworking awkward chapters. In places new introductory sentences have been added to clarify more obscure references, but we have tried to preserve Wickersham's unique voice and style. Furthermore we have added numerous explanatory footnotes, generally drawn directly from Wickersham's diary, which naturally reveal far more about his personal feelings than he allowed to show through in his book.

OLD YUKON WOULD BE the last substantial piece of work that James Wickersham ever finished, as both his energy and his eyesight were fading fast. Only weeks after he received the first copy of the book in June 1938, his eye doctor told him that the growing cataracts in his left eye would soon leave him as blind as he was in his right eye. Nearly fifteen years earlier a doctor had removed the cloudy lens in his right eye; the hope was that use of a "special glass" would restore his sight, but that was not to be.[96]

"My blindness prevents reading," he wrote in March 1939, "but I can still write—badly." A month later his eyes were far worse. "In the office as usual," he scribbled, "but too blind to read or write."[97] Most distressingly, he found that he could not compose his thoughts without putting them on paper. "I cannot work without sight!"[98] A lawyer who could not read, write, or think was next to useless. "I am blind—and busted," he wrote in July 1939. "Our creditors are threatening to cut off our lights. I cannot see to practice law even if I had business. . . ."[99]

The last words he managed to scribble before the world went dark were on October 19, 1939: "Just a shadow—cannot see—blind."[100] The Judge died five days later. The headline in the Juneau paper read:

ALASKA'S 'WICK' BURNS OUT:
BUT HIS LIGHT SHINES ON[101]

And nowhere does that light still shine more brightly than in the pages of James Wickersham's *Old Yukon: Tales, Trails, and Trials.*

ENDNOTES

1 Winfield Scott Downs, ed., *Encyclopedia of American Biography* (New York: American Historical Co., 1948), p. 95.
2 See page 16.
3 Wickersham Diary, 1 September 1939.
4 Evangeline Atwood, *Frontier Politics: Alaska's James Wickersham* (Portland: Binford and Mort, 1979), p. 2; Gay Wickersham Davis, comp. and ed., *The Wickersham Family in America*. (Westminster, MD: Heritage Books, 2004).
5 Jerri Garofalo, "Meet the Wickersham Family," http://www.argenweb.net/marion/photos/wickershamfmly.html.
6 *Encyclopedia of American Biography*, p. 92.
7 David Donald, "Getting Right with Lincoln," *Lincoln Reconsidered*, 2d ed. (New York: Alfred A. Knopf, 1961), pp. 3–18. Thanks to my friend, historian Michael Carey, for bringing the supposed likeness between Lincoln and Taft to my attention.
8 Wickersham Diary, No. 37, inside front cover, 24 August 1926.
9 *Encyclopedia of American Biography*, p. 92.
10 Herbert Hunt and Floyd C. Kaylor, *Washington: West of the Cascades* (S. J. Clarke Publishing, 1917), p. 323.
11 See page 2.
12 Wickersham Diary, 4 May 1900; 17 April 1900.
13 Wickersham Diary, 4 June 1900; 6 June 1900; 7 June 1900.
14 Wickersham Diary, 8 June 1900. See page 2.
15 See page 4.
16 *Fairbanks Daily News-Miner*, 1 September 1939; *Encyclopedia of American Biography*, p. 91.
17 Wickersham Diary, 27 May 1915.
18 James Wickersham, "The Forty-Ninth Star," *Collier's*, 6 August 1910, p. 17.
19 *Daily Alaska Dispatch* (Juneau), 13 February 1911.
20 U.S. Senate, *Government of Alaska: Statements Before the Committee on Territories, S. 5436* (Washington: Government Printing Office, 1910), p. 62.
21 *Tanana Miner*, 18 January 1909; *Fairbanks Daily Times*, 8 January 1907; Jeanette Paddock Nichols, *Alaska: A History of Its Administration…* (Cleveland: Arthur H. Clark, 1924), pp. 279–280.
22 Wickersham Diary, 24 July 1912.
23 Wickersham Diary (clipping), 27 May 1915; 24 October 1939; *Seattle Times*, 4 May 1930; Terrence Cole, *The Cornerstone on College Hill* (Fairbanks: University of Alaska Press, 1994), p. 3.

24 Wickersham Diary, 19 November 1904.
25 *Fairbanks Daily Times*, 13 August 1908.
26 *Fairbanks Daily Times*, 11 August 1908.
27 U.S. Senate, *In the Matter of the Confirmation of James Wickersham as District Judge of the Third Division of the District of Alaska*, Confidential Report, 59th Congress, 1st Session, Ex. Doc. No. 7 (Washington: Government Printing Office, 1906), p. 41; Atwood, *Frontier Politics*, pp. 406–414.
28 *Tacoma Daily Ledger*, 27 February 1889; Murray C. Morgan, "J. Ham Lewis, the Best Dressed Politician of His Day," *Tacoma News Tribune*, 4 November 1993.
29 Atwood, *Frontier Politics*, pp. 412–414.
30 Ibid., p. 34.
31 Wickersham Diary, 1 August 1904.
32 Wickersham Diary, 14 December 1915.
33 Wickersham Diary, 27 December 1902.
34 *Daily Alaska Dispatch* (Juneau), 13 February 1911.
35 Wickersham Diary, 1 April 1905.
36 Wickersham Diary, 12–13 February 1901.
37 Wickersham Diary, 15 February 1901.
38 See page 76.
39 Alfred H. Brooks, "The Alaskan Range: A New Field for the Mountaineer," *Bulletin of the American Geographical Society* 37(8) (1905):478.
40 Wickersham Diary, 14 January 1914.
41 Wickersham Diary, 15 January 1914.
42 Wickersham Diary (clipping from *Grays Harbor Washingtonian*), 18 January 1914.
43 Wickersham Diary (clipping from *Washington Times*), 19 February 1914.
44 *Fairbanks Daily Times*, 11 August 1908.
45 See for instance: Wickersham Diary (clipping from "The American"), 27 January 1914.
46 Wickersham Diary, 4 April 1907.
47 Wickersham Diary (clipping), 27 October 1939.
48 Melody Webb Grauman, "Kennecott: Alaskan Origins of a Copper Empire, 1900–1938," *Western Historical Quarterly*, Vol. 9, No. 2 (April 1978), p. 202; Robert Stearns, "The Morgan-Guggenheim Syndicate and the Development of Alaska, 1906–1915" (University of California, Ph.D. dissertation, 1967), pp. 313–328.
49 S. Hall Young to James Wickersham, 25 February 1911, Box 38, Alaska Coal Lands, Wickersham Papers, Alaska State Library. Reprinted in

Phyllis J. De Muth, *A Preliminary Inventory of the James Wickersham (Family) Papers* (Alaska Historical Library, 1987), p. 58.

50 *Fairbanks Daily Times*, 11 August 1908.

51 U.S. House of Representatives, *Contested Election Case of Wickersham v. Sulzer (Deceased) and Grigsby* (Washington: Government Printing Office, 1920), 66th Congress, 2nd Session, p. 348.

52 U.S. Senate, *In the Matter of the Confirmation of James Wickersham as District Judge of the Third Division of the District of Alaska*, Confidential Report, 59th Congress, 1st Session, Ex. Doc. No. 7 (Washington: Government Printing Office, 1906), p. 39; Atwood, *Frontier Politics*, p. 21.

53 *Seattle Post-Intelligencer*, 25 April 1906.

54 Wickersham Diary (clipping from *Congressional Record*), 28 February 1921.

55 *Seattle Post-Intelligencer*, 24 February 1911.

56 *Fairbanks Sunday Times*, 26 February 1911; Wickersham Diary (clipping from *Washington Post*), 24 February 1911.

57 *Seattle Post-Intelligencer*, 24 February 1911.

58 Wickersham Diary, 25 February 1911.

59 Wickersham Diary, 23 February 1911.

60 Kermit L. Hall, "Hacks and Derelicts Revisited: American Territorial Judiciary, 1789–1959," *Western Historical Quarterly* 12(3) (July 1981):275; Gary Lawson, "Territorial Governments and the Limits of Formalism," *California Law Review*, Vol. 78, No. 4 (July 1990), p. 894.

61 Wickersham Diary, 14 May 1907.

62 Hall, "Hacks and Derelicts Revisited," pp. 273–275, 286–288.

63 Wickersham Diary, 26 August 1905.

64 Wickersham Diary, 15 March 1905.

65 Wickersham Diary (clipping), 13 July 1907.

66 See page 278.

67 Wickersham Diary, 22 May 1912.

68 Wickersham Diary, 18 December 1904; 28 January 1904. In addition to Knute Nelson, Wickersham claimed his other main foes were the two senators from McKenzie's home state of North Dakota, Henry C. Hansbrough and Porter J. McCumber, as well as Sen. Levi Ankeny of Washington and Sen. Weldon Heyburn of Idaho. See Wickersham Diary, 6 June 1905.

69 "Judge James Wickersham," *Alaska-Yukon Magazine*, November 1907, p. 266.

70 Wickersham Diary, 10 February 1904.

71 Wickersham Diary, 25 June 1906.

72 Wickersham Diary, 4 March 1907.
73 Wickersham Diary (clipping), 13 July 1907.
74 "Judge James Wickersham," p. 266.
75 Wickersham Diary (clipping from *Fairbanks Daily News*), 7 November 1907.
76 Wickersham Diary, 4 November 1907.
77 *Nome Gold Digger*, 21 March 1900.
78 Wickersham Diary, 1 January 1903.
79 Wickersham Diary, 24 January 1903.
80 Wickersham Diary, 9 March 1907.
81 Wickersham Diary, 28 February 1907.
82 Wickersham Diary, 11 December 1905.
83 Charles W. Smith, "Review of 'A Bibliography of Alaskan Literature, 1724–1924,'" *Washington Historical Quarterly* XIX (1928):232–233.
84 Wickersham Diary, 5 March 1934.
85 Wickersham Diary, 18 March 1917; 31 May 1918; 8 December 1923.
86 Wickersham Diary, 7 July 1924.
87 Wickersham Diary, 28 December 1926.
88 Wickersham Diary, 27 April 1927; 9 March 1928.
89 Wickersham Diary, 15 August 1931; 20 September 1931; 30 October 1931.
90 Wickersham Diary, 7–9 October 1933.
91 Wickersham Diary, 3 January 1934; 7 January 1934.
92 Wickersham Diary, 20 October 1934.
93 Wickersham Diary, 31 October 1937.
94 Wickersham Diary, 22 February 1938.
95 Joseph Henry Jackson, "A Bookman's Notebook," *San Francisco Chronicle*, August 1938, in Wickersham Diary, 11 August 1938; 4 June 1938.
96 Wickersham Diary, 28 June 1938.
97 Wickersham Diary, 12 March 1939; 17 April 1939.
98 Wickersham Diary, 16 July 1939.
99 Wickersham Diary, 21 July 1939.
100 Wickersham Diary, 19 October 1939.
101 *Daily Alaska Empire* (Juneau), 25 October 1939.

The frontier judge appointed by President William McKinley in June 1900.

(Alaska State Library, Wickersham State Historic Sites Photograph Collection, ASL-PCA-277-019-024)

1

THE GENESIS OF AN ALASKA COURT

All ye icebergs make salaam
You belong to Uncle Sam.
And above the wild ducks' clamour,
In his own peculiar grammar,
With its linguistic disguises,
Lo, the Arctic prologue rises—
* * *
Rocks, too, mebbe quartz; let's see—
'Twould be strange if there should be—
Seems I've heerd such things told—
Eh! Why, bless us,—yes, it's GOLD!

—Bret Harte

AT THE GENERAL ELECTION in the fall of 1898 the people of Tacoma elected me to the Legislature to assist in procuring the return of a local candidate to the office of United States Senator. After a strenuous campaign the Hon. Addison G. Foster of Tacoma was elected to that office. William McKinley was president, Marcus A. Hanna was the leader of the Republican party in the Senate, and Senator Foster became one of their supporters. In due course it became known that I had been recommended for appointment to a modest state office.

Among those who objected to my appointment to this local post, the most earnest protested that the post was not equal to the obligation the Senator owed me for services rendered in his campaign. They urged my appointment as Consul General to Japan, an office credited to the state of

Washington, or to some other foreign post of equal honor and profit. While that suggestion tickled my vanity, it was not otherwise satisfactory to me. My family had been backwoodsmen for two hundred years—ever since my first Quaker ancestor settled on wild land just west of the Brandywine, and began to people the western wilderness with his sons and daughters. It seemed to me, also, like hitching a very small wagon to a very distant star, and the proposal was declined.*

One of my friends observed that those who were most active in urging my appointment to a foreign post were the attorneys and representatives of certain public utilities against which it had been my duty as a public official to wage several legal battles in support of the public interest. He suggested that they harbored the same thought that President Lincoln once so sagely expressed in a similar case. An inconspicuous and not overly competent resident of President Lincoln's home town followed him to Washington and applied for appointment to the foreign consular service. He became such a nuisance that one day the President mentioned the matter to the Secretary of State and requested him to give the offender the appointment. The Secretary replied, "Certainly, Mr. President, where shall I send him?" The President stood by a large library globe; placing his long, bony forefinger upon the City of Washington, he stretched his arms half around the world, placed the other forefinger on the point farthest away from Washington, and replied, "Send him around there."

Whether that thought actuated any of those who gave me their support I never knew. Anyway Congress passed the Act of June 6, 1900, extending civil government in Alaska and authorizing the appointment of two additional district judges for the northerly parts of the great Arctic Territory.

Upon the recommendation of Senator Foster, supported by my local political friends, President McKinley appointed me district judge for the third judicial division of the Territory, which was promptly confirmed by the Senate. My official residence was fixed at Eagle City, on the bank of the Yukon River, about one hundred miles below the great Klondike mining camp, then at the height of its boom. The honor and responsibility of aiding in founding American courts of justice in a vast new territory was accepted in the spirit that my

* In fact Wickersham said he would have much preferred to go to Japan. See p. xv.

forefathers shouldered their rifles in 1776 to aid in establishing the independence of the colonies.*

Albert R. Heilig, a young Tacoma lawyer, member of the Washington legislature which elected Senator Foster, and a competent accountant, accepted an appointment as clerk of the court. George A. Jeffery went with us as stenographer. We quickly packed our personal belongings, tucked my judicial commission and an unbound copy of the newly printed Alaska codes in a grip sack, and were ready to carry the Law into the unknown wilderness.

Under instructions from the Department of Justice we awaited the arrival at Seattle of Judge Arthur H. Noyes, the newly appointed district judge for the Nome division, in order to jointly fix the boundary between the Nome and the Eagle City divisions before proceeding with our judicial labors. This duty was not concluded until after Judge Noyes' arrival at Seattle on the last day of June, when I met him for the first and last time. The judge appeared to be an agreeable man, though he seemed to be immoderately fond of the bottle. I also had the pleasure of then meeting his charming wife, who was en route to Nome with him, and his colleague Alexander McKenzie, who unbeknownst to me was even then plotting a monstrous legal conspiracy that would stain the American legal system and have a lasting impact on my life.

ON COMPARING THE NOME group with the Eagle City group, it seemed to me that my companions were rather unimportant and probably blessed with only moderate ability. Members of the Nome

* Wickersham believed that originally the seat of the Third Judicial Division was to have been located not at Eagle, but at St. Michael, the deep-water port on the Bering Sea near the mouth of the river. He thought the change was due to politicking over who would be slotted for the post of clerk of the court. Wickersham's sponsor, Senator Addison G. Foster, wanted his son Harry to be appointed, and Wickersham thought the senator had the seat moved to Eagle to forestall a rival candidate put forth by Judge H. C. Wallace of San Francisco.

"Well what fools these mortals be! I was, I have no doubt, really assigned or intended to be [assigned] to St. Michael's. Wallace went on to Washington & pressed Dautrick for Clerk at that place. I was then assigned to Eagle City where Dautrick could not go—and Harry Foster is pushed ahead as Clerk!! Wallace is green!" (June 16, 1900). Eventually Senator Foster relented and allowed Wickersham to choose Tacoma lawyer Albert R. Heilig as his clerk.

Unless otherwise noted, all footnotes in this volume are drawn from the transcription of Wickersham's diary in the Alaska Digital Archives.

group were alert, aggressive, and busily engaged in planning huge mining ventures. The members of my modest party felt that they were being shunted to an obscure place in the Yukon wilderness. The great Nome gold camp was everywhere the main topic of conversation. We were not interesting to the Seattle crowds which stood open-mouthed about those bound for Nome.

Our official party was completed by the arrival of Alfred M. Post, of Nebraska, United States attorney, George G. Perry, marshal, and his amiable wife, and Mr. Plato Mountjoy, a special accounting officer from the Department of Justice, who was to install the official system of bookkeeping in the offices of the clerk and the marshal.

ON JULY 2, 1900, we sailed from Seattle on the S.S. *City of Seattle.* On the Fourth we were off the coast of southern Alaska, and that night our children, on the upper stern deck, shot off firecrackers and watched a practice fire drill by the crew.* We stopped at Ketchikan, Wrangell, Treadwell, and Juneau, and then steamed into the narrow and too-often stormy waters of Lynn Canal, at the head of which lay Skagway, the gateway to Alaska and the Yukon. Early the next morning we tied up at the little dock at Haines, on the Portage Bay side of the long narrow peninsula that separates Chilkat inlet from Chilkoot inlet, which leads to Dyea and Skagway. Here we were fortunate in finding a large number of Indians from these inlets at a

* Wickersham does not delve into any family matters in his memoir and this is one of only two references to his son Howard, age six, who accompanied Mr. and Mrs. Wickersham to Alaska. Howard was the baby of the family, a sickly child who was clearly the Judge's favorite, perhaps all the more treasured because an earlier son had died as a toddler. The Judge was in Nome when he received word by mail on March 4, 1902, that eight-year-old Howard had died some two months earlier. The mournful entry in his diary—later crossed out in despair—read: "Oh my son, my son. Would to God I had died . . . and I would as willingly have done it for the light of my life is gone. . . . Oh Howard—Howard—will I never see your sweet face again." Ever the stoic, Wickersham nevertheless held court that morning, without telling anyone of his loss. He later called Howard's death "the greatest loss of my life . . . almost the end of my home life" (October 27, 1905).

On a steamship headed to Alaska in July 1907, he could not help but think back to his first trip north with Howard in 1900: "Seven years ago I was on the *City of Seattle* in this identical neighborhood on my way into the Interior of Alaska the first time. How different things are today with me & my family. Howard then sat on my lap as we crossed the swells—seasick but clinging to me trying to ward it off—bless his frail but courageous body—his death left me an old man" (July 4, 1907).

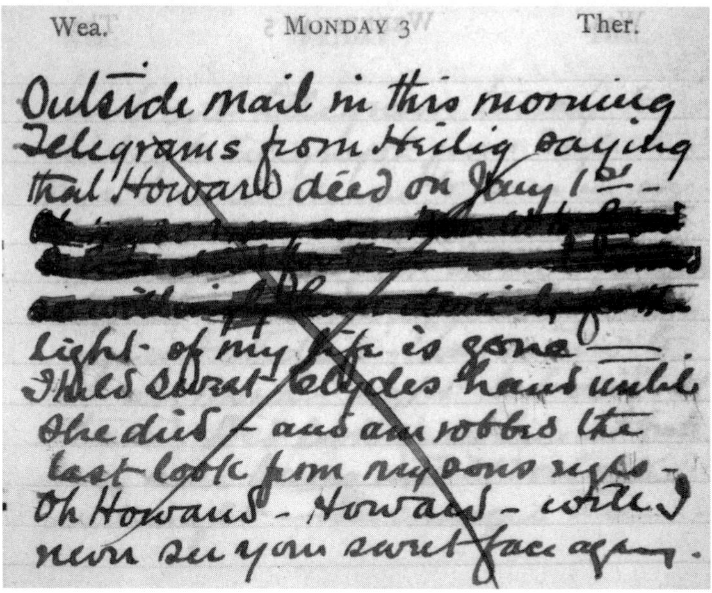

Wea. MONDAY 3 Ther.

Outside mail in this morning
Telegrams from Heilig saying
that Howard died on Jany 1st -
[redacted]
light of my life is gone —
I held sweet Clydes hand until
she died - and am robbed the
last look from my sons eyes -
Oh Howard - Howard - will I
never see your sweet face again.

Howard Wickersham at Eagle in 1900, and the Judge's diary entry when he received word in Nome of Howard's death on March 4, 1902.

(Alaska State Library, Wickersham State Historic Sites Photograph Collection, ASL-PCA-277-004-031 and Wickersham diary March 3, 1902)

The City of Seattle, *the steamship on which the Wickersham party sailed to Alaska in 1900.*

(UAF-1976-0035-00063, Archives, Alaska and Polar Regions, University of Alaska Fairbanks) tribal potlatch, or salmon feast. The Chilkat Indians, and their cousins, the Chilkoots, are members of the Tlingit nation, speak the same language, are divided into the same social clans, and are otherwise so closely related by blood and tribal customs as to constitute one people.

On the 6th day of July our steamer landed us at the White Pass railway dock at Skagway. We were taken in a hack to the Fifth Avenue Hotel, a sprawling three-storied lumber structure, filled with a restless crowd. Some were going "outside" (to Seattle and the States), whereas others were going "inside." There was however, but one topic of conversation—the Klondike gold creeks. We were there at the close of the old Dyea trail days, with all the romance, hardships, and dangers incident to a sixty days' struggle against Arctic blizzards over mountain trails. In Skagway a multitude of railroad laborers were engaged in the erection of shops, engine houses, stations, and warehouses. Terminal switches were filled with loaded freight cars and the wharves with bales of merchandise. Construction work went on night and day. An army of men, with Skagway as their base, were blasting cuts and tunnels in solid mountain walls over the pass and along Lake Bennett. Trains left in the early morning for construction camps along the mountain grades, and over the pass to meet the steamboats at the station on Lake Bennett.

Fortunately the District Court for the First Division of Alaska, Judge Melville C. Brown, presiding, was in session when we arrived at Skagway. At a joint meeting we quickly agreed on a temporary boundary between the Juneau and the Eagle City divisions, and postponed fixing the permanent boundary until we should learn more about the geography of the region. We signed the necessary orders and forwarded certified copies of them to the Department of Justice in Washington.

A gold rush saloon at Skagway, where Wickersham landed in July 1900.
(Alaska State Library, William R. Norton Photograph Collection, ASL-PCA-226-106)

2

DAWSON AND THE KLONDIKE MINES

A million dollar gold bond
could never, never buy,
My memories of the Northland
I'll keep them 'till I die.
I'll treasure them like a miser,
his hoard of gleaming gold—
My memories are my treasure,
and never may be sold.

—Bruce E. Slater

EARLY IN JULY 1900, our party left Skagway over the narrow-gauge railway for our post on the Yukon River. Our train wound its way up the Skagway valley and along the steep mountain sides to White Pass summit, and to a busy town of tents and shacks at the head of Lake Bennett. Since the railway had not yet been completed around Lake Bennett—construction workers were still blasting the grade along the south shore—we transferred to the steamer *Australian*, which carried us to Cariboo Crossing at the foot of the lake. There we were crowded back into small railway passenger coaches and sent on to Whitehorse, where we arrived at midnight. The steamer *Yukoner*, bound for Dawson, was waiting for our train and we were given berths, though many were forced to sleep on the floor or to share berths on the half-time plan.

Our boat left Whitehorse in the early morning. As we steamed northward towards the land of gold and our homes in Alaska, we overtook many belated sailboats loaded with gold-seekers and their supplies.

Late at night we came upon the steamer *Pingree* hard aground on a sandbar in the middle of the river. The crew had worked for two days to get her off, but without success. To lighten ship the cattle on board had been driven into the river and forced to swim to the east bank, and the sheep had been landed on the west bank. The steamer had lifted, only to be forced higher up on the bar by the strong current. Our boat tied up to the bank and heavy cables were attached to the *Pingree* and to the capstan on our boat. Both boats puffed and pulled, the capstan creaked—and the cables broke! All night long both crews worked, and not until ten o'clock the next morning was the *Pingree* freed. When our boat rounded the bar at noon on her way to Dawson, the *Pingree*'s crew were getting the cattle and sheep on board again. It is little wonder that the prices of chops and steaks were high in Dawson.

When our boat landed at the Dawson levee we were informed that there would be no boat going down the river to Eagle City for several days. This enabled us to visit Dawson and the Klondike mines. Our party stayed at a nearby bunkhouse, for all the better hotels were filled. Dawson was then in its heyday as the richest mining camp in the Yukon basin. Its buildings had been constructed the preceding year from logs cut on the ground, or up the river; its streets were quagmires; its waterfront was jammed with hundreds of small boats and scows which had brought its inhabitants from Lindeman and Bennett through the dangers of the Whitehorse Rapids. The Ladue sawmill on the riverbank had furnished as much lumber as its coffee-grinder machinery could cut, and whipsawed lumber from Bennett coming down in the form of boats and scows was used for building purposes. In Government Square, buildings for official use were going up; the Mounted Police barracks, flying the flag of Canada, and the dreaded woodpile hard by, gave warning that a sentence for crime meant hard work; two-story buildings fronting on the levee were covered with signs, which were lighted by kerosene lamps at night, inviting all and sundry to the saloons and dance-halls; large log buildings housed the stores of the Alaska Commercial Company and the North American Trading and Transportation Company; log cabins and tents occupied the back streets.

YEARS BEFORE IN TACOMA I had been appointed city attorney by Mayor Ed S. Orr. Six feet tall, handsome and generous, he was one of the first to join the Dawson stampede, and had established a stage line between Dawson and the Klondike mines. He met my party at the levee with outstretched hand and a happy smile and invited us to visit the mines by his four-horse stage. He introduced us to the Commissioner-Governor, the judges of the courts, other officials and businessmen, many of whom I had known on Puget Sound.*

The next morning the Orr and Tukey stage drawn by four fine horses, driven by Orr, appeared at our bunkhouse at an early hour, and we drove away for a two-day visit to the famous Klondike mines on Bonanza and Eldorado creeks. We followed a bottomless mud road up the Klondike to the mouth of Bonanza gulch, and thence up that stream to Grand Forks. The view up the Klondike valley, as the rising sun tinted the distant peaks of the Rocky Mountain Range, was well worth the early morning trip. Our excitement increased as we entered the gateway of the gold gulches and saw a thousand men mining gold along the famous creeks and on the high bench claims. Gravel dumps, open cuts in the valley, hillside mining, cabins, miners at work casting the rich paystreaks into the long sluice boxes where rushing water carried away the muck, silt, and lighter rocks, leaving only the gold behind, made a picture never to be forgotten.

We arrived at the Grand Forks hotel in time for lunch, and took rooms for the night in that sprawling, and sometimes brawling, log hotel. That afternoon we inspected Clarence Berry's rich claim on Eldorado Creek and others like it. These were the most valuable claims on the creeks; the exposed gravel paystreaks fairly glowed with nuggets and heavy flakes of gold dust. Mr. Berry rather recklessly, it seemed to me, invited us to dig all the gold we wanted from the fully exposed golden paystreak, limiting us, however, to digging with our hands. Two greatly excited six-year-old boys, my son and Mr. Heilig's, and his young daughter Florence, at once began to hunt and dig like terriers after rats. Each child soon had a fistful of bright yellow gold nuggets, while the elders of the party were

* In 1910 Ed Orr would be the Republican nominee for delegate against Wickersham. Therefore the Judge had to run under the banner of the "Insurgent Republicans." Wickersham thought Orr had renounced his American citizenship in Dawson, but claimed the former Tacoma mayor "is probably the most dangerous opponent they could have given me as he is big, strong, good humored, silent, obedient—an ideal candidate for the 'big interests'" (June 29, 1910). Nevertheless, Wickersham beat Orr handily.

The Wickersham party in the Klondike in the summer of 1900. From left to right: Stenographer George A. Jeffery, Mrs. Deborah S. Wickersham, Judge James Wickersham and his son Howard, Court Clerk Albert R. Heilig and his son Reed, Mrs. Heilig, and her daughter Florence.

(Alaska State Library, Wickersham State Historic Sites Photograph Collection, ASL-PCA-277-004-043)

satisfied with one or two larger nuggets of the value of ten dollars or so. It was an exciting hour for the three children, who greatly pleased the owner and other miners by their happy cries as they dug out some particularly bright nugget. When they had recovered all the nuggets their hands could hold, and quite as much mud as their hands, faces, and clothes could hold, they were dragged out of the paystreak by their equally happy and excited mothers and taken to the creek for cleaning. We had dug gold in the richest part of the richest paystreak in the Klondike, and the result was interesting to us as chechacos (newcomers), a delight to the children and their parents and quite evidently a pleasure to the on-looking miners.

The Grand Forks roadhouse was a typical wild-west saloon and gambling house, without pistols or bad men. The main room on the ground floor had the office in one corner, the bar along one wall, gambling tables and games—said to be on the square—in the center, and the dancing floor at the rear. The second story, where guests' rooms were located, was supported by cross-beams which rested on a row of upright round logs along the center of the lower room. After a good dinner we viewed the dancing and gambling as nonchalantly as if we were quite used to such things. The strident music of the fiddles, the calls of the dance director, the whirling-dervish performances of some of the dancers, the promenade of the miners and their partners to the bar after each dance, the hazard of large sums on the turn of a card, the drop of a ball or the fall of dice stirred us, but official position and the presence of wives kept us merely spectators.

IN THE WINTER AND early spring before our visit to these creeks the miners were engaged in cutting timber and dragging the logs down into the gulch for use on their creek claims. When the spring thaw sent water through the trenches cut by the logs, prospectors soon discovered indications of gold on the hillside far above the paystreaks in the creek gravels. Finally the source of all the gold was found to be a high gravel deposit called the "white channel." Chechako Hill, Gold Hill, and other hillside mines soon added to the wealth of the Klondike. We were allowed to go far underground in these excavations and were greatly interested in the removal of the frozen paystreak by means of woodfires and steam points. These two days along the Klondike gulches filled our envious souls with the hope that somewhere on the Alaska side of the line prospectors might find equally rich diggings and that we might aid in developing an American Klondike.

For two more days we enjoyed Dawson, its people and their strange frontier mining camp, their saloons, dance halls, churches, banks, tent stores, and the excited polyglot mob that milled in and out by day and night seeking for something to inflame their jaded appetites, always under the watchful eye of redcoated policemen. We visited the newspaper offices, heard the tales of new strikes and stampedes to faraway creeks, met the camp's famous characters, Big Alex McDonald, Swiftwater Bill Gates, Tom McGowan, and many others. In one of the banks a gentlemanly clerk named Bob Service was introduced, smilingly, as a writer of poetry.*

Tales of suddenly acquired fortune by all sorts of men in all kinds of ways, and of cunning schemes to despoil them of it, were current, as in other great mining camps. The Dick Lowe fraction was pointed out to us as we passed up the gulch, and the story of the owner's luck as a locator was related to us with gusto. It seemed that Dick had a fair and legal preference to locate a full claim at another place on the creek, which everyone believed to be rich. Through some unfair scheme he was not permitted to locate there, but, finally, to get rid of his constant complaints about official injustice, he was informed that he might have this small fraction in lieu of his full claim. Grumblingly he accepted the fraction as better than nothing. Some peculiarity on the bedrock of the fraction, or possibly the formation of a small side gulch from the mother paystreak into the main creek at this point, had filled this spot "plumb full of gold," as the narrator told it. The full claim he had cried for turned out to be of little value.

Another miner who had struck it rich became infatuated with a singer and dancer on the Dawson stage. He spent his gold dust freely to gain her favor but with little success. Becoming desperate, he proposed marriage; she coyly murmured her acceptance conditioned on receipt of the simple wedding gift of her weight in gold dust; he agreed but stipulated that she should live with him

---

* Wickersham is mistaken, because Robert Service did not come to Dawson until years later.

for one year. The betrothal concluded, the fiancée weighed in on the theater stage before a full house. Her "lover"—not, of course, her future husband—had cunningly filled her corset with twenty pounds of fine bird shot, which enhanced her value by about five thousand dollars. The wedding gift, based on the displacement of the bride—and ballast—was promptly paid and the marriage ceremony was performed on the stage to the delight of the spectators who spent the night drinking champagne at twenty dollars a bottle at the groom's expense. Love's young dream lasted for only a brief period, the woman and her lover skipping outside on the first spring boat downriver.

A Forty Mile prospector strongly addicted to drink, as most Yukon prospectors were in those days, had located a claim on upper Bonanza Creek which a group of crooks concluded must contain a rich paystreak. Three of them got the owner drunk, and persuaded him to sell his claim to them for eight hundred dollars, and a worthless wildcat claim on the west branch of the creek. He delivered a deed to the sharpers, accepted the eight hundred dollars and a deed to the wildcat claim, and continued on a glorious drunk until he had spent every cent of the money. In the meantime the sharks had conveyed his mine by deed, duly recorded, to a confederate who posed as an innocent purchaser for value. The prospector begged the swindlers to give him back his claim and offered to return their money and the claim they had deeded to him, but they refused to do so. He told his story to the police and then to a lawyer, but failed to get his upper Bonanza claim back. Finally he concluded to work the wildcat claim. His first hole struck a golden paystreak on Eldorado Creek, the richest creek in the Klondike. The upper Bonanza proved worthless.

EVERY WESTERN MINING CAMP has its quota of derelicts. They are generally chair warmers, or swampers in saloons. Almost always one of these men will be known familiarly as "the old man" and be allowed, along with better customers, to have a regular dram of liquor on first appearing in the morning. Of course, he is expected to be on hand when some tipsy miner is throwing his poke on the bar with a loud "come on boys and have a drink on me," and in these ways he does not often lack for drinks, though he may sometimes want bread. An "outside" barkeeper, who had been employed in one of the numerous Dawson saloons, had brought with him some new ideas about running such a resort, and when "the old man" came for his regular morning's "morning," he was ordered to clear out. The old man determined upon a speedy and public revenge. That night when the saloon was crowded the old man furtively entered and took up a position at the end of the bar near the door. Suddenly he stood on the bar rail, waved a stick of dynamite with a burning fuse, and shouted at the barkeeper, "I will blow you to hell, damn you." In a minute the room was empty, the barkeeper being the first to go through the front door into the sixty below zero weather outside, with only his linen coat to shield him from the wintry blasts. The crowd fled in terror from the front of the saloon expecting momentarily to see it crash into the street.

The barkeeper ran up the street shouting for the police and quickly a redcoat policeman appeared. The policeman either had more courage or less sense than the scared barkeeper, for he ran to the front window and entered the saloon. The old man was behind the bar with a bottle in his hand pouring out his third drink of the best liquor in the house. As the officer entered the old man shouted, "Come on, sergeant, and take a drink on the house with me." What had appeared to be a stick of dynamite was a ten-inch cut of bologna sausage, into the end of which the old man had forced a six-inch fuse. The whole town laughed, the new barkeeper was discharged, and the old man had his regular morning dram thereafter.

Volumes of romantic stories with a basis in fact might be collected from these Klondike prospectors and miners. Every mile of trail between Skagway and Dawson had its own stories of hardship and adventure, of heroic service by generous men and women, of defeat, of injustice, and of crime. Every stampeder over the high mountain divides and down the unknown rivers, every prospector and trader in this wilderness of the Arctic, related experiences worthy of preservation in song and story. Only the few rare experiences will be remembered. Heroism is commonplace, success is rare, disappointment and defeat are the rule. We could not take the time to gather this wealth of romance, for our thoughts were on the Alaska wilderness far below the Klondike, whither our duty called us. Our boat was at the levee, our friends had wished us success in establishing American courts and law and order in the Alaska-Yukon basin. They were particularly interested in the development of mining there, and spoke hopefully of finding in that vast wilderness a great mining camp equal to Dawson and the Klondike. They promised to follow us into the Alaska mountains as soon as our prospectors should make the big strike that would justify their coming.*

* When Wickersham returned to the Klondike for a visit a decade later, the sad changes were ample proof of the transience of mining camp prosperity.

"Arrived in Dawson this morning early. We went up to the poor old 'Regina' [hotel]—with its gilt rubbed off, unpainted & poorly kept it is a hobo reminder of the early days of 1900. The town is going to rack and ruin. It is a pitiful sight to see a town die" (October 2, 1910).

North American Trading and Transportation Company (NAT&T Co.) store at Eagle on the bank of the Yukon River.

(North American Transportation and Trading Company Collection UAF-1995-190-41, Archives, Alaska and Polar Regions, University of Alaska Fairbanks)

3

PLANTING AMERICAN COURTS IN THE WILDERNESS

A greenwood isle in the Yukon's flow,
lies 'neath an Arctic mountain crest;
Eagles fly north when south winds blow,
and raise their young in the old crag nest.

ON SUNDAY, JULY 15, 1900, we arrived at Eagle City on the steamer *John Cudahy*, via Dawson. At the steamboat landing we were met by the entire population headed by the acting mayor, a Mr. Querry, who undertook to get us settled. For temporary sleeping-quarters we were given possession of a furnished log cabin on the military reservation and we took our meals at the Eagle log-cabin restaurant.

Above a beautiful clear-water stream called Mission Creek rises the rocky wall of Eagle Bluff. Upon the summit of this peak eagles had built their nest. In midstream opposite the town there is a small island covered with evergreen trees, which suggested to Moses Mercier, a French-Canadian and the first fur trader on the upper river for the Alaska Commercial Co., the name for the post established by him there in 1874—Belle Isle. When American prospectors in 1886 found gold on the Forty Mile, the Belle Isle trading station was moved to the mouth of that stream; and not until the United States created a military reserve below Eagle Bluff and built Fort Egbert in 1899 was the site again occupied by white men. A company of infantry under the command of Colonel P. H. Ray then occupied the reserve. The town was established alongside the military post; a forest of spruce interspersed with white birch, covered the beautiful townsite and the surrounding rolling hills.

The Alaska Commercial Company and the North American Trading and Transportation Company each maintained a large store there with good stocks of merchandise supplied by summer boats via St. Michael. A custom house, in charge of a deputy, took toll of the trade between Alaska and Canada; a Presbyterian church under charge of Rev. James W. Kirk; a Catholic hospital and church in charge of Father Francis Monroe, S. J.; two restaurants; and four or five log cabin saloons made up the business part of the town.

Purchasing a set of house logs from George Dribelbis for seventy-five dollars and a town lot from a squatter for one hundred dollars, with Dribelbis' assistance I soon erected my log cabin. It was sixteen feet wide, twenty-four feet long, seven feet high to the top of the side walls and ten feet from the floor to the center ridge pole, and, across the back, a lean-to kitchen eight feet wide, completed the structure. The roof consisted of closely-placed poles running from the ridge pole to the side walls, covered with a foot of moss, eight inches of turf and lastly gravel. The side walls were well caulked with moss; rough boards salvaged from an old Yukon River boat were used for flooring; half-windows were installed and front and rear doors. We made some of our furniture, bought a bedstead and some chairs, an air-tight heating stove for the large room, a cheap cookstove for the kitchen, made our shelves and a kitchen table, put down some carpets we had brought from the outside, moved in and had one of the best and warmest cabins in town. It was always comfortable, even when the temperature outside was sixty degrees below zero. For our office the clerk rented a small log cabin with two half-windows, the marshal rented another for his office and a jail, and in a short time we were ready for pioneer court work.

THE THIRD JUDICIAL DIVISION was sparsely peopled, for within its wide boundaries there were fewer than fifteen hundred white persons according to the 1900 census just then completed. The area of the division, however, was enormous. Its northern boundary extended along the Arctic Ocean easterly from the 141st meridian to the mouth of the Colville River; thence southerly to Mount McKinley and Lake Clark to 60 degrees north latitude; thence west to Bering Sea. Its eastern boundary was the 141st meridian from the Arctic coast to Cape St. Elias, and the Pacific shore. Its greatest length from the northeast corner on the Arctic coast to Attu Island was more than

Judge James Wickersham with his wife Deborah (left) and an unidentified woman in front of the Wickersham's log cabin home in Eagle.
(Alaska State Library, Wickersham State Historic Sites Photograph Collection, ASL-PCA-277-019-022)

two thousand miles, and it contained about three hundred thousand square miles.

It contained no courthouse, jail, school or other public building. There were only four log churches within its widespread boundaries. There was not a mile of public wagon road or trail. No money had been appropriated or promised by Congress for any of these purposes, except that the district judge had been authorized to reserve two town lots and build a courthouse and a jail out of license funds.

Our personal finances were in even a worse plight. After our appointment in June, we had paid our traveling expenses from the States to the Yukon, built our cabins, supported our families, and paid official expenses. Our paychecks covering the period from June to November were not received until the following February, and were always three to four months late. One of the officials, gazing at his last silver dollar with its legend—"In God We Trust"—sighed and suggested that it ought to read: "In the A. C. Co. We Trust." That company financed us and thereby loyally aided in establishing American government in the Alaska-Yukon basin, as it had aided the American fur trade and the efforts of prospectors to open the country to mining development.

We also had to contend with another financial handicap which affected all our court collections for government licenses, fees, fines, and other business. Practically all the money in circulation in this part of Alaska was Canadian currency. All the United States gold and currency coming into Dawson was retained by the Dawson banks for their own remittances to the States, and in lieu of American money they handed out worn Canadian bills to all persons coming down the river into Alaska. In this way they effectually barred all United States gold or currency from coming into our part of Alaska but flooded us with their own Canadian bills. These Canadian bank bills were so heavily discounted in the United States that they would not be accepted in Washington. The clerk of our court, however, was obliged to accept them or stop public business. At the close of each quarter the clerk appealed to the mercantile companies and businessmen—for there was not a bank, national or private, in this district—for United States currency to make his remittances to the Treasury. It took five years to get enough United States gold coin and currency into our district to enable us to carry on the public business with United States money.

The act of Congress of June 6, 1900, establishing our court empowered the district judge to reserve a tract of public land, forty by one hundred feet for a courthouse site, and another of equal size for a jail. The court was further authorized to cause a courthouse to be constructed at an expense not to exceed five thousand dollars, to be paid for out of local license funds when collected by the court. Public spirited citizens in Eagle procured the abandonment of two squatters' lots for these two public buildings and they were reserved by order of the court for that use.

The day after our arrival at Eagle City the clerk and I immediately began to collect mercantile and saloon license fees. There were then in Eagle five saloons doing a flourishing trade and three stores. Each saloon was required to pay an annual license fee of one thousand dollars, and each store paid a fixed percentage upon its annual sales.*

We soon collected enough license money to justify the erection of public buildings. There being no architect in the country, after much talk and more wasted paper, we drew and agreed upon plans and specifications. We determined to use sawed lumber manufactured

* Another source of license fees came from a "tax" on prostitution. Due to the chronic lack of funds for law enforcement, a common practice in most early mining camps, including Eagle, was to fund the police department by levying a fine on prostitution. Though both prostitution and the government kickback were clearly against the law, most officials—including Judge Wickersham—thought this officially sanctioned extortion scheme a necessary evil.

The Judge would learn of at least "two notorious . . . houses of ill fame" in Eagle and explained the local commissioner had instituted a plan "to fine them a reasonable amount each quarter in vindication of the law and as an aid to the fund to maintain the police department." Apparently the pimps refused to pay the fine and the Judge wanted to teach them a lesson.

"Last year they were arrested . . . and they engaged [a] lawyer and owing to the lax conditions procured the jury to acquit in the face of overwhelming evidence, and this they are now again to attempt. . . . I have instructed [the commissioner and the marshal] . . . that they must employ the whole power of the government to convict since it is a case of defiance of the courts by the criminal class" (December 7, 1900).

When the saloon men and gamblers realized that Wickersham was not a judge with whom they could trifle, they immediately surrendered and agreed to pay all fines and costs. The Judge was both pleased and disgusted.

"The War [between the bars, the brothels and the courts] is over: I have been much surprised at the weakness and cowardice of the men of Eagle in this matter. Men who ought to have stood by the courts have joined in abusing them, and have [been] in the most flagrant violation of the law and their oaths" (December 11, 1900).

at the military post's sawmill, but here we met one of those bureaucratic nightmares with which Alaskans were all too familiar. The commander informed us that he was not permitted to furnish lumber, even at commercial rates, for any use other than the construction of the post buildings. He suggested that the only way the Department of Justice could procure lumber from the War Department sawmill was for us to apply to the Department of Justice in Washington, D.C., and secure a permit from the War Department to use the mill, and that if we succeeded in securing such a permit we must buy our own logs from loggers who would cut them in the public forest along the upper river and float them down to the mill. We could then employ mill men and saw and dress the lumber at our own expense. It would take at least four months by the slow dog team mails via Dawson and Skagway to get the permit, but since there was no other way to secure the much-needed lumber, we were obliged to adopt this suggestion. The letter asking for the use of this idle mill to saw lumber for the public buildings at Eagle started on its long journey to Washington in the next month's mail bag.*

CHIEF CHARLEY, HEAD OF the Charley River band of Tena Indians, was the first litigant to appeal to the new court officials for justice. He came up the Yukon in a birch bark canoe which he had paddled a hundred miles against the current, escorted by a dozen other fighting men of his band, each in his own birch bark canoe, with a determination to get justice if he had to get it by force. When this hostile fleet landed at Eagle someone directed him to the clerk of the court, who sent him to interview the marshal. That officer advised him to consult the prosecuting attorney and this official sidestepped by directing him to consult the judge. To each of these officials the old chief had told the same straight story, but none of

---

* Due to the bureaucratic mind-set of Fort Egbert commander Capt. Charles Farnsworth, who refused to allow the Justice Department the use of the post sawmill to build a courthouse and jail until he heard from Washington, D.C., the red tape stalled the project all winter. Not until December did Wickersham hear by letter that his sawmill request to the War Department the previous July had been approved. He drew up plans for the buildings in January, let the contracts in February, and oversaw construction through the end of April. On May 10, 1901, Wickersham dedicated the first U.S. courthouse in the Yukon basin, which he proudly called the most northerly in the world. His son Howard raised the flag (May 10, 1901).

Chief Charley (right) of the Charley River band, with Chiefs Roderick (left) and Issac (center). Wickersham said Charley was "his first litigant" in a case that involved Eagle Jack's theft of Charley's dog.

(Alaska State Library, Wickersham State Historic Sites Photograph Collection, ASL-PCA-277-4-95)

them did anything about it. So the big Indian came striding up to my cabin and knocked on the door. On being admitted and given a seat he looked me straight in the eyes with a level and steady gaze which betokened both honesty and courage and told me what he had come for.

He introduced himself by saying, "Me Chief Charley from Charley River. You big chief here?"

Yes, I told him, I was; whereupon he added, "Any odder chief big as you?" No, I modestly admitted. I was the biggest chief in Eagle, all the time wondering what important tribal matter he was bringing to me. He seemed anxious to have my status as the big chief settled, and later I learned that each of the other officials had at first admitted he was the biggest chief in Eagle, but failed to qualify when Charley stated his business.

Having concluded that I was the big chief he was looking for, he then stated his business, "All right, you big chief, I tell you. Eagle Jack steal my dog at Nation River. He got my dog at Eagle village, one mile. You big chief you get my dog; bring him me. If you not get my dog I get my dog. Maybe some Indian get hurt. Maybe you get my dog?"

I HAD STUDIED THE old chief as carefully as he had studied me, and by this time I would have approved his bond for any reasonable amount, for his fearlessness, simple speech, and apparent honesty had won my confidence. There was no doubt in my mind of the truth of his statement and reaching for my hat I said, "Come with me, Charley."

He walked uprightly by my side as one big chief should walk with another down to the A.C. Co. store. "Wait here, Charley, and we will get your dog." He sat on the store step while I found a deputy marshal who knew just enough law to obey without question any order a superior officer might give him. Charley described the dog and the Indian who had stolen it, and I instructed the deputy to carry a folded paper in his hand to the Eagle village, about a mile upstream from the town, find the dog, and deliver him to the Chief. In the meantime I sat on the store step with the Chief and we talked about fishing and building a schoolhouse for Indian children.

Within an hour the deputy brought in the dog and Charley returned to his canoe leading the animal with the full assurance that he had found the biggest chief in Eagle. Whatever may be said about the want of regularity in this action it prevented an unhappy quarrel and probably a fight between the Eagle and the Charley River people, and possibly the death of Jack, for we learned that each Charley River Indian had his gun hidden in his canoe, and the old chief was in a fighting mood.

PROSPECTORS ARE INVARIABLY OPTIMISTS. Most of them then in Alaska, having gazed enviously upon five-gallon tin cans filled with placer gold in the Klondike, hoped to locate an equally rich camp on this side of the border. They were searching the hills between the Yukon and the Tanana, using Eagle, Circle, and Rampart as bases of supplies. We expected to aid them by promptly deciding all controversies and by establishing recorders at favored points.

Though there was no pressing court business downriver that first summer, I declared a special term of court to be held at Rampart on August 20 in order to collect license fees and to see the country. On August 17 we took passage on the A. C. Co. sternwheeler *Susie*, a palatial steamboat constructed after the style of those running on the Mississippi River, a large, flat-bottomed, light-draft boat, with two smokestacks, high decks, and a gallant display of cabin lights. She made a strange but beautiful spectacle as she sped downstream in the Arctic twilight, like a fairy palace floating noiselessly through the dark green forests.

Between Eagle and Circle there were no towns or permanent settlements, but here and there on the bank of the river was a roadhouse, or a mail carrier's or a woodchopper's cabin. Circle City is situated on the left bank of the Yukon just below where it breaks from the highlands and floods the many channels that thread the flats for two hundred miles. It was a bleak, log-cabin town, except for one or two recently constructed corrugated iron warehouses, which were the only signs of late improvement. Prior to the discovery of the Klondike, some four years before, it was a busy port of entry, but since that event, it had been almost abandoned. However it was still the supply camp where prospectors outfitted for the Birch Creek mines, twenty-five to fifty miles to the westward. While our boat lay at the levee front, the clerk and the marshal visited the saloons and the stores on a license-collecting tour, and with some success, though many promised to pay on our way back from Rampart.

Rampart is located below the Yukon flats in the Rampart Canyon, where the great river is again gathered between two banks. Minook Creek empties into the river just above the long line of log cabins that comprised the town at that time, and a trail led out to the mines up the creek. In addition to the two big mercantile companies, there were small stores tended by Al Mayo, the old-time fur trader, and John Minook, the half-breed prospector and miner. Most of the cabins were then empty, their owners having gone to the new Nome strike the preceding fall.

I held court at Rampart on August 20 in one of the North American Trading and Transportation Company's (NAT&T Co.) warehouses. I sat behind a lumber counter; the clerk had a table; but there was little business to be transacted. Two or three miners were trying to get into a lawsuit, but fortunately for them there were no lawyers in Rampart to prepare their case for trial, so they settled it among themselves instead!* The clerk and the marshal collected license fees, and I signed a few orders. A prisoner, charged with the larceny of a dog and food supplies from a trapper's cache, was bound over to the grand jury at the Circle City term to be held the following month; some papers in a civil suit were filed with the clerk, who also gathered in a few license fees, and court adjourned.

MY FIRST JURY TERM in the third district court was set to convene at Circle City on September 3, 1900, but thanks to the vagaries of river travel and the hazards of sandbars, it proved an eventful journey both going and coming. After our brief excursion to Rampart we had returned to Eagle, and departed downriver once again on August 31, this time on the sternwheeler *Sarah*, which was soon high and dry on a sandbar.

Sticking on sandbars was an inevitable fact of life in those early days. The best story I ever heard about this peril involved the Rev. Hudson Stuck, archdeacon of the Yukon. One of his admirers tells this story of the archdeacon's trip to Fairbanks on his launch, the *Pelican*. He was going up the Tanana River but missed his course and ran the

* Wickersham said Rampart had "many messy controversys [*sic*]—but nothing ready for court" (August 20, 1900).

The sternwheeler Sarah *at the dock in Eagle. She was stuck on a sandbar in the Yukon Flats for three days in the late summer of 1900, forcing Wickersham and his court party to travel the last sixty miles to Circle City in rowboats.*

(Alaska State Library, William R. Norton Photograph Collection, ASL-PCA-276-537) boat into shallow water and grounded. The water was falling and he remained there two days before a steamboat came along to which he made signals of distress.

The captain of the larger craft brought his boat opposite Dr. Stuck's small launch—now almost out of water—some two hundred yards from the steamboat channel, and shouted through his megaphone.

"Ship, ahoy! Who are you?"

The distance, and probably his deafness, rendered the reply indistinct, for the choleric skipper caught only the word "stuck."

He repeated his inquiry in a louder voice and again the word "stuck" reached his ear.

"Yes, any damn fool can see you are stuck, but what's your name?"

When for a third time his ear caught the word "stuck" he impatiently rang the engine-room bell for full speed ahead and left the little launch and the kind-hearted missionary stuck on the bar!

During our trip on the *Sarah* in the summer of 1900, about sixty miles above Circle the steamer ran out of the channel and grounded in shallow water. For three days she stirred the shifting sands with her wheel and sparred off with her poles and tackle without moving a hundred feet or getting back into the river's current. On Sunday afternoon the court party, including myself, other court officials and jurors, set off in two small rowboats sixty miles downstream to Circle where court was set to convene the next day.

It was to be an all-night trip, and as we were none too warmly clad, I had instructed the deputy to take a large hamper of food supplies from the boat, sufficient for a generous midnight lunch and for next morning's breakfast. As a precautionary measure, I also recommended he purchase from the steward a quart bottle of Cyrus Noble Kentucky whiskey, so that in case of accident or other necessity, there might be some stimulant along. With the aid of this hamper and bottle and general good luck, we reached Circle the next day.

I advised the deputy to add the sum paid for the whiskey to his subsistence account for that trip, charging the Department of Justice for "one bottle of subsistence, five dollars!" Suspicious officials in the Washington office wasted much time and good paper in communications addressed to the accountant, making inquiries about it, questioning his integrity. He had the entire sympathy and assistance of the other Circle officials who offered suggestions, but none seemed to satisfy the Washington clerks and he never was paid for "one bottle of subsistence, five dollars."

THE FIRST CIRCLE CITY court term met in the Episcopal log church and hospital, a squat, one-story building rented from the mission for that purpose. A grand jury was impaneled; it returned three indictments, one for murder, another for rape, and a third for larceny of a dog and supplies from a trapper's cache. The man charged with murder was found guilty of manslaughter and sentenced to ten years in the penitentiary; the larcenist pleaded guilty and was sentenced to two years; the man charged with rape was acquitted.* The court concluded all its business, civil and criminal, and adjourned after a session of only seven days.

---

* The defendant in Wickersham's first murder case was Charles Hubbard, a man from Dawson City who freely admitted he shot and killed Thomas McNamee at Fort Yukon on May 20, 1900. Many in the Yukon Valley believed it was "justifiable homicide."

McNamee owed Hubbard five thousand dollars and had skipped out of Dawson into Alaska after promising he would repay the debt. Hubbard trailed McNamee all the way down the river to Fort Yukon. "I was aggravated and I hardly knew what I was doing," he admitted. "I helped him at Juneau and also in Dawson.... I had no money left so I followed him, borrowing from friends at Fortymile. I caught up with him at Fort Yukon and demanded the money.... He replied insultingly. I then drew my revolver and fired, but missed. McNamee ran into a cabin and just as he was closing it I fired again.... I then went to Beaumont's saloon and gave up the revolver" (*Daily Klondike Nugget*, May 30, 1900).

Newspaper reports in Dawson concluded that Hubbard had ample cause to kill McNamee. "When Hubbard reached Circle... he was penniless and... his very clothing was in rags. He had no shoes, and the old moccasins he wore hardly sufficed to cover his feet. Under these conditions it is not to be much wondered at that he shot the man who, though having plenty of money, merely insulted him when asked to pay what had been loaned him as an act of friendship" (*Daily Klondike Nugget*, August 25, 1900).

While a miners' meeting would have probably cleared Hubbard of any wrongdoing, Judge Wickersham would not take such a lenient attitude, especially since it was the first capital crime in his court. "Grand jury... utterly refuse to indict Hubbard for the murder of McNamee. Called them in and gave them very pointed instructions as to their duty. Will hold Hubbard over to next grand jury if no indictment found. There is an evident inclination on part of the grand jury to refuse to return indictments. Stringent measures may have to be resorted to" (September 4, 1900).

Wickersham never thought that Hubbard's conviction for manslaughter and ten-year sentence at McNeil Island Penitentiary was unduly harsh, even though the Judge would be hounded for years by friends of the defendant pleading for commutation of the sentence (January 21, 1903). Ultimately he would acquiesce

The two convicted men were sent on their way to the United States penitentiary at McNeil Island in the state of Washington. I was obliged to remain at Circle for a few days longer, to write up and sign the records and to settle the accounts for the term.

And then an Arctic snowstorm came roaring out of the leaden skies. The A.C. Co. agent assured us that a boat going to Dawson was due in three days, but it did not arrive. We impatiently waited and watched the northern skyline for smoke for many days.

On Sunday we attended church services held by Episcopal Bishop Peter T. Rowe in the room in which court had convened the previous week. Two incidents particularly attracted my attention. The first was that while the Bishop was dressed in his beautiful church canonicals, he wore at the same time a pair of Indian-made moosehide moccasins. We heard later that he had forgotten his shoes at some trail roadhouse where he had changed to moccasins as a rest for his sore feet. While those who saw smiled at his rough footwear, they loved the good bishop just a little more for his disregard of the conventionalities of dress.

Another incident, which occurred while the church offering was being collected, I did not understood until later. Charles Claypool, a young attorney passing the contribution plate, paused upon reaching a young merchant, and conversed with him in a low tone. Though the man in the pew had already put a five-dollar gold piece on the plate, Deacon Claypool whispered "come again" and stood with arm and plate outstretched as if no contribution had been made. As he put another five dollars on the plate, he said, "What do you want, you blackmailer?" The deacon replied in a stage whisper, "I want the whole twenty-five dollars you beat me out of in the poker game last night," and remained patiently waiting with outstretched plate in his face. Everybody in the church turned to see what had caused

---

in 1906, apparently to win the favor of Washington Senator Levi Ankeny, when the Judge was in the midst of his unsuccessful three-year struggle for reconfirmation by the U.S. Senate.

"I...called on Senator Ankeny," Wickersham wrote on February 16, 1906, "and informed him that I would now approve the pardon of Charlie Hubbard whom I sentenced at Circle in 1900 for 15 [actually only 10] years for killing [McNamee] at Ft. Yukon. Senator Ankeny has been trying for three or four years to get Hubbard pardoned but so far without success owing to my refusal to recommend it." In spite of Wickersham's change of heart, however, the Justice Department denied the request (May 7, 1906).

the delay. Blushing like a schoolgirl, he took out an additional fifteen dollars and dropped it on the plate, whereupon the now smiling deacon passed on his way. Deacon Claypool later explained that "Joe needed a little Christian chastening; the church needed the money; and I needed the happy glow of righteous satisfaction which I failed to get in the poker game."*

DAYS PASSED—A WEEK—TEN DAYS—AND winter came shrieking on northeast Arctic blasts, carrying clouds of snow and clogging the river current, but no boat arrived. We prepared to go up to Eagle in a poling boat, with tents and hired boatmen, but postponed the trip one more day hoping for calmer weather.† And, then, on September 22, an Indian boy from the top of the great woodpile gave out the happy signal "steam b-o-a-t!" Far down the Yukon slough we saw white puffs of steam, and in a few hours the *Susie* and the *Rock Island* blew their whistles and landed in front of the A. C. Co. store. The mail bags were hurriedly exchanged, the Circle freight piled on the bank, the gang plank was hauled in, and we were off upriver under a full head of steam, for both boats and cargoes had to reach Dawson before the freeze-up.

ON ARRIVING AT EAGLE every official went to work to bank up his cabin and get in a supply of wood for our first winter. I spent two weeks in splitting and piling wood in a tent at my back door, and another week in banking up the walls of the house to keep the cold from getting beneath the floor.

In the fall a prudent Yukon pioneer always killed a moose or a caribou, or both, and stored the meat in an outdoor cache, where it froze and remained fresh all winter. Captain Charles S. Farnsworth, the commander of Fort Egbert, had established a hunting camp on the divide between Mission Creek and the Forty Mile River, about fifty miles from Eagle, and had sent hunters and a squad of

* Fearful of revenge, Claypool explained to Wickersham that when it would be his rival's turn to pass "the plate next Sunday . . . I'll not be there" (September 9, 1900).

† "No steamer yet. Making arrangements to go up the river afoot: will take a boat & two men to pole her along shore to carry provisions, tent, & etc. Snowing hard, and will wait day or two until weather settles. Will take 10 to 15 days to Eagle!" (September 21, 1900).

Wickersham's desk and legal library in Eagle City.
(Alaska State Library, Jack Allman Manuscript Collection, ASL-MS-220-01-04-09)

soldiers there to kill caribou for the post. He invited me to go with him on a hunting trip to kill my winter's meat. Early in October we followed the post pack train over the hills near great herds of browsing caribou.

Frank Lee and Charley Webb, packers and hunters employed to shoot for the post, had been on the range for several days, and when we arrived they had fifty or more caribou carcasses hanging on their racks. With Lee as a guide we went out to get a caribou. The captain killed one but my gun was evidently "out of focus" for it missed a fair broadside of a big bull at close range!* A day later four caribou fell from my gun's muzzle, and not far away either, for the first shot stampeded the great herd which almost ran us down in their mad flight. From a small butte on the divide we could see literally thousands of these fine fat animals. We also saw big timber wolves among these herds. Wolves hover about the caribou herds, subsisting on the young, the old, the sick, and the wounded, though a single wolf can run down and kill the strongest and fleetest bull in the band.

On returning to Eagle with my four caribou a friendly butcher cut them up into steaks, roasts, and other cuts ready for cooking. We placed these cuts on a board in a tent thirty degrees below zero, and froze them separately, then piled them into a big box in the outdoor cache, where they rattled like boards. When we wanted a steak or a roast, we picked it out of the box, put it into a skillet, pot, or pan, and cooked it. It was just as fresh as when the animal was killed. A quarter of a fat moose, purchased from a hunter, was cut, frozen, and cached in the same way.

---

* Charley Webb would be one of the five members of Wickersham's Mount McKinley expedition in 1903, and his partner Frank Lee was an equally tough frontiersman, not an easy man for the Judge to keep up with on his first caribou hunt. "We rode over mountains, along precipices, over snowfields and a thousand places where a Sioux Indian would have hesitated. Cap [Farnsworth] saw band of caribou feeding on a high steep mountainside, and Lee conducted us around and near them on horseback. We dismounted and [Farnsworth] and I approached them creeping, while Lee held the horses. We had to climb mountain. Lee gave me his gun—not used to it and nervous—I missed but the Capt. killed one buck caribou. If I had kept my own gun think I could have shot the whole herd with buck shot—they were so close" (October 7, 1900).

THE TOWN OF EAGLE is built on a beautiful tract of gravely bench land, lightly forested with small spruce and birch. It lies thirty to fifty feet above the river, which washes the edge of lower Front Street. When the river freezes for the winter in mid-October, a hole is cut in the ice over the main channel and a box or barrel set in the hole to prevent those coming for water from slipping into the dangerous current beneath. As the ice grows thicker the hole is kept open with an axe. When the first snow falls the local waterman brings out his dogs and sled, with two barrels, fills them at the waterhole and becomes a welcome public utility delivering water at your kitchen door at so much per bucket. This beats carrying two dripping buckets of freezing water from the waterhole, through an Arctic blizzard, up an icy bank and sidewalk to the top of the street. Anyway, the waterman was a welcome visitor at our back door that winter.

REPORTS REACHED US THAT the Seventy Mile River bars, and those on its side streams, disclosed the presence of widespread placer grounds of a low grade. It was hoped that careful prospecting might unearth a rich paystreak similar to those on Eldorado and Bonanza at Dawson. More particularly a friendly hunter at Eagle reported that the rugged peaks at the head of the Seventy Mile were the habitat of the beautiful but wary white sheep, the *Ovis Dalli*, so I determined to go prospect for both placer gold and Dall sheep with several companions.

Soon after New Year's day we loaded our blankets and supplies on two light sleds, each drawn by three dogs, and set out for the Seventy Mile River across a well-used trail above Mission Creek. Prospectors' cabins were along the river, and we found a latchstring hung on the outside of every door. Any traveler was welcomed to pull the string, which raised the inside wooden bar, walk in, make a fire, and make himself at home. By the unwritten law of the trail each empty cabin had a square block of matches in sight, and a pile of shavings and wood in the small sheet-iron Yukon stove ready for a quick blaze, so that one coming in, sometimes almost perishing from cold or wet, could start a fire immediately.

INSTEAD OF GROWING MILDER as the days went by, the weather became excessively colder. On the second day, at the falls of the Seventy Mile, the thermometer stood at thirty degrees below zero. The next day it fell to forty-three degrees and the following day to sixty degrees below. The sky, however, was clear and bright, for such exceeding cold actually freezes the moisture in the air and it falls in the form of frost or fine snow, and there was not a cloud in the sky. We carried two thermometers with us on this trip, and at the same hour that the instrument in the valley camp registered sixty degrees below zero, the one with us on the summit registered only forty-five degrees below. The next morning as we began our journey to the cabin farthest up the river the thermometer had risen to thirty-five degrees below zero, which we thought good weather for the trail.*

We saw footprints of four large timber wolves and followed them upstream for five miles until they were lost in trails made by caribou herds. These great herds surrounded us at close range and we could have killed any number as easily as if they had been cows in a farmer's pasture.†

The next day, Sorenson, the guide, led me towards the summit of the highest peak in the range, some six thousand feet above sea level. The presence of old Indian camps on the mountain slopes gave proof that the Indians had long hunted the white sheep here. We saw signs of white sheep, and finally the sheep themselves, but, alas, they saw us first and ran out of sight round the mountain far ahead of us. We followed but were unable to pass over the narrow pathway where a slide had carried it away.

We returned to the mountainside, and climbed to the summit of the peak from which we had a fine view of the surrounding region. We saw the Seventy Mile gorge from its head in the range to its junction with the Yukon. To the north and west the Charley River canyons lay spread out before us. Far away the Yukon stretched northward like a gigantic white serpent until it disappeared in the flats. To the eastward across the Yukon rose the distant white summits of the Rocky Mountains, and to the southeast we could trace the great river

---

* This trip was the Judge's first experience with both snowshoes and moccasins. After ten miles tramping through the snow, he knew he had done a day's work. "I had no trouble with snowshoes, and kept up—but my two second toes are blistered and sore" (January 7, 1901).

† "We saw great bands of Cariboo on the mountains just above us—the river was beaten like a highway and trails ran across it like heavy cattle trails on the Prairies of the West" (January 13, 1901).

to the boundary line above Eagle City. Our lookout was the highest point in the surrounding mountain mass, and in honor of the Seventy Mile prospector who led me to its summit it gave me great pleasure to name it Mount Sorenson.*

* Though thrilled at the "sublime" view from the top of Mount Sorenson, Wickersham was disappointed not to get a trophy on his first Dall sheep hunt.

"The country lay before me like a great relief map, but not a sheep could we find. We found tracks and fresh sign in abundance, but the day is too short to give time to reach the summits and hunt before night. I cannot hunt longer—business is being neglected and I must go home tomorrow. I only came to stay seven days, and am now out fourteen, but the frightful cold has prevented us from reaching the summits except for the last two days. . . . We start home in the morning" (January 17, 1901).

4

COMMON LAW OF THE TRAIL

Lottie went to the diggins;
with Lottie we must be just.
If she didn't shovel tailings—
where did Lottie get her dust?
—Hamlin

CIRCLE CITY WAS SO NAMED because its founders believed it was located exactly on the Arctic Circle, in which they erred for it stands about seventy-five miles south of it. In the early summer of 1893 a Russian-Indian named Pitka, accompanied by a bronze-colored companion by the name of Sorresco, floated down the Too-whun-na (Birch Creek) to its junction with the Yukon River, thence down the Yukon to the Tanana station, and there reported they had found placer gold in a stream far across the Yukon flats, southwest of Fort Yukon, and exhibited a fat poke of gold dust as proof of their tale. There were three American prospectors at the station at that time waiting for an opportunity and a guide to cross the mountains to the Koyukuk River, in search of a mythical "preacher's creek," said to contain fabulous wealth of coarse gold, but Pitka's story and his poke of gold dust persuaded them the creek had at last been located in another direction.

THE LEGEND OF THE "Preacher's Creek" originated in this manner. It was the custom of the priests of the Church of England to follow the Hudson Bay traders to the most distant posts in northern and western British America, and thus it came about that Archdeacon McDonald arrived at the Hudson Bay post at Fort Yukon one summer day in 1862 as chaplain at that station and missionary to the Tena Indians. This Christian gentleman and scholar was an industrious worker in the Arctic vineyard. He taught the Kotch-a-Kuchin or lowland people, the Tena of the Mun-na plain, and the Gens de Large of the Chandalar, and even the visiting Gens de Butte, or the "mountain men" from the distant Tanana, the first principles of civilization and Christianity. He translated the scriptures, the church services, and songs into their tongue; taught them to read the Holy Book, to conduct the ceremonies of his church and its services with understanding and decorum. They listened with respect and interest when he talked to them of the land from which he came which existed vaguely in their imaginations far beyond the mountains that bounded their horizon, and they confided to him their secrets of the mountains, forests, and streams.

The influence of the priest long survived his death. For example, an Indian family from the Tanana River came to Eagle City in the fall of 1900 to visit some relatives at the Tena Indian village located about a mile upstream from Fort Egbert. That winter the head of the family died, and was to be buried on a Sunday.

Out of sympathy for these poor people two of us went to the burial ground back of the Indian village to attend the funeral. When we reached the spot we found the Indians gathered round a rough box-coffin resting on two poles laid across an open grave.

I was, of course, interested in how these apparently ignorant and certainly poverty-stricken creatures would conduct a burial service and in what view, if any, they might have of life after death. Much to my surprise a young man, probably twenty-eight or thirty years of age, came forward to conduct the funeral ceremonies. He held a book in his hand and read from its pages at some length in the Indian tongue. At regular intervals the whole band of his Indian auditors would respond in unison apparently in complete understanding. I was amazed to discover that it was a Christian service, conducted as decorously and with the same ease and intelligence as if a Bishop were carrying on the service in his cathedral.*

At the conclusion of the ceremony, after attempting to console the poor Indian mother and her three small children, I asked the young Indian what book he had used, and what church he represented. He

* The funeral was for "Ketchumstock Billy" and Wickersham said he was one of only two white men to attend the service. "The widow, with a child on her back—simply knelt in the snow. I was sorry . . . she looked so poor and unhappy" (December 2, 1900).

informed me that it was the book of common prayer and administration of the sacraments, and other rites according to the use of the Church of England, translated into the Takudh tongue by Archdeacon McDonald, and printed in 1873 for the use of the Tena (Takudh) people residing in the Fort Yukon and the Mackenzie River districts. He had been taught to read it by the missionaries of that church at Fort Yukon, and it was generally used in the region on all proper occasions.

WHEN THE FIRST GROUP of American prospectors invaded the wilderness of the Yukon in search of gold, the gentle and unambitious Tena Indian was mystified. When, however, he was paid for a few days' service as guide or packer with goods for which he had formerly given to the Hudson Bay or Chilkat trader his winter's catch of furs, he wished to learn more about the wonderful yellow sand that the white man craved more than leisure or even life itself. He soon learned the rude art of separating the fine grains of gold from the gravel, and on his journeys to his hunting grounds, or along his fishing streams, he practiced the white man's art and often found gold in small quantities in regions where the white men had not yet penetrated. Some Indian informed Archdeacon McDonald that he had found grains of gold on a stream southwest of Fort Yukon. An American miner heard the whisper of that confidence and the "preacher's creek" story grew as it spread, until every miner on the Yukon became a hunter for its fabulous riches.*

IT WAS THIS STORY, in different versions, that set all the early miners at Forty Mile and along the Yukon River searching for the "preacher's creek" in the '80s. And then, thanks to Pitka and his companion, Jack Gregor and Pat Kinnaley found it! The stampede began. How the story of a strike could spread so quickly the length of the Yukon in those preradio days is past finding out. Stampeders

---

* *The Klondike Official Guide* by Wm. Ogilvie, 1898, records the whispered confidence as follows: "The existence of coarse gold was known in this district as early as 1864, for in a letter dated 'Fort Yukon, 2nd October, 1864' written by a clerk in the service of the Hudson Bay Company at that post, to his father in Ontario, it is said; 'There is a small river not far from here that the minister, the Revd. McDonald, saw so much gold on a year or two ago, that he could have gathered it up with a spoon. I have often wished to go, but can never find the time. Should I find gold in paying quantities, I may turn gold hunter, but this is merely a last resort, when I can do no better.'"

came from Forty Mile, from Stewart, and from Juneau; from far-off Cassiar and more distant California. Mines were located that winter on Mammoth, Mastodon, and Preacher creeks, and the foundation stone of American institutions was laid in interior Alaska on the grave of the buried rumor of the "preacher's creek."

From the date of the strike in the fall of '93 until the greater gold stampede to Dawson in 1896, Circle City flourished after the manner of its kind. The proud municipal boast was that it was the greatest log cabin town in the world! Every building was constructed of round spruce logs cut in the nearby forest. The Grand Opera House was of the spread-eagle type of architecture, the only double-decker in the city. The saloons, the stores, the church, and the sanctum of the *Yukon Press*, the dance halls, and the Indian rancheries, miners' cabins and dog houses were all one-story and squat, with every flat pole roof covered a foot deep with sod. In its heyday, when Birch and Mammoth and Mastodon creek miners were sledding heavy pokes of gold dust to squander for wine, women, and faro, its inhabitants were a cosmopolitan lot. Bearded and roughly dressed miners from the creeks, gamblers, actresses, prospectors, preachers, merchants, prostitutes, dog-mushers, hunters, dance-hall fairies, and dogs—a frontier gathering from every land, drawn together by the lure of a mining camp stampede.

Circle City was also proud of its beautiful early spring lawns and flower beds, which like the hanging gardens of Babylon, grew on the flat rooftops of the dwellings and business houses. When the combined heat of the rising spring sun without, and the oil-tank stoves within, melted the winter's snow off the flat rooftops, the lawn grass and flower bulbs rooted in the roof sod, sprouted and thrust their leaves upward, as if growing beneath tropic skies. In the month of May these beautiful lawns and flower beds, covering the one-storied flat-roofed town, gave the approaching traveler the illusion that he was entering a raised but wide field of green crops and flaming flowers. Many a vegetable garden grew on the housetops when the earth supporting them was solidly frozen many feet in depth.

AN ACT OF CONGRESS prohibited the importation and sale of intoxicating liquor in the territory, but it was freely and openly sold over every bar, in every dance hall, and in every saloon. Harry Ash opened a saloon and gambling house on the corner next to Jack

Jack McQuesten's store at Circle City, the town that prided itself as the "greatest log cabin town in the world."

(Charles E. Bunnell Collection UAF-1958-1026-766, Archives, Alaska and Polar Regions, University of Alaska Fairbanks)

McQuesten's store. Jim Chronister established another next door. Burke's dance hall and Bob English's Monte Carlo and a dozen more offered a square game of faro—any game—with the sky as the limit. Transportation was slow and difficult, and liquors could be brought in only by the summer boat from St. Michael, but every merchant brought in barrels of sugar, dried fruits, and other supplies, from which Hootch Albert and Black Sullivan distilled fiery liquors by means of rude stills. A keg of outside liquor could also be watered for quantity and doctored for quality until it was a barrel, nor did the Act of Congress ever restrict sales over the bar.

It has been noticed that whereas the devil gets his agents on the front sleds in a mining stampede, the followers of the Meek and Lowly are generally a close second at the finish. The Episcopal Church having special charge of this diocese promptly established a large and well-equipped log hospital and church, and entered into active competition with the saloons and dance halls to "beat hell," as one of the clerics put it.

Notwithstanding the want of organized government, justice was not unknown. A young woman appealed to the miners at one of the camps to compel a dance-hall fiddler to marry her and to pay hospital and other bills resulting from her surrender in reliance upon his promise and his subsequent repudiation of it. A miners' meeting was called at which the miners from the nearby creeks appeared in numbers and elected a judge and a sheriff. A warrant was issued and the fiddler was brought before the assembly. The trial was prompt. The plaintiff told her story and the defendant was heard in ominous silence. At the close of all the evidence a miner from the creeks offered the following verdict which, without debate, was unanimously adopted:

"Resolved, that the defendant pay the plaintiff's hospital bill $500, and pay the plaintiff $500, and marry her as he promised to do, and that he have until five o'clock this afternoon to obey, this order; and, Resolved further, that this meeting do now adjourn till five o'clock."

There was no notice of appeal, no bill of exceptions, no stay of execution. The saloons did a rushing business that afternoon, but the miners from the creeks were orderly and not unusually intoxicated. The records disclose that when business was resumed by the court at five o'clock, the Committee, headed by the sheriff, reported satisfaction of judgment and marriage. Whereupon this frontier court, led by the judge and the sheriff, escorted by the jury, adjourned to the bar to congratulate the happy couple. It would have taken my court two years, with many pleadings, hearings, and arguments, instead of two hours, to give judgment, which in all probability would have been reversed on some technicality!

ANOTHER MARITAL CONTRACT PERFORMED on the Koyukuk trail some few years ago was just as remarkable. In the absence of both Church and State, recourse was again had to the Common Law of the Trail, and one French Joe performed the ceremony, wrote the contract, and made the public record. The ceremony took place at a night camp of a group of stampeders en route over the mountains to the distant Koyukuk River gold camp. The record is preserved in the society columns of the *Yukon Press*, March 17, 1899: "On the evening of November 10, 1898, a romantic union took place between Frank McGillis and Aggie Dalton, near the mouth of Dall River. Splicing was done by 'French Joe' (J. Durrant), and the form of the contract was as follows:

Ten miles from the Yukon, on the banks of this lake,
For a partner to Koyukuk, McGillis I take;
We have no preacher, and we have no ring,
It makes no difference, it's all the same thing.
Aggie Dalton

I swear by my gee-pole, under this tree,
A devoted husband to Aggie I always will be;
I'll love and protect her, this maiden so frail,
From those sour-dough bums, on the Koyukuk trail.
Frank McGillis

For two dollars apiece, in Chechaco money,
I unite this couple in matrimony;
He be a rancher, she be a teacher,
I do the job up, just as well as a preacher.
French Joe"

History records that the contracting parties found the pot of gold on the Koyukuk and lived happily together ever afterwards.

THE AMERICAN PROSPECTOR AND miner in the distant Alaska wilderness is almost always willing to fight for what he thinks is just. He may infringe minor laws but he is generally ready to support any combination of his fellows to protect life, liberty, and property against outlaws. His education and early training have usually acquainted him with the forms of law enforcement, and he readily adapts these to the Common Law of the Trail.

Two instances, of many which might be cited, will suffice to show how promptly and courageously he acts on such occasions. In 1885 John Bremner accompanied Lt. Henry Allen's small reconnaissance party up the Copper River and down the Tanana, and thence across to the Koyukuk River, where Bremner remained to prospect for gold. In 1888 Bremner was killed by two Koyukuk Indians about two hundred miles up that stream and robbed of his supplies. As soon as the prospectors on the lower Yukon heard of the murder they formed a party to go to the Koyukuk and avenge the crime. They ascended the river on the small steamer *Explorer* to the Indian village where their guide, Minook, informed them the Indian criminals lived. They were well armed, and as soon as they reached the lower edge of the village they sprang ashore, surrounded the camp, and captured the murderers.

They discovered that Bremner had been shot with his own gun just as he and the two Indians had eaten a meal from his grub box. The young Indian who fired the first shot was commanded to fire while Bremner was loading his supplies into his canoe. Since this Indian failed to kill him, the old Indian, a notorious and much-feared shaman, took the gun and completed the horrid crime. They then threw the body into the river and carried off his gun and supplies. The vigilantes asked the young Indian whether the old shaman had assisted him in killing Bremner, and out of fear of the power of that dreaded being, he said, "No." They took the Indians down to the mouth of the Koyukuk for final trial and punishment, but as they could not agree on hanging both, they hung the young Indian who admitted the homicide, and turned the old shaman loose. He went back up the river, but the young Indian's family, who knew all the facts, attacked the old shaman and his family, and six Indians, including the old murderer, were killed in the family feud. The courage displayed by the white men in punishing these murderers made a powerful impression upon the Koyukuk natives for they never afterward killed a white man.

Lynch law in Alaska during the gold rush of 1898. Before Wickersham arrived in the Yukon basin, miners' meetings dispensed "justice" on the trail in a swift fashion.
(Alaska State Library, Claude Hobert Photograph Collection, ASL-PCA-425-6-01)

In the winter of 1887 Frank Dinsmore, John Hughes, Jim Bender, and John Burke camped on the island opposite Andreafski, the old Russian trading post near the mouth of the Yukon River, which was then occupied by Frederickson, the trader, with a stock of A. C. Co.'s trading goods from St. Michael. Three white renegades who had bought supplies from the trader on credit but refused to pay for them evidently intended to leave the camp without paying. Koyukuk Indians, under the leadership of Old Sport, their chief, and his son-in-law, Minook, were camped nearby and threatened to sack the post and carry off the trader's goods. The white men at the island learned of this threat from friendly Indians and told Frederickson to keep careful watch and let them know if he should be in danger. One morning an Indian ran into the white men's camp about a mile from the post and told them the Koyukuks had battered down the door, captured the trader and his goods, and were carrying the latter away. The white men rushed to the rescue. Being well armed and sufficient in number they easily overawed the Indians, captured Old Sport and Minook, and called a council with the Indians. Minook told the white men that some of their number had told the Indians to attack the post; that these white men said the trader had been overcharging them and that they had the right to rob the trader. He named the three renegades who owed the trader for their winter's supplies as the persons who had persuaded the Indians to attack the store. The Indians were compelled to replace all the goods in the store, and to agree not to attack the place again, and peace was made with them.

The miners then turned their attention to the three renegades. Jim Bender was elected chairman of the meeting, and Burke and Anderson were elected to serve notice on the three delinquents to attend the meeting. They came and after discussion they were directed to pay the trader, which they promised to do. However, they did not act promptly, and, for first one reason and then another, postponed the date of settlement. It soon became apparent to the camp that the debtors were not acting in good faith but were waiting until the main body of miners should leave camp when they would again refuse to pay. Thereupon they were ordered to pay at once. They became impudent and refused to obey the order. They were then notified to attend another meeting, but refused to do so and sent back word that they would pay when they pleased and not before.

On receiving this word the meeting gave them peremptory notice to pay the trader by ten o'clock the next morning. Again they refused and began to cut portholes through their cabin walls so they could use their guns on assailants from any direction. The miners then notified them that if the trader was not paid by ten o'clock the next morning they would come armed in a body to arrest them, and would take such forcible means as were necessary to compel them to pay the trader, and if they resisted they must take the consequences. Before the hour set the next morning one of them came with the money and in company with the committee went to the trader's store and paid all their bills. They were then given short notice to leave the camp ahead of all others and were forced to pack their supplies and blankets on their sleds and travel. Thus ended the first civil action for debt tried on the lower Yukon River, long before the courts were established in the Yukon basin.

WHEN I VISITED CIRCLE City again in early 1903, the arrival of the "white chief" from Eagle aroused keen interest in the Indian rancheries of Circle. Many of them had attended the white chief's court either as defendants, witnesses, or onlookers in whiskey-peddling cases. They again hoped to aid in law enforcement by appearing as witnesses in liquor cases for, it must be confessed, the fees!

Tena had learned the art of getting a bottle of outside red liquor, or of Hootch Albert's best brew, for a dollar, and turning that dollar, through the peculiar wisdom of the law, into a grubstake. A prospector while entertaining some young squaw in his cabin on the outskirts of the city might lose his private bottle only to see it in evidence against him next day when brought into court. This was the only game in which the young Tena squaw could fairly compete with the superior race, but in it she excelled for she knew not the fear of perjury.

Nor had the Tena chief forgotten that it was polite to give his brother, the white chieftain from Eagle Rock, a public reception. A servitor appeared to inform me that the great chief of the Tena would honor me with an official call as soon as he and his braves could prepare their visiting costumes. An hour later came Dayinnun, the medicine man of Toowhunna. He stood before me, a ragged but royal son of the birch-clad hills. Nature created him in fit form, but art had adorned him—savage and mission art combined. His head covering, a marten-skin cap with flowing tail piece, was fit adornment for a Cossack captain; his brown, tanned moose-skin coat was ornamented with Hudson Bay beads from collar to tail; his blue flannel shirt had done long service on some prospector's back before it warmed his perspiring shoulders; his trousers had come from a mission box; his beaded moose moccasins fit him like gloves.

Trailing in behind the shaman came his servitors and retainers, at the head of whom shuffled those ecclesiastical assistants whose duty it is to calculate and collect the value of sorcery in rescuing the drooping sick from the insidious approaches of Tenaranide, the hovering spirit of death. For be it known that such services demand the same high consideration in Tenadom as in Christendom.

After the official amenities were ended came Tena business. Would the white chief hold court in Circle? "No hootch drinkers we; no hootch maker Tena men. Tena got no can, no pipe, no sugar, no hootch makers we. Hootch Albert bad man. A. C. Co. sell plenty sugar, plenty apples, plenty everything. Tena got no money. Plenty hootch Circle; many empty bottles my cabin, smell good but no hootch. Bella she get drunk, plenty hootch. White chief hold court, let Tena talk. Plenty talk, plenty hootch, plenty bottles, hootch bottles one dollar, no got dollar. Plenty white men sell hootch Circle, me talk plenty. What you say?" In discreet and judicial phrase he and his band of ragged reformers were referred to the local U.S. Commissioner, Charles Claypool, and the U.S. Deputy Marshal, my younger brother Edgar Wickersham.*

In Indian vernacular Edgar was "Strongarm," the man responsible for the "Skookum House," the federal jail in Circle City, an institution

* On August 5, 1900, only some three weeks after the Judge had first arrived in Eagle City, his younger brother Edgar Wickersham, who had actually come North several years earlier, was appointed as a clerk and U.S. Deputy Marshal in the Third Judicial District, stationed at Circle City.

When Edgar died in 1936 in Pasadena, where he and his wife Lizzie had lived for many years, the Judge recalled that in the 1880s Edgar "went to sea & made two or three voyages to Asia when he was about 18–20 years old." Subsequently he "went to the Klondike Gold stampede about 1896–7. Edgar was probably the first regular brakeman on the White Pass & Yukon Railroad—one of the first men in surveying & construction work on that line & remained in the Ry. [railway] employ until I was appointed U.S. District Judge at Eagle City, June 1900, when he came down the Yukon & was appointed Deputy U.S. Marshal at Circle City—later at Fairbanks" (December 26, 1936).

Marshal Wickersham's checkered law-enforcement career in Alaska—Edgar had an admitted "weakness for drink"—would prove to be a habitual embarrassment,

The office of U.S. Deputy Marshal Edgar Wickersham in Circle City.
(Alaska State Library, Wickersham State Historic Sites Photograph Collection, ASL-PCA-277-004-080)

---

but the Judge always stood by his little brother. On one drunken spree Deputy Marshal Wickersham jumped U.S. Marshal George Perry, and the Judge had to take away Edgar's star and his revolver until he sobered up and apologized. Then the Judge had the unpleasant task of smoothing things over with the irascible Marshal Perry. "Had talk with Perry about Edgar. He agrees to give him another trial—I don't blame Edgar except for becoming drunk!" (August 7, 1902).

After 1903 Edgar settled in Fairbanks, where he held the office of both town marshal and Deputy U.S. Marshal at the same time. Deputy Wickersham caused another stir when collecting the "city tax" on prostitution. The Judge confided to his diary: "I am having trouble—as usual—with small people [living with women in adultery] trying to attack public officers before the grand jury...for fining the prostitutes! They are also circulating a scandalous story about Edgar and an Indian girl and generally attempting to discredit the officers and prevent prosecutions" (June 17, 1904).

When Marshal Perry took a trip out of town in July 1904, Edgar enjoyed the nightlife of Fairbanks even more than usual. "Perry went away four days ago & Edgar was out all last night drunk—was taken home this morning at 9 a.m. making a fool of himself. Will give him just one more chance & will then force his resignation" (July 22, 1904). Marshal Wickersham finally lost his tin star for good in September 1904 when Perry ordered his resignation. Though disgusted with Perry and disappointed with his brother, the Judge refused Edgar's request to intervene (September 6, 1904).

that had developed some peculiar rules and regulations, not in strict conformity with the United States statutes, but required for the safe custody of its inmates. Posted on the front door of that log Bastille was the following warning:

NOTICE:

All prisoners must report by 9 o'clock PM, or
they will be locked out for the night.
—By order of the U.S. Marshal

Since it was two hundred miles to a point of escape and the thermometer generally ranged from twenty to fifty degrees below zero on the trail, there was but one thing for a poor prisoner to do, i.e., report at nine o'clock and be locked in his warm room with plenty of good food, or suffer on the outside from cold and hunger—hence the rule. It was entirely effective and no escapes were attempted.

5

RIDING THE ARCTIC CIRCUIT

So in seeking for an emblem
for this empire of the North,
We will choose this azure flower
that the golden days bring forth.
For we want men to remember
that Alaska came to stay,
Though she slept unknown for ages
and awakened in a day.
So although they say we're living
in the land that God forgot,
We'll recall Alaska to them
with the blue forget-me-not.

—Esther B. Darling

DUE TO THE LACK of litigation in Eagle in the winter of 1900–1901, I determined to make a winter trip down the Yukon River to hold court at Rampart. Mine owners there were aroused because alleged jumpers had intruded upon placer claims and threatened expensive litigation over their ownership. Too frequently the prospector, generally a happy-go-lucky frontiersman, has failed to comply with the technicalities of mining law. The mining law requires certain forms in location and definite labor in development; lacking these the claims are illegal and open to the first comer who will comply with the law; the jumper appears, and the mining camp quarrel begins. Nor are attempts to evade the mining law always the work of unscrupulous jumpers or tricky lawyers, for even the horny-handed prospector is not above acquiring a larger number of mining claims than the rules and regulations permit.

A prospector of this type heard a whispered story of an unexplored creek, which was to be located immediately by a group of his campmates. Hastily stowing a big carpenter's pencil in his pack and loading a bundle of laths on his sled, he left camp the evening before his friends were to leave at dawn, and reached the creek at daybreak. Beginning at the mouth of the stream he set a lath marked No. 1, for a discovery stake; and a lath marked with a number every 1,320 feet—the length of a mining claim—to the head of the creek, and thus located the creek for a distance of eight miles before noon! When the crowd of stampeders reached the creek that evening they found him in camp on "Discovery Claim," at the mouth of the creek, with every claim lath-staked to "No. 32 above Discovery." The law, of course, required him to make an actual discovery of mineral on each claim before he could legally locate it; but how could they prove he had not? Certainly not more readily than he could swear he had done so.*

EVERY DOG IN OUR team was quivering with excitement and plunging in the collar anxious to be gone. With a highly developed dog team sense they knew that another journey over snowy trails was to be taken and they were ready to start.

---

* The question of what actually constituted a legal discovery of gold would become one of Judge Wickersham's quixotic legal crusades. Knowing the propensity for miners to stretch the truth, and the plague of unscrupulous "pencil miners" like the prospector in this story to claim entire creeks, the Judge became a staunch supporter of what he called the "bedrock discovery rule." This would have required miners to actually sink shafts twenty to two hundred feet down to bedrock—where the paystreak was located—and find gold there before a claim could be staked. In his interpretation the Judge was at odds with most legal precedent and tradition. The law generally favored what was disparagingly known as a "muck discovery," by which a miner could simply claim to have found two or three flecks of gold—called "colors"—in the muck on the surface of the ground. With such flimsy justification, it was next to impossible to ever prove or disprove a "discovery" had been made, and as a result the possibilities for fraud were rich. "It is too strong a temptation for most miners [inviting] a little safe and gentlemanly perjury by saying that when they staked they also—when alone—panned along the muck bank and found colors of gold" by simply dipping a pie plate in the water (November 7, 1906). Though the Judge's "bedrock discovery" theory was overruled by the Ninth Circuit Court of Appeals in 1906 (*Lange v. Robinson*, 1906), he remained certain it was the only way to stop prospectors from perpetual perjury.

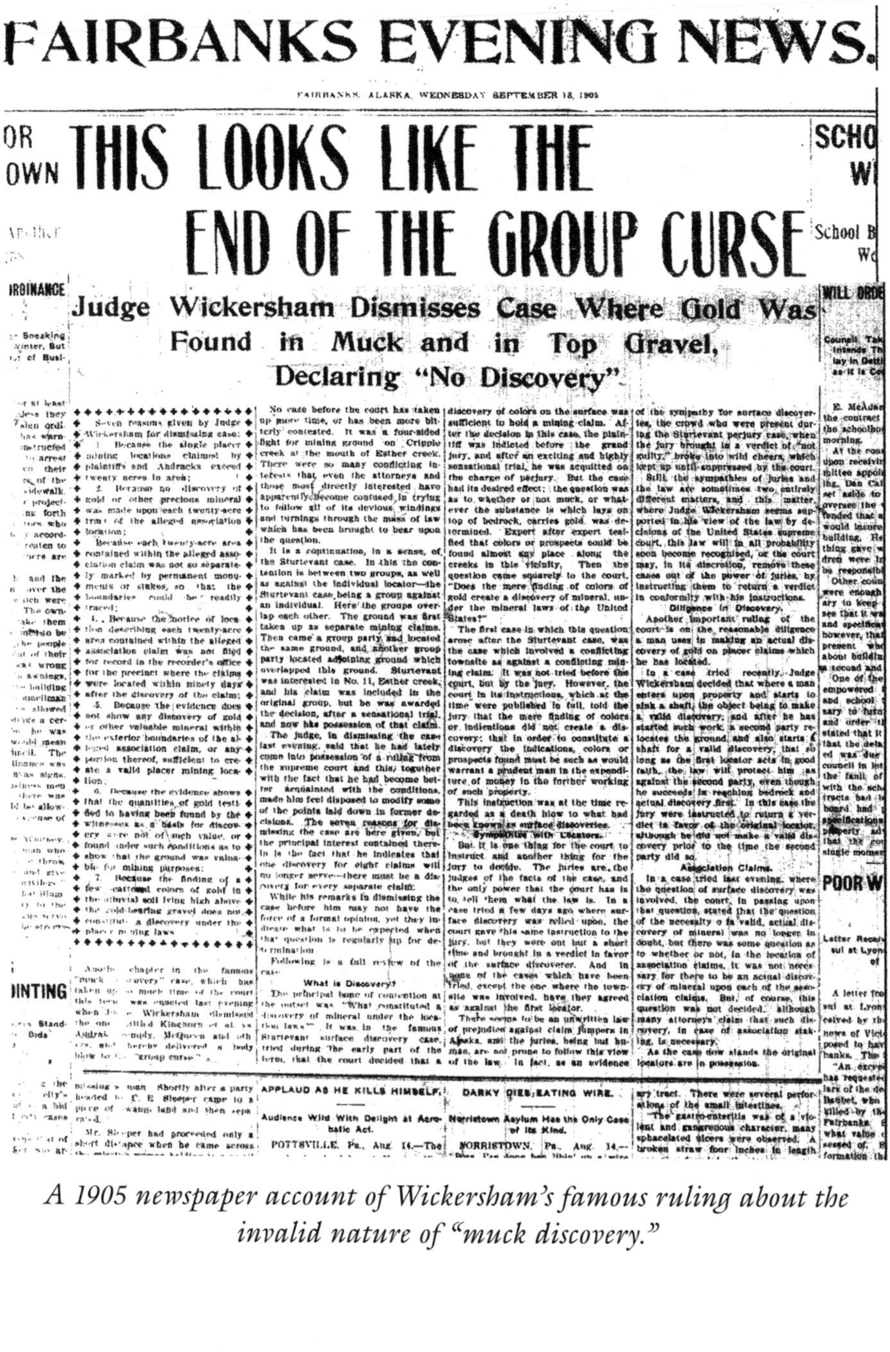

FAIRBANKS EVENING NEWS.

FAIRBANKS, ALASKA, WEDNESDAY SEPTEMBER 13, 1905

THIS LOOKS LIKE THE END OF THE GROUP CURSE

Judge Wickersham Dismisses Case Where Gold Was Found in Muck and in Top Gravel, Declaring "No Discovery"

Seven reasons given by Judge Wickersham for dismissing case:

1. Because the single placer mining locations claimed by plaintiffs and Andracks exceed twenty acres in area;

2. Because no discovery of gold or other precious mineral was made upon each twenty-acre tract of the alleged association location;

Because each twenty-acre area contained within the alleged association claim was not so separately marked by permanent monuments or stakes, so that the boundaries could be readily traced;

4. Because the notice of location describing each twenty-acre area contained within the alleged association claim was not filed for record in the recorder's office for the precinct where the claims were located within ninety days after the discovery of the claim;

5. Because the evidence does not show any discovery of gold or other valuable mineral within the exterior boundaries of the alleged association claim, or any portion thereof, sufficient to create a valid placer mining location;

6. Because the evidence shows that the quantities of gold testified to having been found by the witnesses as a basis for discovery were not of such value, or found under such conditions as to show that the ground was valuable for mining purposes;

7. Because the finding of a few scattered colors of gold in the alluvial soil lying high above the gold-bearing gravel does not constitute a discovery under the placer mining laws.

Another chapter in the famous "muck discovery" case, which has taken up so much time of the court this term, was enacted last evening when Judge Wickersham dismissed the one [illegible] Kinghorn et al. vs Andrak [illegible] McQueen and others, and thereby delivered a body blow to the "group curse."

No case before the court has taken up more time, or has been more bitterly contested. It was a four-sided fight for mining ground on Cripple creek at the mouth of Esther creek. There were so many conflicting interests that even the attorneys and those most directly interested have apparently become confused in trying to follow all of its devious windings and turnings through the mass of law which has been brought to bear upon the question.

It is a continuation, in a sense, of the Sturtevant case. In this the contention is between two groups, as well as against the individual locator—the Sturtevant case being a group against an individual. Here the groups overlap each other. The ground was first taken up as separate mining claims. Then came a group party and located the same ground, and another group party located adjoining ground which overlapped this ground. Sturtevant was interested in No. 11, Esther creek, and his claim was included in the original group, but he was awarded the decision, after a sensational trial, and now has possession of that claim.

The judge, in dismissing the case last evening, said that he had lately come into possession of a ruling from the supreme court and this, together with the fact that he had become better acquainted with the conditions, made him feel disposed to modify some of the points laid down in former decisions. The seven reasons for dismissing the case are here given, but the principal interest contained therein is the fact that he indicates that one discovery for eight claims will no longer serve—there must be a discovery for every separate claim.

While his remarks in dismissing the case before him may not have the force of a formal opinion, yet they indicate what is to be expected when that question is regularly up for determination.

Following is a full review of the case.

What is Discovery?

The principal bone of contention at the outset was "What constituted a discovery of mineral under the location laws?" It was in the famous Sturtevant surface discovery case, tried during the early part of the term, that the court decided that a discovery of colors on the surface was sufficient to hold a mining claim. After the decision in this case, the plaintiff was indicted before the grand jury, and after an exciting and highly sensational trial, he was acquitted on the charge of perjury. But the case had its desired effect; the question was as to whether or not muck, or whatever the substance is which lays on top of bedrock, carries gold, was determined. Expert after expert testified that colors or prospects could be found almost any place along the creeks in this vicinity. Then the question came squarely to the court, "Does the mere finding of colors of gold create a discovery of mineral, under the mineral laws of the United States?"

The first case in which this question arose after the Sturtevant case, was the case which involved a conflicting townsite as against a conflicting mining claim. It was not tried before the court, but by the jury. However, the court in its instructions, which at the time were published in full, told the jury that the mere finding of colors or indications did not create a discovery; that in order to constitute a discovery the indications, colors or prospects found must be such as would warrant a prudent man in the expenditure of money in the further working of such property.

This instruction was at the time regarded as a death blow to what had been known as surface discoveries.

Sympathize With Locators.

But it is one thing for the court to instruct and another thing for the jury to decide. The juries are the judges of the facts of the case, and the only power that the court has is to tell them what the law is. In a case tried a few days ago where surface discovery was relied upon, the court gave this same instruction to the jury, but they were out but a short time and brought in a verdict in favor of the surface discoverer. And in none of the cases which have been tried, except the one where the townsite was involved, have they agreed as against the first locator.

There seems to be an unwritten law of prejudice against claim jumpers in Alaska, and the juries, being but human, are not prone to follow this view of the law. In fact, as an evidence of the sympathy for surface discoveries, the crowd who were present during the Sturtevant perjury case, when the jury brought in a verdict of "not guilty," broke into wild cheers, which kept up until suppressed by the court.

Still, the sympathies of juries and the law are sometimes two entirely different matters, and this matter, where Judge Wickersham seems supported in his view of the law by decisions of the United States supreme court, this law will in all probability soon become recognized, or the court may, in its discretion, remove these cases out of the power of juries, by instructing them to return a verdict in conformity with his instructions.

Diligence in Discovery.

Another important ruling of the court is on the reasonable diligence a man uses in making an actual discovery of gold on placer claims which he has located.

In a case tried recently, Judge Wickersham decided that where a man enters upon property and starts to sink a shaft, the object being to make a valid discovery, and after he has started such work, a second party relocates the ground and also starts a shaft for a valid discovery, that so long as the first locator acts in good faith, the law will protect him as against the second party, even though he succeeds in reaching bedrock and actual discovery first. In this case the jury were instructed to return a verdict in favor of the original locator, although he did not make a valid discovery prior to the time the second party did so.

Association Claims.

In a case tried last evening, where the question of surface discovery was involved, the court, in passing upon that question, stated that the question of the necessity of a valid, actual discovery of mineral was no longer in doubt, but there was some question as to whether or not, in the location of association claims, it was not necessary for there to be an actual discovery of mineral upon each of the association claims. But, of course, this question was not decided, although many attorneys claim that such discovery, in case of association staking, is necessary.

As the case now stands the original locators are in possession.

A 1905 newspaper account of Wickersham's famous ruling about the invalid nature of "muck discovery."

An ever-present hazard on the trail was falling through hidden overflows in river ice. During the gold rush this miner, known only as "Old Charley," was found frozen to death on the trail. His stiff body was strapped to a sled and stood up against a tree for a photo of his corpse.

(Alaska State Library, Claude Hobert Photograph Collection, ASL-PCA-277-425-6-25)

On the trail there is change and exercise, long and exciting races with other teams along the icy surface of the river trails, bells jingling sweet music in the clear and frosty air, warm rations of rice and bacon deliciously boiled over the evening campfire, with every canine eye on the cook and the steaming kettle. Mouths water while waiting for the savory supper served hot in separate pans at the evening meal—the one meal of the day. Then, too, there are friendly meetings with strange teams and sometimes jolly good fighting at the overnight roadhouses, and more often with passing teams crowding in narrow snow trails. Dogs and boys, be they young or old, love Alaskan winter snow trails and the joy of their travel.

Our friends gathered round the official sled to wish us a safe journey and a dry trail. Many of them looked upon the trip as hard and unpleasant, not without danger from overflow and freezing. Often a deep carpet of snow is insidiously invaded from underneath by the constantly flowing water, and the unwary traveler may find himself suddenly floundering knee-deep in water, far from fire or fuel, in a temperature of thirty degrees below zero, or lower. Unless he can quickly start a fire and change his footwear his feet will freeze, and he will be helpless to save himself. Most of the cases resulting in the death of travelers in this region are caused by accidents of this kind. We carried on our sleds a dozen or more flour sacks of heavy drilling, and when we saw indications of water under the snow or crossing the trail, we pulled a sack over each foot and tied them closely about our feet and legs. This enabled us to wade water for a reasonable distance in safety.

Our long, Indian-made spruce-basket sled was filled with dunnage bags, and dog feed, generally rice and bacon, sometimes dried fish; with blankets, dry socks, and warm clothing; with the Alaska Code and blank court records for law and order purposes; with a well-stuffed grub box, extra dog harness, and soft caribou-skin moccasins for trail-sore dog feet. The load was well wrapped in waterproof tarpaulin and lashed down with the diamond hitch. The dogs were hitched tandem, with the wise old leader ahead. On the right side of the front end of the sled the gee-pole extended forward; the driver ran astride the low hanging rope which attached the dogs to the sled; he guided the team with his whip and voice, and the sled with the gee-pole. At the rear of the sled a pair of handlebars, similar to those of a common plow, enabled the rear guide to manage the sled and to keep it in an upright position on sloping ice ways.

Our lead dog was a heavily-thewed female husky, with fine team sense, and a faculty for finding the hard and beaten trail even when covered with many inches of new-fallen snow. Neither a strong wind carrying clouds of snow or sand, nor water, nor hidden underflow could drive her astray. When the danger of overflow and water was met she dragged the team through to dry snow and immediately stopped and lay down, as every native dog will do. An inexperienced outside dog under such conditions will stand and shiver while the wet snow freezes around its feet and legs, but the native or husky dog will instantly lie down in the snow and apply first aid to its feet by licking the snow and ice off, and then drying them with his tongue, as his cousins the timber wolves do, thereby escaping all harmful effects.

All ready! At this warning the leader sprang into her collar and started the load; every dog barked a joyful farewell. Ed Crouch, the manipulator of the gee-pole, guided the heavy equipage down the steep riverbank and lined it up along the north-bound trail on the icy bosom of the mighty Yukon River, and I, the wilderness magistrate, clad overall in blue denim parka, ran behind, hanging to the handlebars.

It was my practice to keep a diary of my journeys on the Alaska trails; and the following notes are copied from the diary for the whole period of the trip, in the hope that the details of daily travel, trails, temperature, weather conditions, and lodgings, may be of interest. These notes are typical of those kept on all such journeys.

February 9, 1901.* It was a beautiful bright morning when we left Eagle at ten o'clock, thermometer 30° below zero. Trail along the

---

* Although much of *Old Yukon* is drawn liberally from his diaries, the Judge seldom quoted himself verbatim. (For good reason he often wrote on the cover of his private journal: "Hands Off!") For publication the Judge revised freely, removing anything he thought too private, impolitic, or embarrassing. For instance, the entry for the first day of his dog mushing trip, February 9, 1901, included more details about flipping the sled and landing upside down on his head in a snowbank:

"It was a beautiful sunshiny morning—thermometer 30° below zero—we left Eagle at 10 o'clock having determined on going only to Star—at mouth of the Seventy Mile River. Trail along side of Yukon River ice, but filled with snow, and broken and bad. We reached Star at 4:00 o'clock in pretty good shape—five dogs with 300 lbs. on sled. We put up with Ed Jesson in his cabin—first class accommodation and splendid supper—beans, bread, [butter] and Hamburg [moose] steak. Distance 20 miles. As we came down the bank of Seventy Mile River I held back on the handle bars, the sled upset, caught me and turned my heels where my head was and threw me several feet out into a snow bank. 40° below zero."

sloping shore ice, broken and bad, but well marked. Reached the Star roadhouse at four PM, five dogs with three hundred pounds on the sled. I had a bad fall when the sled turned over on broken ice near Star. Ed Jesson keeps the roadhouse, good meals; distance covered twenty miles; forty below zero tonight.

February 10. Fifty-two below zero when we left Star roadhouse this morning early; at noon forty-two below, and tonight forty-three below. Bad trail today. It had not been traveled since last fall of snow, and one of us walked ahead on snowshoes and broke trail while the other straddled the line and managed the gee-pole. Much sloping ice in places and we had to lift the sled up and down shelf ice. Distance to Montauk roadhouse twenty miles.

February 11. We determined last night not to leave Montauk roadhouse until late this morning, on account of sore feet and to go only as far as Nation River roadhouse, fourteen miles. The trail is very bad, heavy with snow, and much snowshoeing done to help the dogs. Forty below all day and tonight it is fifty-two below.

February 12. Fifty-six below zero this morning and the trail covered with new snow, no track to follow, so we remained in camp all day. Tonight it is warmer, thirty-five below and we hope for better conditions tomorrow. Trapper here has 150 marten skins, several black and some gray wolf pelts.

February 13. It was forty-five below zero this morning when we left Nation, but within an hour after it had gone down to fifty. It was thirty-five below at noon on the river trail and forty below when we came into the Charley River Indian roadhouse tonight. There was no sign of a trail during the forenoon and one of us had to go ahead of the dogs and snowshoe to get the team along—then we happily met the up-bound mail team at our noon camp. The forenoon trails made a good afternoon trail for each of us, and we traveled much faster in consequence. Traveled thirty-four miles today, according to Ben Downing's mail route distance table. Gave fourteen little Indian children, less than ten years of age, ten cents each and made them happy. Chief Charley was glad to see me, for he remembered that I was the just judge who recovered his stolen dog.

February 14. It was forty-two below zero when we left the Indian camp this morning, only twenty-five below at noon, but forty below tonight. Good trail today. Coal Creek roadhouse tonight—twenty-four miles. My ankle hurt by fall the first day out is paining me badly and is very much swollen. Raised a bad blister on my other foot trying to shield the bad ankle; opened it and filled the hole with coal oil.

February 15. Fifty below zero this morning and we did not leave the roadhouse until ten AM. A prospector here reports he has located good bituminous coal mine miles back from the Yukon. I left the roadhouse half an hour ahead of the dog team and walked twelve miles before they caught up with me. Had noon lunch with "Pete the Pig" at the mouth of Woodchopper Creek. Warmer this afternoon but a bad wind made it more uncomfortable than an extra ten degrees of cold. Came to Webber's roadhouse at two o'clock and, owing to the bitter wind and distance to the next roadhouse, put up for the night.

February 16. Left Webber's late, thermometer thirty-eight below and the wind blowing a gale. Luckily it blew downstream and pushed us along. We made a mistake in not starting early for we could have reached Circle tonight. We stopped at Johnson's roadhouse—twenty-two miles out of Circle. Weather tonight much warmer—only twenty-two below. The trails are good now and well marked; my feet are getting well; and we travel more rapidly.

February 17. Left Johnson's early, thirty below, and reached Circle City an hour after noon—distance twenty-two miles. Visited with my brother Edgar and family. Attended Bishop Rowe's services tonight at the cabin church. Public matters here seem in good shape; two foreigners declared their intentions to become citizens; the delinquent miners' meeting recorder came in to talk things over and went away agreeing to surrender the old records to the new United States recorder.

February 18. Left Circle this morning early, about an hour ahead of the dog team, which overtook us at the 20 Mile roadhouse where we had lunch. We left them there at one o'clock and reached the Half-Way roadhouse after six o'clock, distance traveled forty-five miles. Sun rose at eight and set at four, magnificent day, clear, cloudless, and cold; twenty below zero; trails rough but solid and dry.

February 19. Thirty-five below zero this morning. Left Half-Way roadhouse at seven o'clock and came to Seventeen Mile Cabin at two o'clock. We could have made Fort Yukon but our feet are sore again and we can get in tomorrow before noon anyway. My right foot is badly blistered on the sole. We open the blisters, fill them with coal oil out of our lantern which seems to effect a rapid cure. We have seen wonderful mirages to the westward both yesterday and today. Yesterday the objects seemed to be houses, churches and mills, high, square, and upright. Today the reverse—the objects are elongated—a long flat bridge-like structure with wide arches standing on low piers, a low flat battleship with cannons thrust out at each deck end, and other similar objects. They were so astonishingly like the objects mentioned that we stood gazing at them in amazement. They seemed miles away, and yet connected with the nearby foreground. We passed much open water in the river today, the main river channel is open, running fast and deep; the ice is breaking and falling in and crossings are dangerous. Twenty below tonight.

February 20. We reached Fort Yukon early, thirty-five below, and walked ahead of the dog team to Britt's cabin at Willow Creek, thirty-five miles in nine hours; crippled my ankle again. Good trail and clear weather.

February 22. Left Britt's early, thirty below. Fine sunup; walked twenty miles before dog team overtook me; feel better than any day since we left Eagle. Met the Alaska Commercial Co. party on their way from St. Michael to Dawson—Menzies, the auditor, Hill, Marion, and Trump. They had three dog teams with six dogs in each team. The court party seems rather shabby in comparison with its one sled and five dogs. Two mail carriers and teams at Britt's with us last night; distance Britt's to Julius cabin, twenty-five miles.

February 23. Left Julius cabin early, an hour ahead of my team and walked twenty-five miles before they caught up near Victor's cabin; thirty miles to Victor's. From running astride the rope and handling the gee-pole Ed is about worn out; his ankle is badly swollen. I have walked all the way so far, but swinging freely along the trail is much easier than running astride the rope and managing the dogs, sled and gee-pole. Thirty below.

February 24. Walked twenty-two miles today, from Victor's to Smith's cabin and reached the latter an hour ahead of the team. Thirty degrees below this morning but much warmer tonight; looks like snow. Sent mail back to Eagle by every mail carrier we met, going up the river.

February 25. Snow fell last night and this morning when we left Smith's cabin a keen wind came down out of the north woods. The trail was generally obliterated and traveling very bad. Came to Carsh's cabin—woodchopper, fifteen miles, but as the next cabin is twenty-two miles away we remained with Carsh for the night. Walked fifteen miles and came in an hour ahead of the dog team. Five above zero this morning, the warmest weather so far on the trip, but a bitter north wind is blowing which is in many ways worse than thirty below with no wind. Carsh and his partner cut cordwood for the A. C. Co. steamboats. The contract is signed by both partners and brings in good wages. They live in a good-sized cabin with two front doors. Carsh goes in one door and his partner in at the other. Carsh lives on one side of a line drawn across the middle of the floor, his partner on the other side. They do not speak to each other; each has a sheet iron stove and his own dishes. The grub pile is divided and each cooks his own food and eats it alone on his own board table. Each cuts the same amount of wood and the purser on the steamboat divides the money equally between them. We talked to both and found them pleasant fellows—to us—but on account of some misunderstanding, live solitary and speechless.*

February 26. Left Carsh's at eight o'clock; broke trail through badly drifted snow, high wind and clouds of flying snow. Traveled all day with Salmon, the mail carrier, who drove ahead and broke trail. Met a band of Indians going out on their regular spring moose hunt. Reached Ross' cabin, twenty-two miles from Carsh's, for the night; seventeen below.

---

* Traveling up the Yukon on a sternwheeler in 1910, the Judge found the woodchopper was still chopping, but his silent partner was long gone.

"We stopped at Carsh's cabin at noon to take wood. It was here in the spring of 1901 that I found Carsh & his partner living—one in each end of the cabin—neither would speak to the other. Each had his stove, table etc. and cooked for himself. Though they cut wood together—it was a silent partnership. Carsh is still cutting wood—but now alone.... He looked well & happy—his wood is fine & well corded for delivery upon the boat" (September 25, 1910).

February 27. Left Ross' cabin in company with Salmon and his mail team and came into Fort Hamlin at two o'clock—thirty miles in seven hours. Hurricane of wind and snow at our backs all day, coming off the flats into the ramparts through which the Yukon breaks its way. Schidel, a trader who keeps a store here, gave us good food and a bed.

February 28. Left Hamlin early in a frightful blizzard, wind coming into the water gap off the flats behind us accompanied by dense clouds of fine snow. Five miles down the river we found better shelter behind the bluffs, but a hurricane of wind and snow at our backs, pushed us along all day. Met Jim Oldfield, mail carrier, going upriver accompanied by one of the litigants in a mining case awaiting my arrival in Rampart. He is on his way to meet my party expecting his attorney who was reported to be coming with us. He remained at Fort Hamlin hoping his attorney was yet on the trail, but he was finally disappointed. Distance traveled twenty-three miles.

March 1. We remained last night in an old abandoned cabin, minus doors and windows, at a place called Salt Creek—a fitting name for the frightfully cold and uncomfortable place it was. No landlord, no stove, no bed—we slept in the most sheltered corner on the packs and dog harness, while the dogs huddled on our feet and at our sides for such comfort as our bodily heat gave them. Left there early ahead of the team to get warm by exercise. Ten miles down the river we met the whole band of Rampart Indians going on a moose hunt. Nine large sleds hauled slowly along by a pack of poor dogs hitched to each sled, carried their beds, children, old persons, and such supplies as they have left after a long hard winter in their village cabins. Counted thirty adults. They moved across to the north bank of the river and camped intending to send their hunters out from that camp to kill a much-needed moose. Reached Tucker's cabin for the night, distance twenty-five miles. Oldfield, the mail carrier, and the litigant looking for a lawyer, came back and remained for the night.

March 2. Left Tucker's early; passed Drew's coal mine opposite the south of Mike Hess Creek. Here the team caught up and we came into Rampart early in the afternoon; distance thirty miles.* Secured a

* "People are surprised to see me—say that they had no idea that I would come—that I made a very quick trip, & etc." (March 2, 1901).

room in the rear of the NAT&T Co. store, while Ed and his dogs got into an outside cabin.

March 3. A day of rest, in bed until noon; swollen ankles and blistered heels afflict both of us. The dogs' feet are equally sore but there is nothing the matter with our trail appetites.

March 4. Pursuant to public notice, a special term of the United States District Court convened at eleven o'clock today—the first court ever held in Rampart. James B. Wingate was appointed deputy clerk, and the deputy marshal stationed here served as bailiff. The case of *Allen v. Myers*, a hotly contested mining claim quarrel, involving a rich claim on the Minook Creek, is the most important business before the court. The litigants and receiver are present, but the leading lawyers are not. There is a tangle of injunctions and local matters so we proceed with the case without the leading attorneys. My trip here was largely to straighten out this tangle to enable the miners to work the claims as soon as possible, and to save the litigants greater losses. The Court was held in a vacant log house fronting the river—made arrangements to rent another cabin on a back street for use as a jail.*

March 5. Rendered a written opinion in the case, holding that the court has no jurisdiction as it is presented. Case continued until Saturday on motion to amend, and other business taken up so as to be disposed of by Saturday for court gave notice of adjournment that day.

March 6. Arguments on small motions; orders in license cases, and general business; nothing until Saturday.

March 7. Being anxious to inspect a real Alaska mining camp in my own division, went out to Little Minook Creek today. Visited Idaho Bar, met William G. Atwood, geologist and surveyor; many miners and inspected workings and especially those on claims belonging to [former Washington State] Governor McGraw and Erastus Brainard, my Seattle friends, who dug enough gold here to get back on their financial feet. Saw mammoth tusks nine feet long taken from one of these pits, and the widespread horns on the skull of an extinct Alaska buffalo taken from another. These creeks have yielded considerable gold, but nothing to compare with the Klondike creeks.

* "Business of court in poor way—for want of competent lawyers to handle it" (March 4, 1901).

March 8. Commissioner Balliet and citizens called for a conference about enforcing the laws in relation to selling liquor to Indians. They complain of the want of action by the deputy marshal; promised to take the matter up with marshal on return to Eagle.

March 9. Busy day in court; dismissed *Allen v. Myers* after argument, to clear the record and enable parties to file new suit; granted injunction against removing the gold until case can be tried on merits.

March 10. Spent the day preparing necessary orders and record in cases pending when there are no lawyers present, but only clients, so as to protect them until regular term can be held for trials of civil cases. Appointed J. Lindley Green a notary public and delivered commission sent to me by Governor Brady from Sitka, for use in such cases. Entertained at dinner by Col. and Mrs. Wiggins; several friends called—Lieutenant Rogers, Dr. Tweedle, U.S.A. Pleasant evening. Am packed ready for the return trail in the morning.

March 11. In company with Lieut. B. H. Camden, of the United States revenue cutter, *Nunivak*, now in winter quarters in Dall River, left Rampart early and walked eighteen miles home-bound before the dog team overtook us. Deputy marshal came with mail team to Drew's coal mine to serve papers in some lien cases. We reached Tucker's cabin, thirty miles, for the night, to find the cabin occupied by thirteen woodchoppers on their way to the Dall River. We occupied the floor in an adjoining cabin. Was tired after facing a cold wind carrying drifting snow all day. Our cabin belongs to a man by the name of Clinton who years ago went to South Africa to prospect and mine, thence to the Amur River, where a guard of Chinese soldiers put him out of the country through Korea and Japan. He then made his way to Alaska but failed again to find the pot of gold, and is now in his old age catching fish for dog feed and cutting cordwood on the banks of the Yukon—such is the life of many prospectors—yet the star of hope always shines overhead.

March 12. Left Tucker's early with Lt. Camden and faced a blizzard with cutting snow for twenty miles before the dog team overtook us. Reached Anderson's wood cutters cabin for the night—twenty-two long and weary miles. The storm is increasing in severity, cloudy, dark, and snowing. Slept on the floor again but slept like a log from weariness.

March 13. Camden and I left the cabin this morning to face a fog of snow in our faces. It filled our eyes and clothes and then froze. We walked backwards, when the trail permitted us to do so, for protection. As our cavalcade approached Fort Hamlin roadhouse we could stand erect only by holding to the handlebars of the sleds, while our dogs dragged us into the cabin. Here we met Ben Downing, mail contractor, and one of his carriers and team waiting for better weather. After a warm lunch my team started out to go to the *Nunivak*, in the Dall River, leaving Camden to come the following day with Downing and his mail teams. As we passed through the upper ramparts into the great Yukon flats the gale increased to hurricane force, and the flying snow and small particles of ice cut our faces. We could only hold on to the gee-pole and the handlebars and follow our dogs—at five o'clock we found ourselves floundering in the drifts at the mouth of the Dall River. Once behind the protection of the spruce forests on the bank of the river, we found easier traveling and a mile up the Dall we saw the welcome lights on the revenue cutter, where we were heartily welcomed by Captain Cantwell. His vessel is assigned to revenue cutter service on the upper Yukon to prevent smuggling into or out of Dawson on the Klondike, and is hidden away here on the Dall waiting for the spring break-up. A good supper, a warm bath, and a clean bed after two nights on a pole floor gave us much-needed rest. The storm is howling and whistling over us worse each hour.

March 14. Downing, with his mail team, and Lt. Camden reached the *Nunivak* and reported the worst wind and snowstorm of the winter raging outside of the mountain walls of the Yukon and urged us to lay over until it abated. It did not require much urging. Downing and his mail teams went on up the river half a mile where the A.C. Co.'s steamer *Alice* is in winter quarters, to remain overnight. We will remain here in peace and comfort and go on tomorrow.

March 15. Downing and his dog teams came down by the *Nunivak* early but my team was not ready, so followed them out of Dall an hour later. This is a trick all dog drivers play when they can—follow a trail made by those who will lead and locate the trail. When we got out on the Yukon the wind was still blowing hard but not so fiercely as it did yesterday. Reached Ross' cabin for the night, a distance of twenty-six miles from Fort Hamlin.

March 16. The trail from Ross' cabin to Carsh's was bad—deep snow with a light crust through which we were continually dropping to our waist. At one crossing of the river we broke through into the water but escaped with only a slight wetting. Met Manchester, wood agent for the A.C. Co. traveling in state. He had an Indian ahead with four dogs hitched to a toboggan, locating trail, while he followed in a sled pulled by nine dogs, with a driver. Nothing in his sled but robes tucked in well around his rotund form. Downing and his teams went on four miles to a mail cabin for the night while we remained at Carsh's.

March 17. A beautiful day, morning, noon, and night. Left Carsh's early; reached Smith's cabin at noon for lunch. Met three Indians hauling in to their village four moose and four caribou they had killed. Walked and assisted with sled on rough broken river ice and reached Victor's cabin for the night, a distance of thirty-seven miles. It was a two days' journey as we went down the river. At Victor's we found Ben Downing, with Salmon and Peterson, two of his carriers, who met here—Victor, Lewis, Ed, and I, seven men in a small cabin with one bunk and twenty-six dogs. Dog fights all night.

March 18. Left Victor's early and had a fine day's walk to Julius's cabin—to find three other dog teams, en route from Dawson to the Nome stampede, with eleven dogs—together with our team and the mail carriers' teams, making a total of twenty-eight fighting huskies in a bunch. The cabin is ten by twelve feet square and only six feet high at the eaves. That night it held nine men and three lead dogs as its occupants, while outside, twenty-five howling dogs made the night vocal with their jealous quarrels and fights.

March 19. The weather is settled and warmer. Spent half an hour with the Indians at White Eye village talking about their condition, need of schools, and examining their old-time skin tents.*

* "The tent is oval shaped... about six feet wide and ten feet long. 'Jim,' wife and 4 children occupy one end, and the widow [of 'Old Simon'] and grown boy staying with her occupy the other end. A stove in the center furnish a fire for cooking. Beds of cariboo skin, on the ground. Tent on bent poles, made of old tent cloth and cariboo skin, while door is piece of cariboo skin with heavy stick on bottom. Four dogs also occupied the house with the two families. Smoke hole in center—stove pipe in it. A pile of new moose skins lay on the floor, and joints of meat lay on bed in the pan" (March 19, 1901).

Walked from Victor's to Britt's cabin, twenty-five miles. Met many stampeders from Dawson en route to Nome passing down the river with dog teams.

March 20. Left Britt's cabin at 5:30, had lunch at 12 Mile Island and came into Fort Yukon at four o'clock, thirty-five miles. Appointed Mountfield a notary public and delivered him a commission signed by Governor Brady. Issued declaration of intention to become a citizen to McDonald Wooden, the Episcopal minister, made complaint in writing against Beaumont an Indian fur trader, for unlawful cohabitation with Bertha, a clerk in his store, and asked to have it filed with the United States Commissioner at Circle.

March 21. We left Fort Yukon late, ate lunch at the roadhouse where the Arctic Circle crosses the Yukon River, fourteen miles south of Fort Yukon, and put up at the Half-Way roadhouse for the night. A single man with a loaded sled pulled by two dogs passed us on the trail. The man was pushing with a pole against the rear of the sled to help his two dogs along. When he was opposite I saw it was Bishop Rowe, of the Episcopal church, going to Fort Yukon and his more northern mission stations. We rested on his sled while we visited together. He then went on north pushing his load with the pole, while I walked south. The strong rays of the rising spring sun are affecting my eyes with snow blindness.

March 22. Yesterday and today we met many sleds on their way to the Koyukuk mining district, and among them a Geological Survey party under Peters going up the Chandalar.* Today I am suffering greatly with snow blindness; my eyes feel as if they were filled with sand and I keep them covered with a bandage and hold on to the handlebars of the sled for guidance. Lunch at 20 Mile house; came into Circle in time for supper with my brother. Find there are many public matters here, and on that account and because of my eyes, will remain over a day.

March 23. Commissioner Charles Claypool wishes to go outside on private business for a month, and asks that James Stewart be appointed commissioner during his absence, which was done. Wooden's complaint filed with commissioner, who issued a warrant

* USGS topographer W. J. Peters.

for the arrest of Beaumont and Bertha.* Heard some motions and uncontested court matters. A day's rest and treatment and my snow blindness disappeared.

March 24. Left Circle early and reached Webber's roadhouse at dark—forty miles covering two days' stages on our journey down the river. Good trail and a fine day. Webber is a crank and generally a nuisance.

March 25. From Webber's to the Washington Creek roadhouse, forty-four miles; six miles farther than two days' run in our journey going down. Passed two sleds drawn by horses and several drawn by dogs, some going to the Koyukuk, others to Nome. Also passed Downing mail teams at his Charley Creek cabin. He will be along in the morning and go with us to Eagle.

March 26. Left Washington Creek at six o'clock, the team an hour later; took lunch at Nation. The roadhouse keeper reports a rich strike on Fourth of July Creek; exhibited a glass jar with fifty ounces, about eight hundred dollars, in coarse gold dust which he says came from that creek. Ran into Montauk roadhouse for the night, thirty-four miles. The dogs know we are getting home and travel better.

March 27. Left Montauk early; had lunch at Star at the mouth of Seventy Mile River. Bought a handsome Navajo Indian blanket from Mrs. Matthews; reached Eagle and home at three o'clock; distance thirty-six miles. We were twenty-two days in going from Eagle to Rampart, less one day and two half days not traveling—full time twenty days, a distance of 520 miles one way and an average of twenty-six miles per day. Returning in seventeen days, one day at *Nunivak*, and one at Circle, which left us fifteen days for the return trip—an average of thirty-four miles per traveling day. We were gone forty-five days and traveled more than one thousand miles. The total expense of the trip for dog team, driver, roadhouse expenses, meals, and beds, amounted to $705. Paid driver and sent my vouchers to Washington with report, paid. Found everybody at home well and happy.

* Beaumont was eventually tried and found guilty of adultery and Wickersham gave him the maximum sentence of three months in jail (August 1, 1901).

6

THE YUKON RIVER WINTER TRAIL

O, Land of Gold, I sing of thee,
Alaska, my Alaska;
Thy snow-capped peaks I love to see,
Alaska, my Alaska.
From Arctic Ocean's frozen shore,
To Baranoff of Russian lore,
Thy mighty rivers I adore,
Alaska, my Alaska.

—M. A. Snow

ON OUR TRIP IN the winter of 1901 from Eagle to Rampart we followed the only established roadway in interior Alaska at that time, the Yukon River trail. In the summer season one traveled it in rowboats or sometimes on rafts, or less often on the newly arrived steamboats. These took three weeks to carry provisions and mining supplies from St. Michael to Dawson, serving the Alaska way-ports as they ascended the river. In the winter one followed the main channel iceway generally, though the trail sometimes cut off behind an island or across a wooded portage, thus reducing the distance and sheltering the traveler from the wind. The trail was marked every winter with stakes or branches of trees where it crossed the river, and was thus kept flagged by the mail carriers, who made regular weekly trips in relays both ways from Dawson, via Eagle, Circle, and Fort Yukon, to Fort Gibbon at the mouth of the Tanana River, and thence to Nome, a distance from Dawson of sixteen hundred miles. Mail cabins had been erected by the contractor, about twenty-five miles apart, where there were no woodcutters' cabins, generally in the edge of the timber, on or near the riverbanks, and these afforded the needed shelter to the mail carrier and his dogs, as well as to the traveling prospector or trapper. Provisions and stoves were to be found at each of these mail cabins, and sometimes, shelter for dogs. The dogs generally slept in the open, and many a time at the call for breakfast I have seen what looked like a pile of snow in the yard explode like a small volcano, as a husky broke through the crust of snow which had settled over him during his night's slumber. Not that the dog has a morning meal, for he is fed when the team comes in off the trail in the evening and has no more until the next evening. He seems able, however, to smell the cooking breakfast through his blanket of snow, and shakes himself free in the hope of getting a scrap before being hitched in for the day's journey.

The dogs used in these mail teams are of two kinds, the native or malamute dog and the outside dog. The native dog is a wolfish animal, gray-brown, with an immense, bushy tail which he carries curled high over his back when in harness on the trail. His wolfish nature renders him rather dangerous on occasions when the team is obliged to travel through new-fallen snow, and the driver must go ahead on snowshoes to break trail. If the driver falls and flounders in the snow these native dogs become quickly excited and are liable to attack him, when he must be able to fight them off with a club or a whip to prevent serious injury from their fangs. They are not as gentle and companionable towards their master as the outside dogs. These are, of course, dogs imported into the north from the States, and are gentle and easily managed but not so well adapted to trail work as the native dogs.

Generally each driver keeps a "leader," an outside dog which has learned his ways and his voice, and readily responds to the commands, "gee," "haw," "mushon," and "whoa," by which the team is guided. These words are used with the meaning given to them by ox drivers, except "mushon," which is the dog driver's rendering of the French-Canadian driver's command of "*marche on*"—to go—hence, also the Alaska verb "to mush," meaning to travel, in dog driving.

WHEN THE MAIL TEAM reaches the station or the roadhouse at the end of the day's run, the driver unhitches the team and turns all dogs, except the leader, loose to rustle for themselves. His leader, his parka, gloves, and whip, he brings into the roadhouse; puts the leader under his bunk, hangs his wet garments on the best wires around the stovepipe—and woe unto him who complains about the leader under the bunk!

All other vehicles are required by the United States laws to give the right of way to mail teams, and so the mail driver is the most important personage on the trail, in the mail station, or at the overnight roadhouse. He is given the best seat at the table, the first service of hot cakes for breakfast, and the best bunk at night. He sports a striped denim parka trimmed round his face with wolverine fur which does not gather frost, and a gaudily beaded pair of Tena gauntlet gloves, often prepared for his special use by a beautiful Tena girl resident in the Indian village on his line. Some of these dandies finally marry the native girls, and settle down to managing a wood-yard or buying furs, or in the language of one of our Alaska poets, with—

A cabin, a squaw, and a fish wheel,
a bend in the river's flow,
A band of half-naked breed kids—
he stayed there, a sourdough.

Ben Downing, a tall Missourian, was then the contractor for carrying the mail along the Yukon from Dawson to Fort Gibbon. His division was cut into three sub-divisions, and his teams went no farther than from one of these divisional points to another, when they returned to the starting point. We had met him and two of his teams, when we stayed at the Star roadhouse at the mouth of Seventy Mile Creek. Downing was an old plainsman adept at driving both horses and dogs. From Dawson to Eagle he ran a four-horse bobsled stage on which he carried both passengers and mail but below Eagle his teams were dogs. "Big Ben," as he was known to everybody on the Yukon, was quite deaf though he seemed able to hear better at one time than another. One of his discharged drivers, who was notorious for wasting his money in gambling at Eagle, accosted Ben one day and asked him for the loan of twenty dollars. Ben elevated his right hand like a sail behind his ear and shouted in rather an amiable voice, "What did you say, Shorty?" Shorty took courage from the pleasant tone in Ben's voice, and raised the stakes: "I asked you to lend me thirty dollars. I need it to pay some bills in Eagle." Ben's hand dropped from behind

Ben Downing with his mail team.

(Alaska State Library, Clarence Leroy Andrews Photograph Collection, ASL-PCA-45-1031) his ear as he said; "Oh, I heard you the first time, Shorty; here's ten. We'll split—you lose half and I lose half."

Each mail team is made up of eight to ten dogs, hitched tandem, to sleds specially constructed to carry the mail, and such express matter as the settlers and miners along the river require. A passenger is obliged to run at the handlebars and is permitted to ride only in case he gives out, or the mail is especially light and the trail exceptionally good. These dog teams travel from one station to another in a day, a distance of twenty-five to thirty miles, and the load averages about one hundred pounds to each dog. It is a dangerous life, for in the early fall, before the ice is solid, and in the late spring when it is breaking up, there is always the chance of going through the thin or broken ice, and if the thermometer is low, as it usually is, and the distance to the mail station or a fire is far, as it too often is, there is the added danger of freezing.

On one occasion that winter a mail team failed to come into its station when due. The relay driver coming up the river to meet this team waited a day at the station and then went on up the river thinking he might soon meet the delayed team, but a few miles above the station he found the other driver's hat on the ice at a place where the trail crossed the deep river channel. The ice there had settled on the running water, which was warm enough to cut it out from underneath, so when the downriver team and sled attempted to cross, the whole trail broke through and the driver, dogs, and mail had all gone down and were carried under the ice by the current. No hardier, braver, or more capable men ever drove a stage across the plains to California than these pioneer mail carriers of the Yukon.

ONE INCIDENT OF OUR trip to Rampart might well be included here. We had been on the trail all day. We had followed it down the river, then across a mighty bend through deep snowdrifts; then back to the ice highway which the north wind had swept bare and left as our only guides patches of nicotine that marked the route of stampeders or passing mail carriers. Approaching darkness and a bitter cross-wind made us anxious for the sight of the camp. Finally, our huskies raised their muzzles and sniffed the air. A sudden burst of speed informed us that we were approaching a roadhouse. After rounding a long bend we saw the roadhouse a mile ahead at the edge of the forest. We had never met the landlord, who was by reputation an insolent scamp, with a rough and ready wit, and an ungovernable tongue. The landlord was emptying ashes into the yard as we approached and continued as if unaware of our existence.

I gravely inquired, though I knew there was no other within thirty miles, "Is this Mr. Webber's roadhouse?"

The landlord vouchsafed a truculent stare and an affirmative grunt. The judicial inquiry was then changed to a dignified announcement: "Mr. Webber, I am the United States district judge from Eagle City."

The landlord's face lighted instantly with a grin, as he replied; "Oh, the hell you are!" Shocked surprise prevented an answer, and evidently none was expected, nor time given to utter it, for the worthy host quickly continued:

"Well, this was a good country before the shyster lawyers and grafting deputy marshals began to come through it with their damned law books and commissioners' warrants, but it's going to hell now as fast as it can go."

With this very clear statement of his opinion about court officials he disappeared through the clapboard door into his cabin, and left us standing in the doorway. After a moment's time for recovery, the magistrate, minus considerable dignity, gave the driver instructions to unhitch the dogs, for it was then nearly dark and thirty miles to the next roadhouse, entered the tavern, and inquired in a gentle voice,

"Mr. Webber, have you any water in which to cook dog-feed?"

"Yes, sure, plenty of it," he replied.

After a short pause, and a glance around the cabin, "Well, where is it?" "In the river," was the surly reply.

From his brief but pointed replies to our modest inquiries, he reiterated his inveterate prejudice against magistrates, lawyers, and officials armed with commissioners' warrants. What experience caused such complete loss of confidence in his country's courts he did not disclose. Possibly justice had scourged him before he took up his hermit's abode in the Arctic wilderness; possibly injustice, who can tell?

WEBBER'S ONE-ROOM LOG TAVERN with a dirt floor stood at the edge of a dense forest. The side walls of the cabin, built of small round logs, were head high, and the central roof log was just above the outstretched fingertips. The tavern was about ten by sixteen feet square inside. It was finished with one clapboard door hung on wooden pins, and one window sash. The dining table consisted of boards nailed to poles, about three feet long, driven into auger-holes about four feet apart just below the window. Two pole bunks of similar design adorned the back wall. The dirt floor was spattered with grease from the stove. There was one chair of riven slab set on three pole legs. The two other chairs were boxes, one marked in large letters "Hunter's Old Rye," and the other, "Eagle Brand Milk." A dog stable, much smaller than the tavern, stood alongside. These buildings and their accommodations for travelers were typical of those along the Yukon River trail.

After we had carried water from the hole in the river ice, and fuel from the forest, we cooked the evening meal for our hungry dogs and bedded them down within the frost-encrusted walls of their stable. We then came to our own meal in the tavern without unnecessary dignity or appetite—in fact we begrudged our animals the good hot pan of rice and bacon we had prepared for them.

The fame of Webber's rabbit stew, as well as his disposition,* had spread along the trail. The stew was prepared and simmered all winter long in a large kerosene can on top of an ancient Yukon sheet-iron stove. In this can the famed rabbit stew was always brewing. As hungry guests at the pole table reduced its contents, more water, rabbit, caribou, bear, or lynx was added. From early in November

---

* Nine years later when Wickersham was Alaska's congressional delegate, he came up the Yukon on the steamer *Tana*. Passing by Mat Webber's cabin he did not stop to renew their acquaintance, but he did recall for his diary once again his favorite story from his first long-distance mush in 1901:

"The cranky old fellow still keeps a smoke coming out of the house. I expect I have told you this story before but I'll tell it again. In February 1901 I was on my way from Eagle to Rampart with a dog team & driver. I walked ahead & late in the evening I reach Webber's. As I came up the riverbank he came out of the house to throw out his dish water. I was dressed in rough trail clothes. I had heard what a surly fellow he was and being a young judge thought to suppress any show of his crankiness by the dignity of my position, so I said: 'Is this Mr. Webber?'

He grunted acquiescence, and I then said, 'I am Judge Wickersham Mr. Webber'—and I got no further for he said, 'The hell you are! Well we had a pretty peaceable country here in the Yukon before the damned shyster lawyers began to come in but I suppose it will be different now,' and my dignity wilted" (September 29, 1910).

Rough accommodations in a miner's cabin on the trail, and a game of cards by candlelight.
(Alaska State Library, Claude Hobert Photograph Collection, ASL-PCA-425-6-37)

when the first ice permitted travel on the great river highway in front of his door, until the following May break-up, the odor and steam from this ragout of wild meats permeated the tavern, glazed the half-window with beautiful icy patterns, and filled the two-inch air-hole above the door with frost. But we ate it and paid two dollars each per meal for it.

After the landlord had given us for the second time his personal opinions about the courts and law as administered in the Yukon valley, we spread our blankets on the pole bunks. I was allotted the "bridal chamber," whose knobby ribs and knotty spruce boughs were dry and hard from the heat of the nearby stove, and had evidently been cut and seasoned the previous autumn. But ten hours' tramping from Charley River to Webber's in thirty-below-zero weather on the hard ice of the river trail made sleep easy and sweet.*

---

* As revenge for his cranky disposition, some of the dog drivers foisted a practical joke on Webber, which amused the Judge. "He is irascible and cross, the world is upside down—the mail couriers know his weakness, and have combined to annoy him. He has a fine body of the timber at his cabin that he has been protecting against fire for two years intending to cut it into cordwood next year. They have informed him that Downing the mail contractor intends to establish a mail station and a large wood yard here to cut the timber—a word each trip—some new item of lie carefully and artlessly dropped keeps him in a continual rage—and Downing knows nothing of it and has no intention of taking his place. How much trouble we do borrow in this life" (February 15, 1901).

THE NOME NEWS: NOME ALASKA, TUESDAY, AUGUST 6.

ATROCIOUS MURDER OF THREE PROSPECTORS

Tragic Fate of A Party of Four Miners On Unimak Island

DETAILED STORY OF THE CRIME

The murder and robbery of three prospectors on Unimak Island, as told exclusively in the News last week, has developed into one of the most cold-blooded atrocities ever perpetrated, even in Alaska, which has known so many dastardly outrages of the kind.

There are many conflicting stories about the crimes and the only actual knowledge is that out of a party of four prospectors, three of them, Con and Florence Sullivan, brothers, of Butte, Mont., and P. J. Rooney, of Seattle, lie dead, shot full of holes, and the only survivor, Owen Jackson, found in a dying condition 100 miles from the scene of the crime, is being nursed back to life at Unalaska. Fred Hardy and George Aston, two sailors, deserters from the fishing schooner Arogo are double ironed and guarded charged with the crimes and the authorities are now looking for two natives supposed to have at least a criminal knowledge of the affair.

Thetis Brings News.

The revenue cutter Thetis, that came in yesterday, had aboard Mr. John Reed, deputy clerk in the Nome office, and while at Dutch Harbor Mr. Reed was called upon to transcribe testimony in the case. The one witness heard up to the time the Thetis left Unalaska was George Aston, whose story is said to have been varied and changed three times, so much so that his arrest has followed.

As soon as information of the crime reached Dutch Harbor the Manning, with U. S. Commissioner Whipple, and Special Deputy Marshal Sullivan aboard, sailed for the scene of the crime, found the bodies, and Judge Whipple held an inquest over [illegible] The cutter then found the [illegible] olen from the men, found the w[illegible] men now under arrest, and returned to Unalaska where attempts [illegible] the vicinity, they left their guns, revolvers, their coats, and all the goods brought down at the first load, in the tent at the cape.

Their Camp Robbed.

When they arrived back with the second load, about one p. m. June 7th or 9th, they saw two men carrying away their goods and their tent torn down. They at once landed, and Con and Florence Sullivan, with Owen Jackson, started after the robbers of their camp, leaving Rooney to watch the boat.

They neither discovered the lost goods nor the robbers for some time. Florence Sullivan took the right hand side of the creek, the other two taking left, and being about a quarter of a mile apart. Con Sullivan and Jackson hearing a shot from across the creek, looked over in that direction and saw a man arise from behind a rock and shoot Florence four times; saw Florence fall, and saw the murderer searching the body. Fearing for their own lives they ran back to where the boat was in charge of Rooney, and tried to get it out to sea. The murderer, leaving Florence, came to the edge of the bluff and began shooting at them from close range. They laid down behind the boat, and while in this position P. J. Rooney was shot in the leg.

Finding the place insecure they decided to leave the boat and seek safety behind an adjacent rocky point. In running to this point Con Sullivan was killed by a shot in the back, having not gotten more than 20 feet from the boat. Rooney and Jackson got behind the rocks. Rooney, because of his wound, either could not or would not go further. Jackson went on around another rocky point, some 200 yards further. The murderer here stopped long enough to rob the body of Con Sullivan, and then went up to Rooney and shot him twice.

Crazed By Sufferings.

During all this travelling Jackson was barefooted and without a coat, in fact he had nothing on him except a cap, shirt and pants, and the weather was cold and it was raining, and he was obliged to travel at times for miles over snow banks in his bare feet. Jackson can recollect very little of what occurred from then on. He remembers crawling under a boat at a point which he afterwards found out was on Unimak Pass, and under this boat he was found in a dying condition on the morning of June 24th by Fred Williamson, who was camped near by. Williamson and his comrades nursed Jackson back to life, and on about July 10th he was able to stand on his feet again. On July 15th the mail boat took them off and brought them to Unalaska.

Search for Murderer.

Upon arriving at Unalaska, Jackson at once reported the affair to the Hon R. H. Whipple, U. S. Commissioner at Unalaska, who immediately repaired to the scene of the murder at Cape Lapin, on board the U. S. revenue cutter Manning. He summoned a coroner's jury and held an inquest on each of the dead bodies, decently buried them, and then, with the assistance of the officers and crew of the Manning, began a systematic search for the murderers and the property of the murdered men.

Although Mr. Whipple and his party had at their disposal the revenue cutter Manning with its very accommodating complement of officers and men, the task of finding the murderers was no easy undertaking.

A month and a half had elapsed since the murders were committed. Jackson claimed that the man whom he saw shoot Florence Sullivan was an Indian. The man who looked through the roof of the cabin and said "How do," and who tried to point his gun through the window and shoot Jackson was a native. The native who looked through the window, and who is now held as a witness in the trial, denies that he pointed a gun through the window.

On the other hand the fact that the murderer immediately searched the bodies for plunder indicated that the [illegible] that he was identified, admitted that he was the one who looked through the window of the cabin, but denied pointing the gun at Jackson. Then all the natives admitted that they had been on the island, but that none of them had been so far south or west as Cape Lapin. Their claim in this respect was supported by two white men of the village, Brown, Berson and Charles Rosenberg, who claimed to know of the whereabouts all the time of their absence from the village.

Commissioner Whipple also has got a clue to the real actors in this the greatest and most cold-blooded and unprovoked murders ever committed in Alaska.

Clue of Murderer.

It seems that on June 2d a man by the name of George Aston had deserted from the codfishing schooner "Arago" while lying off Unimak Island in Bering sea and came to Morshova, arriving there on June 5th and remaining there until about June 11th or 12th. He was destitute. He then went to Scott's camp, a party of prospectors then located about 5 miles southwest of Morshova. Here Aston met a former ship mate from the "Aroga," by the name of Fred Hardy, who had deserted from the same boat about June 5th or 6th.

Here Hardy was caught drying a large amount of paper money said to have been $1,300 but the amount now seems to be $650. Hardy said he had been a lieutenant in the army and had just returned from the Philippines. He also said that on his way up the beach he had found a dead man who had been shot by Indians, and had buried the body; that a large amount of supplies were on the beach and that he was going after them. He invited George Aston to go with him. These are the goods found by Commissioner Whipple's party.

They together went to the cave where the goods were and Aston began to suspect that all was not right and, therefore, questioned Hardy about the matter. Hardy told him three different stories about it. One of which w[illegible] he and a man by the name [illegible] deserted the "Arago" [illegible] came ashore in a dory, and just as they landed they heard a shot and saw the men run-

The trial of Fred Hardy for the 1901 triple murder in the Aleutian Islands would be one of Wickersham's most memorable cases.

7

TRIPLE MURDER IN THE ALEUTIANS

A land of surprises and hardships,
Men seek it and hasten away;
They rob it, and curse it, and leave it,
Then bring back their loved ones and stay.
A land of allurement and promise,
Bold venture and strenuous deed,
Where dreams have a chance of fulfillment,
And Almighty God is our creed.

—Isabel Ambler Gilmore

AT THE END OF 1900, six months after my appointment, it became clear to me that there was but little litigation to be expected in my Third Judical District in the immediate future. The greater part of the prospectors and miners had gone to the Klondike and to Nome, and the few people remaining were both busy and law-abiding. Most of the mining claims had been temporarily abandoned by these excited stampeders to Faraway, and the business of the district had been greatly depressed in consequence. Even at the most important term held by this court, that at Circle, the work of the court was concluded in eight days, and that at Rampart in less time. The routine business in Eagle was small and was not likely to increase.

I made a full report on this condition to the Department of Justice at the close of 1900, with the suggestion that the courts in the first (Juneau) division and the second (Nome) division, seemed both to be swamped with litigation; that since the judge at Eagle had little to do at home, he would be willing to assist the judges in the other divisions by holding special terms for them. It may be, too, that the loud rumblings of discontent from Nome had reached Washington, for on March 28, 1901, the attorney general gave me written instructions to go to Unalaska, which is in the second (Nome) division, and hold a term of court, provided Judge Noyes made no objection.

ON AUGUST 3, 1901, the court records and official accounts having been signed and approved, I took passage on the A. C. Co., steamer *Leah* for St. Michael, en route to Unalaska via Nome.* We changed from the *Leah* to the *Herman* at Andreafsky, where we spent a day while the crews changed the cargo from one boat to the other.† As our steamer drifted slowly to her anchorage at St. Michael, a man perched on the outer edge of the dock shouted to the Captain in a loud voice, "Is Judge Wickersham aboard?" He recognized me when I waved my hat, and hastily climbed off his dangerous perch on top of a barrel.

---

* On this, his first trip down the Yukon River, Wickersham was awed and impressed by the vastness of the country. "The Yukon is . . . a lordly river—greater than the Mississippi. . . . In a century from now, I predict, this great valley, rich in its lands will contain a population of a million people—they will raise wheat, and other hardy grains, and there will be railroads, mines, &c.—a live portion of our great country" (August 8, 1901).

† At Andreafsky the Judge encountered Eskimo culture for the first time, and commented how he thought it superior to that of the Athabascan Indians. "Soon after we landed at Andreafsky a Malemute (Eskimo) came alongside in his 'Kiack' or one-holed-skin boat and I bought a spear thrower from him together with a spear. He threw it for me several times, from his boat, and I was surprised at the skill and dexterity with which he used it. At 50 yards he could strike a small chip in the water, and his exhibition was a practical demonstration of the value of this unique weapon. I can well understand, from his use of it, what a serious menace it must have proved to Cortez and his Spanish conquistadors, when thrown in clouds by the active desperate and courageous Aztecs. Went down to Pitka's village in the afternoon in canoe with two Eskimo boys. Pitka is a half-breed Russian from Sitka who came here, as he puts it, 'to stay tree mont [3 months]—twenty thee year ago'—he is here to stay & He has built a small Russian (Greek) church at his village, where he rules with patriarchal sway. . . . Bought 10 or 12 beautiful baskets—a spear thrower & a large mammoth tooth. As well as some small carvings in ivory. The difference between the culture here and at 'Holy Cross' Mission—the last Tinneh camp coming down the river, is as marked as that between night & day. The Tinneh use the birch bark canoe, (it may be an attempt to copy the Kiack), make no baskets and do not carve—they are thriftless and wandering in their life, without settled abodes. On the other hand the Malemutes (Eskimo) make the beautiful Kiack, splendid baskets (both the spiral roll-work and woven patterns) and are splendid carvers in ivory and wood" (August 10, 1901).

Everybody on the boat wondered why he was so excited and anxious to see me. When we landed he quickly drew me aside and told me his story. He was to be married at three o'clock; his bride and her parents were waiting in St. Michael; a party of friends had come from San Francisco with the bride to attend the wedding; they were all obliged to leave St. Michael at four o'clock on the steamer *Sarah*, the last Yukon River steamer of the season en route to Dawson, and there was no minister or official in St. Michael to perform the ceremony! All this while the perspiration was running down his face—and would I marry them? At three o'clock Miss Adeline A. Hill became the wife of Stewart Menzies, one of the officials of the A. C. Co. in the presence of a group of family friends, other officials of the company, and the officers from the military post. They departed on their honeymoon trip at four o'clock with many expressions of relief and happiness.

WE CROSSED OVER FROM St. Michael to Nome on the steamer *St. Paul.* At Nome I was surprised to learn that Judge Noyes had left on the steamer *Queen* for San Francisco four days before my arrival, to answer contempt proceedings pending against him before the United States Circuit Court of Appeals for his refusal to obey that court's orders in certain Nome mining cases. There was a bitter feeling against Judge Noyes and those connected with him. The Nome lawyers and businessmen had held a meeting after his departure and had forwarded a petition to the President asking for his removal.

He had left Nome without making any provision for holding court, and lawyers and litigants were hopelessly adrift; the docket was full of important mining cases ready for trial, many of long standing. However, my instructions from the Attorney General required me to hold a term at Unalaska, and I could not remain in Nome for even a day. The Unalaska term was made more imperative when I learned at Nome that several mining prospectors had been murdered near Unalaska. The witnesses in those cases were officers and sailors on the United States revenue cutters stationed at Unalaska, who could not be called away from their vessels—the court must go to them. I was also informed by the local officials that there were but few competent jurors at Unalaska, the majority of the people being Aleuts; that it would be impossible to get enough competent persons there to act as grand and trial jurors.

We finally determined that it would be necessary to summon both juries in Nome and take them and the Nome officials to Unalaska on the *St. Paul*, which would sail that night. I made and entered an order of court instructing the United States marshal to summon a special venire of sixteen men as grand jurors and eighteen to serve as trial jurors, and provided for their passage. We sailed at midnight for Unalaska, 750 miles from Nome.*

ON THE MORNING OF August 19, 1901, at eleven o'clock, court convened in the first session ever held in the Aleutian Islands. In addition to myself as the presiding judge, the others in attendance included: John T. Reid, deputy clerk; Frank Richards, United States marshal, with two deputies; and John L. McGinn, the assistant United States Attorney. Court met in a large room over the A. C. Co.'s bath-house and laundry, one well adapted to the purpose, and outside rooms were rented for the juries. The grand jury was impaneled, sworn and instructed, and went at once to work on two murder cases, including a charge of murder against an old Aleut—Gregorie Yatshimnoff†—for killing his wife, and a charge against Fred Hardy and George Aston for the murder of Cornelius (Con) Sullivan, Florence Sullivan, and P. J. Rooney, on Unimak Island on June 7 of that year.

Sullivan was an Idaho prospector and miner, who in company with other prospectors located the famous Bunker Hill and Sullivan lode mines in that territory in 1885, out of which he made a small fortune and a greater reputation. In the spring of 1901 he determined to go to Alaska to prospect, hoping to find another fortune. He was accompanied on this Alaska prospecting trip by his brother Florence, P. J. Rooney, and Owen Jackson, all Idaho prospectors. They left Seattle

* Wickersham was never a good sailor and suffered from seasickness his entire life. Though he had no discomfort on the trip down to Dutch Harbor, the return to Nome was a different matter, recording his condition as follows: "Noon—Sicker; Evening—Sickest; Midnight—Dying; Morning—Still dying;...Still trying to die; Night—still have hopes of dying" (September 11–12, 1901).

† Yatshimnoff was found guilty of manslaughter, and sentenced to twenty years in the McNeil Island penitentiary. The Judge felt no conviction would have been possible if the death sentence had been on the table. "The Indians in the case of the Indian murderer are about to fail as witnesses for fear that if he is found guilty he will be hung. They would be willing to tell the truth if he was only to go to the penitentiary but if he is to hang they will be dumb" (August 26, 1901).

early in April in a small schooner which landed them at their desired camp on the north shore of Unimak Island near Cape Lakin. They had a good outfit including a boat, guns, mining tools, and food supplies sufficient for the summer. They first stayed in the vicinity where they had landed. On June 6 they took a full boatload of their supplies, including their guns and revolvers, to a new camp ground, erected their tent, put the supplies, mining tools, and their guns and revolvers in the tent, and all four men returned in the boat to the old camp for the remainder of their supplies.

When they returned to the new camp the next day they saw that someone had stolen their guns and revolvers. They separated to search for the thieves. Suddenly they heard shots and saw a man standing behind a big boulder shooting at Florence. As the other three men ran to the boat, the murderer turned the gun on them at a distance of a hundred and fifty yards. His first shot wounded Rooney, the second killed Con Sullivan.

Jackson urged Rooney to come with him and they ran down the beach under the rapid fire of the gunman. One bullet went through Jackson's rubber boot top. Behind a high bluff, out of sight of the murderer, Rooney fell and said he could go no farther. Jackson ran on a little distance, and found a hiding spot, crawling into a cave-like hole underneath an overhanging bunch of tundra. Soon after he heard two shots below him, where he had last seen Rooney, and he knew that his three friends were dead.

Jackson remained hidden until dark when he crept out of the hole to the top of the bluff and started overland across the island, hoping to reach some friendly camp. He had no food and no gun. He walked by night and hid by day until fatigue and hunger drove him insane.

Some twenty days after the murder of the three men other prospectors landed on the shore of the island. They drew their boat above the tide, turned it over, and went off prospecting. They returned in two or three days to find a starving crazy man under their boat. They dragged him out, fed and nursed him back to life, when he told them the story of the killing of his partners.

As soon as he was sufficiently recovered to travel, they took him to Unalaska, more than a hundred miles away, to a deputy marshal. The commander of the United States revenue cutter *Manning* offered to take the civil authorities and Jackson to the camp on Unimak Island where the Sullivans and Rooney had been killed, and to assist them in gathering evidence to trace the murderer.

Arriving at the camp they found the skeletons of the three murdered men lying where they fell, the foxes, ravens, and other wild things having stripped the flesh from the bones leaving them white and bleaching on the hillside. These they buried and then took up the search for traces of the murderer.

Some miles east of the camp where the tragedy occurred they visited an Eskimo fish camp, where they were told that two strange white men had been along that way soon after the date of the murder and were then at a fish saltery at the east end of the island. The *Manning* stopped at the saltery and the officers found the two strangers there. The men gave their names as Fred Hardy and George Aston. The latter declared his innocence of any connection with the murders, gave the officers all the assistance he could in uncovering the property belonging to the dead men, including Con Sullivan's watch, and talked freely about his acquaintance with Hardy. Both were brought to Unalaska and confined in jail.

WHEN THE HARDY CASE came up for trial, C. P. Sullivan and John W. Corson, two very competent attorneys from Nome, appeared for the defense, and John L. McGinn, deputy prosecuting attorney, conducted the case for the United States.

Owen Jackson testified to the facts about the shooting of his three companions on the 7th of June, the attempt to kill him, and much of his wanderings across Unimak Island after his escape. He said that while he saw the murderer shoot his friends he was so far away and so excited that he could not say positively that Hardy was the man who shot them, but that he resembled him in size and other ways. He testified that the watches and other things found in the possession of Hardy and Aston belonged to the murdered men and that Con Sullivan had about twelve or fifteen hundred dollars in money on his person when he was killed. Other witnesses, including the United States commissioner and deputy marshal, and the sailors on the *Manning*, told the story of the arrest of Hardy and Aston, of finding the dead men's watches and a large sum of money in Hardy's possession.

ASTON WAS CALLED AS a witness for the prosecution. He said he met Hardy first in San Francisco, that both sailed from that port on the codfishing schooner *Arago* in April as fishermen bound for the Bering Sea. That about June 2, he left the schooner off the north shore of Unimak Island in one of the *Arago*'s dories to fish. He drifted away from the schooner some distance; in the fog he lost sight of his vessel and finally came ashore on Unimak Island where he found the Eskimo camp and remained several days. Aston swore that he was at the Eskimo camp on the 6th and 7th of June, the latter being the day of the murder of the Sullivans and Rooney. He heard of the saltery where there were white men, and there he met Hardy on the 17th. Hardy told him he had found a cache containing miners' supplies near the beach after he came ashore from the *Arago* and had given him a watch to carry, saying he had found watches, guns, and pistols. Hardy had exhibited a large roll of money to Aston and other witnesses at the saltery, but had not explained where he got it.

HARDY OFFERED HIMSELF AS a witness in his own defense. He told the same story that Aston had related with reference to coming to Bering Sea as a fisherman on the *Arago*, except Hardy claimed he had only come ashore on June 10 (three days after the murders) with other members of the crew to kill a bear. Hardy stayed behind when he discovered he had lost his gloves and by the time he returned to the beach the boat had disappeared without him.

According to his version of events, soon after he had landed he met Aston at a cabin in a nearby gulch, where there were also three other men, strangers to him, who bragged about the miners' supplies, watches, revolvers, and guns they had found in a tent on the beach. Hardy said that during the night he and Aston had stolen these things while the three strangers slept.

He explained the bankroll in his possession by claiming it was the balance of his army lieutenant's salary from serving in the Philippines, receiving a lump sum of more than eighteen dollars upon his discharge in San Francisco. Finally he swore that Aston had admitted to him that he and the three strangers had robbed and murdered the Sullivans and Rooney on June 7th.

HARDY TOLD HIS STORY about meeting Aston and the three strangers at the cabin in the gulch with such positive certainty and specific description that it was at least certain he was fully acquainted with the surroundings, and it became the very groundwork of his defense. But unfortunately for him the prosecution produced witnesses who had occupied that very cabin on the night of the tenth, and they declared very positively that neither Hardy nor Aston, nor the three strange white men were there that night, nor at any time about that date.

In reply to Hardy's story about having been a lieutenant in the army, the prosecuting attorney found four witnesses, sailors on the *Manning*, who testified that they had been inmates with Hardy at Alcatraz military prison in San Francisco harbor—where Hardy was serving a sentence for larceny—and that during his time in the Philippines Hardy had never been an officer, only a private.

ONE OF THE MOST dramatic incidents in this trial occurred when the prosecuting attorney called the old Eskimo chief from the fish camp on Unimak Island by whom he proved that Aston was at his camp on June 7th, when the murders took place some fifty or more miles away.

He said Aston had come to his camp in his fishing dory about the second day of June; that he was there on June 7th, because "me lote (wrote) it in me log." Having proved the exact date and the fact he wanted, the prosecuting attorney turned the old man over to two of the best lawyers in Alaska for cross-examination.

The old Eskimo was the pivotal witness against the defendant, but everybody in the courtroom felt that his testimony would be utterly destroyed by cross-examination. One of the lawyers for the defense, certain the old man could neither read nor write, picked up a piece of paper from the clerk's desk, placed it with a pen and an inkstand on a small table before the jury, and said in a sharp and rather boastful tone: "So you can write, can you; well come over here and let the jury see you write."

The witness moved to the table facing the jury—and wrote his name in a clear and legible script—in Russian! The old chief looked up with his everlasting smile and the attorney said, "That will do," and sat down. The cross-examination was over!

City Official Paper: The Nugget

THE NOME NUGGET

An Alaskan Newspaper For All The People

AN AWFUL CRIME EXPIATED

Hardy Was Hanged at 9.40 O'Clock, | Died Protesting Innocence to the Last.

Gallows on Which Hardy Paid the Penalty.

FRED HARDY

Arrest of Hardy, His Trial and Conviction.

Fred Hardy and the Stories That He Told.

How Hardy Spent His Last Day and Night on This Fair Earth.

The Sullivan Brothers and Rooney, the Victims.

STORY OF THE CRIME FOR WHICH HARDY PAID THE DEATH PENALTY

Fred Hardy in 1901 was the first person to be legally executed in Alaska.

The officers and crew of the U.S. Revenue Cutter Manning *helped in the investigation of the murders and the capture of Fred Hardy.*

(Seward Community Library Association, Robert McEaneney Collection, SCL-38-6)

A DOZEN OTHER WITNESSES told where Aston was located every hour from June 2 to June 20, clearly disproving Hardy's attempt to make Aston out to be the murderer of Con Sullivan. On September 7, 1901, exactly three months after the crime, the jury returned a guilty verdict against Hardy for three counts of first-degree murder, with the sentence to be death by hanging. Hardy unsuccessfully appealed to the Supreme Court of the United States. A year after his conviction he was hung in Nome, the first legal execution in Alaska.*

* Because the Hardy trial was Wickersham's first case of capital punishment, he was touched by the praise he received from Hardy's lawyers. "Sullivan and Corson were very flattering in their commendation of my instructions to the jury—Sullivan's commendation is particularly gratifying to me—both from Tacoma—longtime warm personal friends—it was a real satisfaction to have him say 'I am proud of you.' On a matter of so much importance—where a human life is at stake, to have as good a lawyer as he is speak so strongly is very gratifying—and especially to a young judge" (September 7, 1901). When the Judge sentenced Hardy to death by hanging, the defendant defiantly "chewed gum and was the least moved person present" (September 10, 1901).

Fred Hardy was hung on September 19, 1902, the first man to be legally executed in Alaska. He went to his death proclaiming his innocence to the end. "My case at Dutch Harbor was railroaded through," he said a few days before his sentence, "and I was convicted entirely on the evidence of Aston." In the meantime George Aston—a "hard drinker" of "many aliases" including William Donahoe, Donovan, and James Gates—had been sentenced to the insane asylum in Oregon because he claimed to be a "receiver and transmitter of wireless telegraphic messages" and had received a "flash" message saying Hardy was innocent of the murders (*Nome Nugget*, August 2, 1902).

8

THE ANVIL CREEK CONSPIRACY

There's never a law of God or man
runs north of Fifty-three.

—Kipling

UPON THE CONCLUSION OF the Unalaska term of court in the late summer of 1901, it had been my intention to go to Puget Sound and spend my vacation with my family at Tacoma, but three days before we were ready to adjourn the U.S.S. *Seward* came into Dutch Harbor. On board was General Randall, Commander of the Department of Alaska, bringing a peremptory letter of instruction from the Attorney General of the United States directing me to return at once to Nome and hold such terms of court there as seemed necessary for the public welfare.

When I opened court at Nome on September 16, 1901, as the successor to Judge Arthur H. Noyes, the inflamed passions of angry men cheated by the scandalous corruption of the court lashed like a Bering Sea blizzard round the seat of justice. Tremendous political influences threatened to destroy any official who sought to turn the stream of justice into ordinary and peaceful channels and cannot be fully understood or appreciated without a brief review of the facts and circumstances that led the United States Circuit Court of Appeals at San Francisco to convict Alexander McKenzie and Judge Noyes for their contumacious refusal to obey the orders of that court and their brazen disregard for the law in the Nome mining cases.

The Nome gold strike, out of which these controversies arose, occurred on the bleak and distant Bering Sea coast in September, 1898, at the time the Klondike excitement was approaching its height and was drawing the attention of the world to the Yukon region as a probable source of inexhaustible

The "Three Lucky Swedes" who struck gold on Anvil Creek at Nome in 1898. The attempt to rob them of their rightful riches was the origin of the great gold conspiracy.

(Alaska State Library, Alaska Purchase Centennial Photograph Collection, ASL-P20-088) free gold. The Nome discoveries were made quite unexpectedly by a group of Scandinavian prospectors and Lapp reindeer-herders, who were induced to examine the gravel deposits in the streams near their camps by reason of the rumors they heard from the Klondike. To their surprise they found gold on a stream about three miles back from the beach, near Cape Nome, which they named Anvil Creek. They located claims, marked their boundaries, and began mining in good faith. They were in peaceable and unchallenged possession of their respective claims in compliance with the United States laws. In 1899, the claims were deeded to the Pioneer Mining Co. and the Wild Goose Mining Co., California corporations formed by the locators and friendly California capitalists.

The 1898 Anvil Creek discovery attracted little attention until the summer of '99, when the extent and richness of the claims became generally known. Few miners came to the new camp the first summer except those along the Yukon River, from Dawson, St. Michael, and the surrounding country. Two weekly newspapers, however, were established, saloons were opened, a small crowd of gold seekers came in, and a half-dozen lawyers gathered for the expected feast. Naturally, there were not enough rich claims to go round, even in '99, and those who had missed securing a bonanza sat round the camp stoves and quarreled with Fate because of their ill luck. Gradually their quarrels extended to the original locators of the rich Anvil Creek mining claims, and it seemed wickedly unfair that the rich claims, so few in number, should fall to a few "lucky Swedes" and Lapland reindeer-herders, and loud protests began to rise about the warm stoves in the straggling new town. Then some "sea lawyer" raised the question whether these aliens could legally locate and hold mining claims in Alaska. The dissatisfied element decided promptly that they could not, whereupon their protests grew into threats and finally into direct action.

A miners' meeting was called for July 10, 1899, to consider how they might evict these first and original locators, so they might relocate the claims for themselves! A resolution declaring the claims illegal and open to relocation was prepared for adoption at this meeting. The crafty leaders stationed their associates near the claims on Anvil Mountain, which was in plain sight from Nome, about three miles away, with instructions that when they saw a signal fire at Nome they would know the resolution had passed and that they should

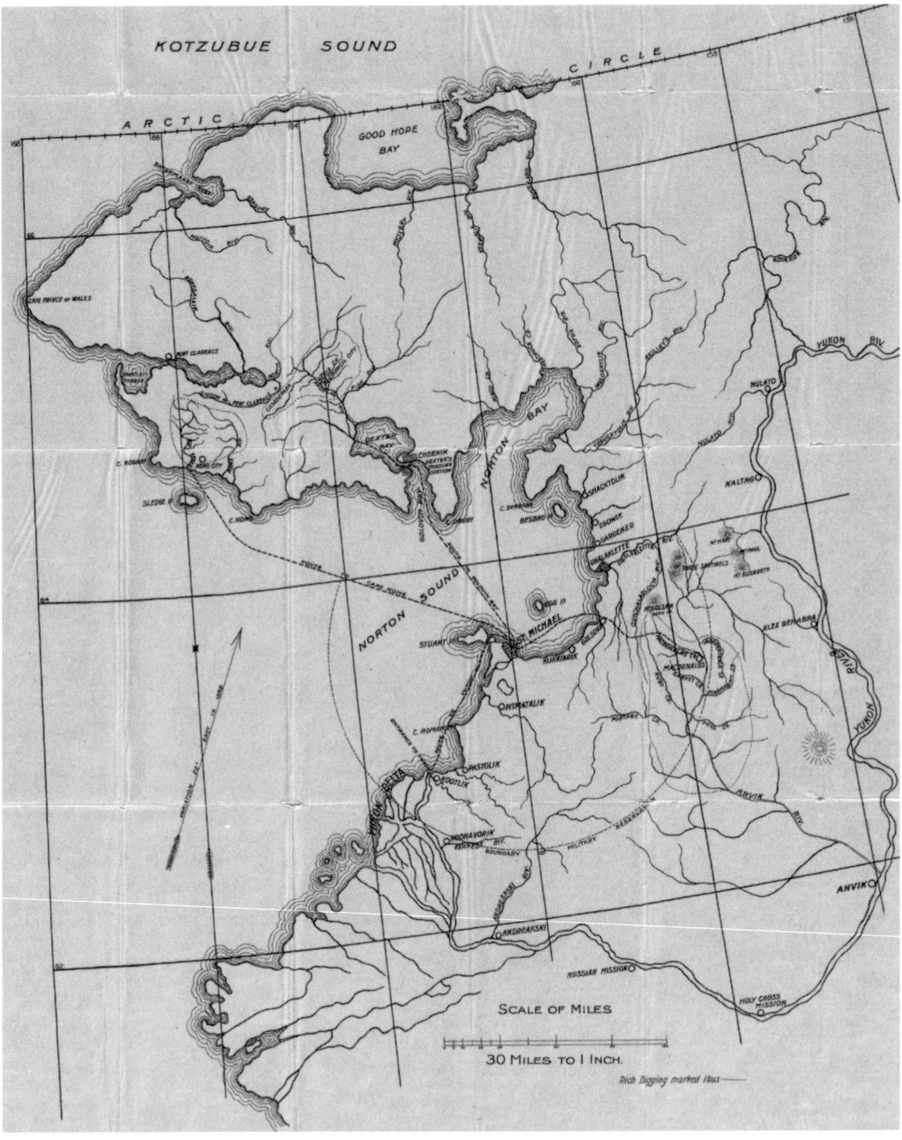

An 1899 map of the "new goldfields of northwestern Alaska."

(Rare Maps Collection G4371-H2-1899-M32, Archives, Alaska and Polar Regions, University of Alaska Fairbanks) then immediately relocate the claims; and take possession of them for themselves and their fellow conspirators. In the meantime news of the proposed violence had been sent to the military authorities. Lieutenant Spaulding, an army officer from Fort St. Michael, came to Nome with two or three soldiers, attended the meeting, and prevented the adoption of the resolution by moving and enforcing an adjournment. The signal fire was not lighted and the scheme failed.

AS THE IDEA OF capturing these rich claims by direct action through local miners' meetings died down, it was privately taken up by a group of shrewd Nome lawyers, who determined to carry it forward by applying to Congress for a change in the United States mining laws which would bring about the desired result, with themselves and their Washington associates as the beneficiaries. They sent one of their number to Washington in the fall of 1899 to present their plan to influential members of the United States Senate, and certain national politicians with whom they were acquainted.

Now the scene changed from the mining camp on the Bering Sea to the nation's capital. The actors were no longer prospectors and "lucky Swedes," but senators of the United States, national politicians, senator-makers, and a group of their jackals, seeking to secure the fortunes in the Anvil Creek gravel beds.

A bill was then pending in the United States Senate to create a better form of civil government for Alaska. The Alaska Organic Act of 1884 had explicitly provided as part of the Oregon code that became the law of the land in Alaska that "Any alien may acquire and hold lands . . . as if such alien were a native citizen" and furthermore that "the title to any lands heretofore conveyed shall not be questioned, nor in any manner affected, by reason of the alienage of any person from or through whom such title may have been derived."

Those two sections of the civil code, then in force in Alaska, had been copied into Senate bill 3919. Someone conversant with the United States mining laws called attention to them as being a bar to the plan to capture the Anvil Creek claims. When the sections came up for consideration before the Senate in the Alaska government bill, Senator Hansbrough from North Dakota moved to strike them from the bill and offered in their place a substitute called the "Hansbrough amendment," which was intended to invalidate the Anvil Creek claims and permit their relocation by "jumpers." The motion met with instant opposition from Senators Stewart, of Nevada, Spooner, of Wisconsin, Nelson, of Minnesota, Teller, of Colorado, and others. As the opponents of the first draft of the Hansbrough amendment made their objections known, supporters soon discovered that it was not sufficiently drastic to accomplish what they wanted anyway, and on April 4th the senator from North Dakota offered a modification of his amendment as follows:

> Persons who are not citizens of the United States, or who prior to making location had not legally declared their intention to become such, shall not be permitted to locate, hold, or convey mining claims in said district of Alaska, nor shall any title to a mining claim acquired by location or purchase through any such person or persons be legal. In any civil action, suit, or proceeding...it shall be the duty of the court to inquire into and determine the question of the citizenship of the locator.

This modification of the Hansbrough amendment contained every vicious feature of the first draft and was in plain violation of the most fundamental principles of justice. Objections to it were renewed with vigor on the floor of the Senate; the debate grew personal and the long Alaska government bill with its intricate code system was practically forgotten. For weeks the extraordinary and sinister provisions of the Hansbrough amendment occupied the attention of the United States Senate. Petitions, affidavits, letters, and briefs of interested parties were read in the open Senate; the alleged facts relating to the original locations of the mining claims by supposed aliens, and their want of citizenship were alleged, denied, debated; angry charges were hurled back and forth across the Senate floor, personal friendships were sundered, the amendment was attacked as retroactive in its effect, and intended to rob honest Scandinavian miners of their legally acquired property and prevent them from having their day in court. One day's *Congressional Record* was filled with such violent language and recriminations that after senators had cooled off it was withdrawn and reprinted so as to exclude the bitter language.

The fight over this remarkable attempt to try a lawsuit before the United States Senate became so personal, acrimonious, and stubborn that cooler heads, not personally interested on either side of the controversy, saw it would result in the defeat of the Alaska government bill if continued, and finally they prevailed upon the angry and stubborn contestants to compromise their differences so as to allow the passage of the bill in the Senate. This agreement was effected on May 1, whereby the Hansbrough amendment was withdrawn, the two Oregon sections were stricken from the bill, and it was passed and approved by the President without any of these controversial sections in it.

THE CONTEST FOR THE Hansbrough amendment in the Senate had been organized and carried on in Washington by Alexander McKenzie, a powerful political leader and Republican National Committeeman from North Dakota, whom the attorneys for the Anvil Creek "jumpers" had retained to represent their interests. McKenzie had much political influence, especially in the states of Minnesota, North Dakota, and Montana. He had been receiver for the Northern Pacific Railroad during its financial troubles in years gone by, and later the chief lobbyist for that and other railroads in the capital. He now determined to use his great power and influence in the Alaska project, which appealed to his imagination and cupidity. He was a large and vigorous man, physically and mentally, and a past master of the art of controlling weaker men in high office. While he lost the benefit of the Hansbrough amendment in the Senate fight, he had excluded the Oregon sections of the law that had protected alien interests up to 1900 and felt certain he could still win the Anvil Creek mines if he could procure the appointment of his nominees as court officials at Nome. With the aid of his senatorial friends from the Northwest he prevailed upon President McKinley to appoint Arthur H. Noyes, of Minnesota, judge; C. L. Vawter, of Montana, United States marshal; and Joseph K. Wood, of Montana, district attorney at Nome. The other and minor offices were also filled at his dictation, and thus he and his followers were placed in power in the Nome court.

WITH A VIEW TO capitalizing and managing his proposed activities at Nome in a business-like way before leaving Washington, McKenzie organized a corporation under the laws of the State of Arizona, with an authorized capital stock of $15 million, named it the Alaska Gold Mining Company, and became its president and general manager. Through Hubbard, the senior member of the firm of Hubbard, Beeman & Hume, the Nome attorneys for his Anvil Creek jumpers, he arranged to purchase from the "jumpers" their "titles" to those mines, to be paid for with company stock! Some of this stock was transferred to friends who could assist the enterprise, some was reserved to purchase other interests, but McKenzie is said to have retained for himself a majority of the total authorized stock of the company. Having thus procured the appointment of court officials of his own choosing, and the "jumpers'" paper titles to the valuable Anvil Creek claims for stock in his Alaska Gold Mining Company, McKenzie sailed away to Nome, accompanied by Judge Noyes and their group of chosen followers, intent on capturing a fortune by piratic force from a few simple-minded Lapp reindeer-herders and hard-digging Scandinavian miners. It looked to the boss like an easy job!

9

THE CORRUPTION OF THE COURT

We join with you in praise today, and raise a joyful shout
In honor of the righteous laws, that knocked the jumpers out.
Let's celebrate in dry champagne, the powers that wield the rod—
You thank the U.S. Circuit Court, while we give thanks to God.
—Sam C. Dunham

JUDGE NOYES WAS AN old friend of Alexander McKenzie. They had known each other in Minnesota; they had been in Washington together during the Senate debates on the Alaska bill and the Hansbrough amendment, and they journeyed together to Nome, where they arrived on the steamer *Senator* on the 19th day of July, 1900. Robert Chipps, the "jumper" claimant of Discovery claim on Anvil Creek, was also a passenger on that boat; he and McKenzie landed as soon as the vessel cast anchor in front of Nome. Judge Noyes remained on the steamer until the 21st.

While Judge Noyes rested quietly in the seclusion of his staterooms on board the steamship, at anchor a mile off the Nome waterfront, the active and versatile McKenzie, on shore, proceeded vigorously to complete his plans for obtaining the ownership of the Anvil Creek mining claims for his company. On the day of his arrival at Nome, McKenzie went to the office of Hubbard, Beeman & Hume.

The contingent interest of Hubbard, Beeman & Hume was a one-half interest in the Anvil Creek claims in case the "jumper" plaintiff prevailed. Hume testified (in the subsequent court proceedings) that McKenzie said to him and to Beeman that he controlled the appointment of the judge and the district attorney, and that if they desired to have their cases heard it would be absolutely necessary to transfer their interests to his corporation, in exchange for stock. McKenzie also demanded a one-fourth interest in the business of Hubbard, Beeman & Hume be transferred to Joseph K. Wood, the district attorney, making Wood a silent partner in the firm, and in exchange Hume would become deputy district attorney.

All this was done on Thursday, July 19th, McKenzie's first day in Nome. Finally McKenzie took Hume and Beeman aside and demanded that an entire one-fourth interest in the firm be placed in his, McKenzie's name, and that he receive one-fourth of the profits. This was assented to on the next morning, after much objection and hesitation, and only after McKenzie had threatened that if Hume refused, his business and the interest of his clients would be ruined.

McKenzie was now ready to take possession of the Anvil Creek mines. He had purchased them from the "jumpers" and their attorneys and paid for them with stock in the Alaska Gold Mining Company! He had compelled Hubbard, Beeman & Hume to give his United States district attorney a one-quarter interest in their law business and profits, including their contract for contingent fees in the "jumper" cases, and to give him a quarter interest, and he still owned more than a majority of the stock of the Alaska Gold Mining Company! Judge Noyes was at last enabled to leave the steamship and come into Nome, which he did on Saturday, the 21st. The trap was set; the next move, naturally, was to get actual possession of the mines.

WHILE MCKENZIE WAS PHYSICALLY a powerful man and had remarkable influence over other men by reason of his pugnacious and fearless disposition, he now found himself face to face, in these cases, with another man of courage—Charles D. Lane, frontiersman and a successful miner from California. Mr. Lane was six feet tall, physically intimidating himself, and willing to fight in or out of court. Jafet Lindeberg, a former reindeer herder, lacked the physical prowess and courage of Lane, but he was a shrewd businessman and had an intimate knowledge of the facts relating to the mining locations, and full acquaintance with the witnesses necessary to defend the cases. Lane's Wild Goose Mining Company and Lindeberg's Pioneer Mining Company now legally owned the original locators' titles and were set to do battle with McKenzie and his men.

Mr. Lane had been in Washington during the contest in the Senate over the Hansbrough amendment and knew about McKenzie's power over Judge Noyes. He and Lindeberg had prepared for the anticipated

The two chief co-conspirators of the Nome gold scandal: Alexander McKenzie (top) and Judge Arthur H. Noyes (bottom).

(Alaska State Library Photograph Collection, ASL-Arthur Noyes-1)

attack by bringing to Nome two active and competent young lawyers—Samuel Knight, a junior member in a prominent law firm in San Francisco, and W. H. Metson, also from San Francisco, to appear for them when hostilities should begin.

Both sides had well developed plans of action. McKenzie and his attorneys depended on Judge Noyes to put their plan over, and defend them long enough to enable them to work out the claims. Knight and Metson and their clients knew they had no chance for success before the Nome court and prepared to protect their interests by appeals to the United States Circuit Court of Appeals at San Francisco, the United States court having appellate jurisdiction in such cases over the district court at Nome.

On Monday, the 24th, at six PM, in Judge Noyes' private room at his hotel, Hume presented applications to the Judge attacking the right of the original locators to five of the most valuable claims on Anvil Creek, and asking the court to appoint receivers for these five claims. Without notice to the defendants, and without even reading the papers or the orders he signed, as his first judicial act at Nome Judge Noyes appointed McKenzie receiver for these five claims, with instructions to take immediate possession and extract the gold therefrom. All persons in possession were ordered to deliver possession to McKenzie and were strictly enjoined from in any manner interfering with him in working the claims. The receiver's bond was fixed at $5,000 in each case, though the output from one of the claims alone was stated to be $15,000 a day. The receiver had two wagons ready and he and his men raced to Anvil Creek that night and took immediate possession of the claims and all personal property thereon, to the surprise of the owners who had not expected such quick work.

The next morning, after the appointment of McKenzie as receiver by Judge Noyes, the attorneys for the defendant mine owners applied to him to revoke the orders appointing the receiver, but day after day he refused to hear them, until August 10, when he denied their applications. A few days later they applied to Judge Noyes for orders allowing their appeals, and accompanied their applications in each case with bond, assignments of error, bill of exceptions, and other necessary papers on appeal. These applications were also denied by Judge Noyes.

HAVING THUS BEEN REFUSED the right to appeal, attorneys for the defendants sailed immediately for San Francisco to present the

The tent city of Nome in the summer of 1900 crammed on the shore between the Bering Sea, the mouth of the Snake River, and the soggy wet tundra.

(Terrence Cole)

records to Judge William Morrow, one of the judges of the United States Circuit Court of Appeals. Seeing it was an obvious miscarriage of justice, Morrow ordered appeals in all five cases, commanding Noyes to desist from any further proceedings, and commanding McKenzie to restore to the defendants all property which he had taken as receiver. When the attorneys made it back to Nome by steamship with these clear instructions, Noyes and McKenzie both refused to comply, and Judge Noyes even boldly denied the right of the Circuit Court of Appeals to even allow the appeals or to issue the writs of supersedeas.

The rightful owners of the Anvil Creek claims sought by every legal means available to get the judge and the receiver to comply with the orders of the Circuit Court of Appeals, but without success. Failing to get McKenzie to submit to the orders of the higher court, the defendants' attorney returned once more to the Circuit Court of Appeals in San Francisco, where the judges recognized that no time could be wasted. The last boat for the season would soon leave for Nome, meaning that no further communication could be had with the gold camp until the spring or early summer of 1901; therefore the Court immediately ordered its marshal to proceed to Nome, enforce its writs of supersedeas, arrest the offending receiver, McKenzie, and produce him at the bar of the Court of Appeals in San Francisco.

When the marshal arrived at Nome and attempted to enforce the writs of supersedeas McKenzie and his advisers flatly refused to comply with the writs. When the marshal undertook to secure the large amount of gold dust deposited in the Nome bank in McKenzie's private deposit boxes a violent altercation arose at the bank counter between the marshal and McKenzie. The marshal thereupon called upon the army at Fort Davis for aid, and a guard of soldiers arrived at the bank to keep order and protect the marshal. With the help of the armed guard, the marshal broke open the deposit boxes in the bank by force and extracted the gold dust, which he delivered to the defendants as the Court of Appeals had ordered. Thereupon he arrested McKenzie and boarded the last boat for San Francisco with the defiant prisoner.

On February 11, 1901, the Circuit Court of Appeals found McKenzie guilty of contempt and conspiracy and sentenced him to imprisonment in the Alameda county jail for one year. In sentencing McKenzie the court condemned "the high-handed and grossly illegal proceedings initiated almost as soon as Judge Noyes and McKenzie had set foot on

Alaskan territory at Nome, and which may be safely and fortunately said to have no parallel in the jurisprudence of this country. And it speaks well for the good, sober sense of the people gathered on that remote and barren shore that they depended solely upon the courts for the correction of the wrongs thus perpetrated among and against them."

The three judges of the Circuit Court of Appeals in the Nome-McKenzie case were shocked at McKenzie's prostitution of the district court to rob the Anvil Creek miners of their property. Their scathing denunciations left no doubt they believed he deserved no leniency. After the U.S. Supreme Court refused to intervene, McKenzie's only recourse was an application to the president of the United States for a pardon, where his prospects were undeniably better.

McKenzie had long been a prominent Republican political leader in North Dakota, Minnesota, and Montana and was a valuable ally of many men of national reputation in local contests, as well as in Republican national conventions. Many of these associates now came to his assistance. In May 1901 President McKinley commuted his sentence on the grounds that confinement in jail had so impaired his health that he might not live to serve out his sentence if forced to remain in prison.

He returned to North Dakota, where his health quickly recovered its normal condition and continued in his activities as a leading citizen.* His notorious criminal activities as the head of the most flagrant prostitution of American courts known in our history, and his other offenses were all forgiven by the President's pardon.

ON THE OPENING OF navigation to Nome in July 1901, citations from the Court of Appeals were served upon Judge Noyes, District Attorney Joseph K. Wood, and also on McKenzie's legal advisers, Dudley DuBose, Thomas J. Geary, and C.A.S. Frost, the latter an official of the Department of Justice, requiring them to appear before the Court at San Francisco on contempt charges. While

* After leaving prison, McKenzie had a miraculous recovery in the crisp, fresh air of North Dakota, and lived for another twenty-one years.

McKenzie was always a secretive man. Fearful of leaving a paper trail, he seldom wrote anything down, so many of his activities remain shrouded in mystery. Upon his death even his "intimate friends" were surprised to learn the North Dakota–Minnesota man had a second family in New York, including two sons and a daughter living in Yonkers (*New York Times*, June 30, 1922).

Geary was acquitted, all the others were found guilty by the Circuit Court of Appeals.

In particular the court condemned Noyes' actions as "extraordinary in the extreme" and found that his appointment of McKenzie as a receiver and the Judge's subsequent refusal to allow appropriate appeals "was so arbitrary and so unwarranted in law as to baffle the mind in its effort to comprehend how it could have been issued from a court of justice."

The majority of the court determined on fining Judge Noyes one thousand dollars for his contemptuous disregard of the court's orders, but Judge Ross, the third member, was not satisfied with that light penalty. He believed conspiracy charges were in order, rather than just contempt of court. "For these shocking offences it is apparent that no punishment that can be lawfully imposed in a contempt proceeding is adequate. But a reasonable imprisonment may be here imposed, and I am of the opinion that, in the case of the respondent Arthur H. Noyes, a judgment of imprisonment in a county jail for a period of 18 months should be imposed."

Though Noyes was spared a jail sentence and was never tried for conspiracy, the others were not so fortunate. Wood was sentenced to four months in jail, DuBose to six months, and Frost to twelve months. Either their health was better than McKenzie's or they had less political influence in Washington, for each served out his designated term in jail. Judge Noyes and district attorney Wood were removed from office; the dream of fortunes to be suddenly acquired by the conspirators by robbing the Nome miners faded away as McKenzie and his duped officials disappeared from Nome forever, but my struggle with the legacy of the gold conspiracy was only just beginning.*

---

* While he detested Alexander McKenzie and considered McKinley's commutation of his sentence a gross violation of justice, Judge Wickersham felt sympathy for Noyes. "I have talked with both the friends and enemies of Judge Noyes . . . from all I hear I conclude that he is an honest but a careless and rather weak man—one easily led by designing people who assume the tone and character of friends for sinister purposes. He has been imposed upon—and has weakly yielded to the plots and designs of persons who have not even defended him after imposing upon his weakness and credulity" (August 16, 1901).

EXTRA

COURT OPENS ON MONDAY

Judge James Wickersham Arrived Today from Unalaska.

Fred Hardy Convicted of the Murder of the Sullivan Brothers and P. J. Rooney on Unimak Island, June 8 Last---Hardy Sentenced to be Hanged in Nome on December 6, Next.

A special term of the district court will open in Nome Monday morning at 10 o'clock.

This is the statement made by Judge Wickersham to a NUGGET representative this morning.

Judge Wickersham, United States Marshal Richards, Assistant Prosecuting Attorney McGinn, Deputy Clerk Reed, Court Stenographer Hawkins, Deputy Marshal Griggs and the petit jury arrived on the steamship Senator at 6 o'clock this morning.

On board the steamer also was Fred Hardy, the convicted murderer of Con and Florence Sullivan and P. J. tenced to 20 years in the penitentiary at McNeil's island. He will be sent from Dutch Harbor to the island penitentiary.

The Murderer.

Fred Hardy says he was born in Lexington, Ohio, and is 25 years of age. He claims to have enlisted in the Second United States Cavalry, and when the Spanish war broke out he was appointed second lieutenant in the First Tennessee Volunteers.

Hardy made affidavit after affidavit before his trial, and on the witness stand repudiated almost every statement he had formerly made. Hardy

An "extra" from the Nome paper announcing Wickersham's arrival in September 1901 and his first court date.

10

LIARS AND THIEVES

Oh, every year hath its winter,
and every year hath its rain,
But a day is always coming
when the birds go north again.
—Ella Higginson

When I landed at Nome in mid-September 1901, it became apparent to me that a bad state of feeling existed.* The many bitter controversies over the Anvil Creek mining claims jumped by McKenzie and those who followed his example, had split the camp into warring factions, each of which took an opposite view about the mining laws in relation to locating mining claims.

Many were of the opinion that the jumpers were in the right because Judge Noyes held the law to be with them. Most persons assume that the judgments of their courts are based upon well-established principles of law and upon that assumption many persons at Nome supported the court. During this early period other persons, ignorant of the law applicable to such cases, jumped other claims because of the alleged want of citizenship by the original locators or other supposed defects in the locations.

* Wickersham realized immediately what was at stake for himself and the country. "I have been very kindly received by the people here and if I am not mistaken I have an opportunity to make a high and honorable record for myself as judge—if I am permitted to clean up the very bad condition which exists here.... Whether Judge Noyes is to blame or not for the unfortunate condition here, the fact exists that the Nome court tangle has annoyed and distressed the National administration—and I have a chance to correct the evil—if I am of such weight and character as to manage the immense and wide spread questions and interests involved. I feel absolutely equal to the emergency and intend to take hold with an iron hand—encased in silk. My greatest task so far in life, begins Monday morning and I feel no fear" (September 14, 1901).

The anger of the original owners was increased because, generally, they were given little or no opportunity to defend their rights, and the court too often aided the jumpers without notice to the owners. In this way, also, a large number of lawsuits between jumpers and owners had begun and now clogged the court's records awaiting trial. When Judge Noyes' view of the law was reversed, miners whose claims had been jumped demanded their return. They grew desperate when they were compelled to stand idly by and watch the jumpers continue to extract fortunes from their claims, without any way to recover their wealth through the courts.

No one had a clearer view of the desperate situation at Nome at that time than Judge Morrow, the able jurist who presided over the Court of Appeals at San Francisco, who said conditions were "deplorable in the extreme" due to the "judicial menace" hanging over Nome. When the court reversed Noyes' rulings, this situation grew more acute. Some even took the words of praise of their patient reliance upon the courts, uttered by the judges in the McKenzie contempt case, as an intimation that they would have been justified in taking the law into their own hands—and they did so.

After Judge Noyes had gone to San Francisco in early August, and I had followed to Unalaska, leaving Nome without a judge and with no promise that the court would convene there until next summer's boat arrived, some of these exasperated owners gathered in force, and equipped with firearms attacked the jumpers on their claims on Glacier Creek, and drove them off. They recovered immediate possession of their claims in this way, but shot one man seriously, injured others, placed themselves in opposition to the law, and brought military guards upon the ground. If the court had not returned that month the vigilantes and the "jumpers" would soon have been at civil war.

ON THE DAY AFTER my arrival at Nome in September 1901 to hold court for the winter, I conferred with General Randall on board the U.S.S. *Seward* to discuss the condition of affairs in the camp. We concluded that there was a sufficient force at Fort Davis to preserve the public peace and to aid the court in the enforcement of law and order.

Major Booth, the commander at Fort Davis, came to my office in the courthouse on Monday morning, prior to the opening of court. He gave me the details of the riot which had occurred on Glacier

Creek between the mine owners and the "jumpers." As soon as these acts of violence occurred, and others were threatened, the army had practically declared martial law in the mines by posting sentries on the claims to preserve the peace. As soon as court was convened and I was satisfied that civil authorities could control the situation and protect life and property, he would call in his armed military guards, but the forces under his command would be available at any time to defend the court and civil officers in the performance of their duties. After a full discussion of the situation I requested him to withdraw his soldiers and allow the civil authorities to resume the full responsibility of keeping order in the mines, but with the assurance of military support if necessary.

The soldiers were withdrawn from the mines that day, and no occasion arose thereafter for their services in support of the court. But without the military force at Fort Davis, under officers of courage and good judgment, there would most certainly have been other armed clashes between mine owners and "jumpers" and probably a serious loss of life.

THE MOST FREQUENT COMPLAINT heard against Judge Noyes was that being convivial by nature and easily approached by designing men, he allowed attorneys of that type to approach him up the "back stairs" and talk privately to him about cases pending in his court. In this way, it is said, mine owners were sometimes ejected from their mines without notice, or opportunity to defend or appeal their cases. To make it generally known that this manner of approaching the court was recognized as an evil and would not be tolerated, a public statement was made by me from the bench before a crowded courtroom on the opening of court the first day of the term, and published in the columns of the daily press in Nome:

> I respectfully request that no member of the bar shall in my private office, or any other place, except in the court room or in the presence of the opposing counsel, speak to me at any time upon any matter connected with the litigation in this court. It will be my endeavor to be in court publicly every day and give counsel every opportunity for a full hearing of any cause pending before the court, and the court earnestly requests that no member of the bar will presume upon his good nature by trying to engage him in private conversation in relation to any matter pending before the court.

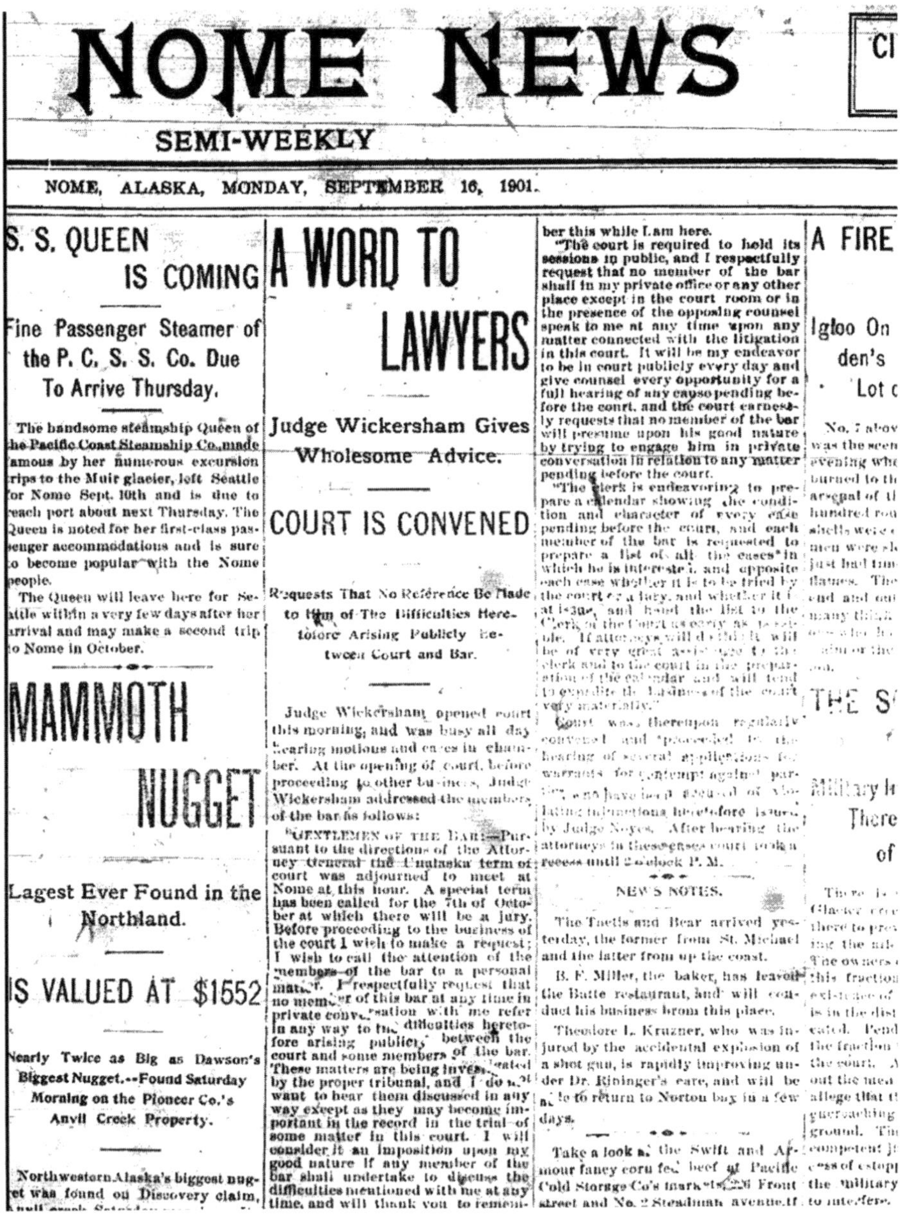

NOME NEWS

SEMI-WEEKLY

NOME, ALASKA, MONDAY, SEPTEMBER 16, 1901.

S. S. QUEEN IS COMING

Fine Passenger Steamer of the P. C. S. S. Co. Due To Arrive Thursday.

The handsome steamship Queen of the Pacific Coast Steamship Co., made famous by her numerous excursion trips to the Muir glacier, left Seattle for Nome Sept. 10th and is due to reach port about next Thursday. The Queen is noted for her first-class passenger accommodations and is sure to become popular with the Nome people.

The Queen will leave here for Seattle within a very few days after her arrival and may make a second trip to Nome in October.

MAMMOTH NUGGET

Lagest Ever Found in the Northland.

IS VALUED AT $1552

Nearly Twice as Big as Dawson's Biggest Nugget.--Found Saturday Morning on the Pioneer Co.'s Anvil Creek Property.

Northwestern Alaska's biggest nugget was found on Discovery claim, Anvil creek, Saturday ...

A WORD TO LAWYERS

Judge Wickersham Gives Wholesome Advice.

COURT IS CONVENED

Requests That No Reference Be Made to Him of The Difficulties Heretofore Arising Publicly Between Court and Bar.

Judge Wickersham opened court this morning, and was busy all day hearing motions and cases in chamber. At the opening of court, before proceeding to other business, Judge Wickersham addressed the members of the bar as follows:

"GENTLEMEN OF THE BAR:—Pursuant to the directions of the Attorney General the Unalaska term of court was adjourned to meet at Nome at this hour. A special term has been called for the 7th of October at which there will be a jury. Before proceeding to the business of the court I wish to make a request; I wish to call the attention of the members of the bar to a personal matter. I respectfully request that no member of this bar at any time in private conversation with me refer in any way to the difficulties heretofore arising publicly between the court and some members of the bar. These matters are being investigated by the proper tribunal, and I do not want to hear them discussed in any way except as they may become important in the record in the trial of some matter in this court. I will consider it an imposition upon my good nature if any member of the bar shall undertake to discuss the difficulties mentioned with me at any time, and will thank you to remember this while I am here.

"The court is required to hold its sessions in public, and I respectfully request that no member of the bar shall in my private office or any other place except in the court room or in the presence of the opposing counsel speak to me at any time upon any matter connected with the litigation in this court. It will be my endeavor to be in court publicly every day and give counsel every opportunity for a full hearing of any cause pending before the court, and the court earnestly requests that no member of the bar will presume upon his good nature by trying to engage him in private conversation in relation to any matter pending before the court.

"The clerk is endeavoring to prepare a calendar showing the condition and character of every case pending before the court, and each member of the bar is requested to prepare a list of all the cases in which he is interested, and opposite each case whether it is to be tried by the court or a jury, and whether it is at issue, and hand the list to the Clerk of the Court as early as possible. If attorneys will do this it will be of very great assistance to the clerk and to the court in the preparation of the calendar and will tend to expedite the business of the court very materially."

Court was thereupon regularly convened and proceeded to the hearing of several applications for warrants for contempt against parties who have been accused of violating injunctions heretofore issued by Judge Noyes. After hearing the attorneys in these cases court took a recess until 2 o'clock P. M.

NEWS NOTES.

The Thetis and Bear arrived yesterday, the former from St. Michael and the latter from up the coast.

B. F. Miller, the baker, has leased the Butte restaurant, and will conduct his business from this place.

Theodore L. Kruzner, who was injured by the accidental explosion of a shot gun, is rapidly improving under Dr. Rininger's care, and will be able to return to Norton bay in a few days.

Take a look at the Swift and Armour fancy corn fed beef at Pacific Cold Storage Co's markets, 226 Front street and No. 2 Steadman avenue.tf

A FIRE

Igloo On ... den's ... Lot ...

THE S...

Military ... There ... of ...

Wickersham's warning to the "Gentlemen of the Bar" that he would carry on the business of the court only in public court, and not make the back-room deals to which they had been accustomed under Judge Noyes.

This public announcement from the bench, the reports carried to Nome by the members of the grand and trial juries in service at Unalaska, and our daily progress with trials, seemed to bring about an increased confidence in the court, and a growing sentiment of friendly support of law and order by the people of the district.

DURING HIS ENTIRE YEAR of service, Judge Noyes had not issued a single written decision; not an opinion on any subject was to be found in the files. On inspecting the court records I found about two hundred cases were substantially ready for trial. Practically no cases, except the notorious Anvil Creek cases, had been concluded by final judgment, and the whole of last year's business with such additional cases as might thereafter be filed confronted the court. In other words, the court work was a whole year behind, and badly muddled by court orders made and entered *ex parte*, including those locally known as Noyes' "deep sea orders," signed by him after he had embarked on the steamer the night he left Nome.*

Owing to the exodus from Nome to be made on the last boats that fall, many lawyers wanted to procure a continuance of cases until the next summer. I notified the attorneys, however, that no continuances over winter would be allowed, and they must be ready to try their cases when they were called, or they would be dismissed. The clerk of the court arranged a trial calendar containing all cases at issue and a motion calendar to get others ready. Cases were peremptorily set for trial beginning on October 7, and continuing from day to day thereafter.

---

* The accumulated backlog of court cases demanded long days of intense concentration if the Judge would be able to clear the docket by the end of the winter. For instance on October 3, 1901, he heard and disposed of *U.S. v. Conant* in a fourteen-hour marathon court session. While he could have sentenced Conant to ten years for embezzlement, he decided to go easy on him, in contrast to pickpocket James Campbell, who was convicted about the same time.

"Will give Conant light sentence, for it is his first offence, so far as the evidence shows: it was simply a failure to stand up like a man—he yielded to whiskey & spent his employer's money. He has a wife and child—but [Campbell] is a hardened pickpocket—a thief—and I regret that I can only give him 2 ½ years in the penitentiary—for he deserves ten." Meanwhile his hours were filled with noncriminal work as well. "Civil cases are crowding hard these days and I work in the office and court room from 9 a.m. to 10 and 11 p.m. The only way to clean up the business of this country is to '*push hard*' and I intend to clean it up before spring" (October 5, 1901).

This forced the attorneys and their clients to be hard at work before referees and stenographers taking depositions of all clients and witnesses who intended to go outside for the winter. Almost day and night this went on until the last boat left Nome in the latter part of October. The result was that many cases were prepared for trial which otherwise must have been dismissed or continued until next summer. There were also some cases which could be tried by the court without a jury before the boats left. These were set and such trials went on early and late.*

THE MOST TRAGIC NEWS that fall of 1901 was the assassination of President William McKinley. It was only on the 18th of September that we first heard the news in Nome that the president had been shot twelve days earlier in Buffalo, New York. Not until September 28 did we learn that he had died two weeks previous on September 14.

I delivered an address in his memory at a public meeting. A great crowd gathered and general expressions of sorrow were heard from all classes of people. We realized, too, that a change of President might bring about a change in the cabinet and the appointment of a new attorney general of the United States, as well as a change of court officials at Nome. This thought was exciting to those who were aggressively interested in the appointment of Judge Noyes' successor, and had induced a renewal of complaints and charges against other officials of the court.

When the grand jury was impaneled on October 7th a prominent lawyer attempted to indict Judge Noyes, McKenzie, and even certain United States Senators for conspiracy in the Anvil Creek cases. I was opposed to this maneuver. McKenzie had already been convicted and sentenced, though pardoned by the President after not four months'

* Wickersham determined that despite the massive amount of work he faced, the legal problems would not be too difficult, and he relished the opportunity to make his own precedents. "After looking over the docket and studying the conditions here I am satisfied that there is no serious trouble ahead of me in the management of their litigation. The conditions are all new—there is no long line of local precedents to follow. I will be able to blaze out the trails myself, and with new conditions, new country, a population gathered from the ends of the earth, and a bar from every state and territory, and a new code without any binding decisions under it, I am at considerable liberty in my movements. It will only be necessary to be careful. Keep within the limits of the statute and the rules of equity—and work like a slave" (September 16, 1901).

incarceration. Judge Noyes, district attorney Wood, and others, were about to be tried before the court in San Francisco. In all probability none of these men would ever come back to Nome, their power was broken, and their conspiracy had not succeeded. We thought, also, it might have a bad influence locally in case the Glacier Creek rioters were indicted—that generally, the quicker the people of Nome and the court forgot those black days the better it would be for the administration of justice.*

AS I HAD HOPED, no indictments were returned on the court officials, but as I had feared, the grand jury did indict Jafet Lindeberg, J.W. Griffin, Till Price, and others of the Glacier Creek rioters. Lindeberg was one of the original Anvil Creek discoverers and locators; Griffin was a prominent lawyer and he and Till Price and the others mentioned in the indictment were all wealthy mine owners, though their claims were in possession of the McKenzie "jumpers." Being, as they supposed, without any other means of obtaining justice from the "jumpers," one night after Judge Noyes' departure they gathered a force of mine owners and friends, armed and masked themselves, and drove the "jumpers" off their claims. Unfortunately some nervous member of the party in the excitement shot one of the jumpers, wounding him seriously. This was the riot that had induced the military authorities at Fort Davis to put guards on the mines to prevent further disorder.

They were indicted for riot and had to stand trial on a serious charge. All gave bond for their appearance in court—all but Lindeberg. The story was that as soon as the grand jury concluded to bring in an indictment against him, some member of that body conveyed the information to Lindeberg. On hearing the news Lindeberg hastily put on his coat, took a poke of gold dust from his safe, hired a small boat, and caught the steamer *Queen* just as she was hoisting anchor—and went to San Francisco to spend the winter.

Two weeks later Griffin's case was the first to be heard. After two or three days' trial the jury failed to agree and I discharged them. My sympathies were with Griffin, and if he had been convicted my determination was to assess only a moderate fine as penalty. Later, on

* Albert Fink was the attorney who wanted to indict Noyes and McKenzie (October 19, 1901).

the application of Griffin, his case was continued for a new trial until after the boats returned to Nome the next summer. The case against Price resulted also in a hung jury, and feeling sure that the prejudice of the camp's jurors was so pronounced that none of the rioters could be convicted, after a time I dismissed all the cases.

R. N. STEVENS WAS one of McKenzie's appointees from North Dakota. He had come to Nome with Judge Noyes and McKenzie and was immediately appointed United States commissioner for the Nome district, which made him ex officio the justice of the peace, recorder, probate judge, and coroner for that district. Stevens was a shrewd and clever lawyer, and McKenzie made a mistake in not procuring his appointment as district judge instead of Noyes, for Stevens would have kept the boss out of much of his trouble. However, he had the same craving as the rest of McKenzie's followers, to get all the traffic would bear as quickly as possible. Stevens occupied a house opposite the courthouse, kept his court and recorder's office in the front room and lived with his family in the rear rooms. He had not made any report of his official receipts and expenditures since his appointment by Judge Noyes on July 23, 1900, though the law required him to do so quarterly. On being ordered to file his official accounts he presented one covering the period from July 23, 1900, to June 30, 1901, showing receipts of $22,895.65, and running expenses of the office for $22,700.45. The report showed that he paid—or charged the government—one hundred dollars per month for the front room in his dwelling house for use as courtroom and recorder's office. All coal, oil, heat, and general supplies for the whole house were also charged as official expense. Enough was charged for his house and family salaries to cover the balance of the total receipts. His expenses were so grossly irregular and excessive that I issued an order removing him from office and sent it to Washington with his accounts, which I refused to approve.

About a year previous, the town council of Nome had passed an ordinance creating a municipal court and appointed Stevens municipal judge. This made him the sole depositary of all judicial power at Nome except that held by his chief, Judge Noyes. A person convicted of some alleged violation of a town ordinance brought a writ of habeas corpus in the district court to test the authority of the town of Nome to create a municipal court, and it became my duty to decide that the town had no such power and the municipal court no legal existence.

The evidence disclosed that Stevens had taken in about $9,000 in fees and fines as municipal judge and had received a good fat salary and heavy expenses, in addition to the salary, fees, and expenses he had received as commissioner, justice of the peace, recorder, probate judge, and coroner. In essence the municipal court had taken $9,000 that would have been earned by the district court, and by so doing Stevens got the additional salary and expenses as municipal judge! It was a smart trick, and my judgment declaring it illegal was cause for more loud and angry complaints and charges. From his two offices Stevens made twice as much as Judge Noyes, his erstwhile boss. There could be no peace or public confidence in the courts while he held the next most important judicial office in the camp. Therefore I ordered him to be removed from office and appointed in his place Thomas M. Reed, a prominent, capable, and honest attorney.

I SOON ASCERTAINED THAT other officials had also been collecting grossly padded or false accounts from the government, charging two or three times the actual sums paid for official expenses, defrauding the government with the approval of the court. The quarterly account of Marshal Frank Richards was presented to me for approval. On examination it disclosed he had charged twice as much as I had paid for the same service at the same hotel.

I called in the hotel keeper who frankly admitted that it was the custom to sign bills or vouchers against the government for the marshal and other officials for larger amounts than were actually paid. When I called in the marshal and laid the matter before him he had nothing to say.* I suggested he withdraw the present account, so falsely verified, and present another stating the account truthfully. He did so without a word. The corrected account was approved, minus hundreds of false items contained in the first one. Richards was another of the

* "Marshal Richards is 'ugly' about his 'padded' accounts, and seeks to get even with the Golden Gate Hotel people by taking the juries to a downtown restaurant to eat, at a saving of twenty-five cents per meal. As the change would involve sending the juries through the crowded streets, filled with every class (including the criminals and their friends and sympathizers), and would take juries away from the eyes of the court I will not allow it. Still the incident shows the Marshal's disposition—I am making the record on him & fixing him so he cannot hurt anyone as much as he may try" (October 17, 1901).

CATCHY Job Printing of all Kinds Promptly Executed at the News office

The Nome News

SPRING is Here at Last and the Wise Merchant Now Begins to Advertise

Vol. 4, No. 33 — NOME, ALASKA, FRIDAY, MAY 30, 1902 — Price 25 Cents

U. S. MARSHAL F. H. RICHARDS UNDER ARREST

District Attorney McGinn Charges Him With Fixing the Jury in the Joseph H. Wright Embezzlement Case Last April.

THE HEARING SET FOR MONDAY

Defendants Permitted to Go on Their Own Reconizances Until That Time.

A Big sensation was sprung yesterday afternoon at 2 o'clock when Assistant District Attorney McGinn appeared before Judge Wickersham and filed a lengthy complaint charging United States Marshal Frank Richards and City Councilman Joe Jourden with conspiracy and contempt of court in connection with the jury in the Joe Wright embezzlement case.

Upon the reading of the complaint an order of arrest was issued and placed in the hands of Deputy Marshal A. C. Griggs for immediate service, and the time of hearing was fixed at 10 A. M. Monday, June 2.

The court room was almost deserted when District Attorney McGinn filed his complaint and asked for the arrest of the defendants named. It came like a flash of lightning out of a clear sky. No one outside of the Wright trial, and that there is a great mass of evidence.

Marshal Richards and Mr. Jourden spent the greater part of the afternoon with their lawyers, P. C. Sullivan and Albert Fink. In legal circles nothing else was discussed last night.

The complaint filed by District Attorney McGin yesterday is quite a lengthy one. Its preamble sets forth that John L. McGin, Assistant United States Attorney, prosecutes for the United States against the defendant, Frank H. Richards, for contempt of this Honorable Court, for misbehavior in office and wilful neglect and violation of duty, and impairing, impeding and obstructing the administration of Justice in a cause pending, and for the unlawful interference with the process and the proceedings of this Court, and against the defendant, Joseph D. Jourden for contempt of the author-

THE ORDER OF ARREST

IN THE UNITED STATES DISTRICT COURT FOR THE SECOND DIVISION, DISTRICT OF ALASKA.

UNITED STATES,
PLAINTIFF
vs
FRANK H. RICHARDS AND
JOSEPH D. JOURDEN,
DEFENDANTS.

To A. C. Griggs, United States Deputy Marshal For The Second Division Of The District Of Alaska, Greeting

An affidavit having been this day presented to me in open court by John L. McGinn, Assistant United States District Attorney for the Second Division of the District of Alaska, charging the above named defendants with contempt of the authority of this Honorable Court,

You are therefore commanded forthwith to arrest the above named defendants, Frank H. Richards and Joseph D. Jourden and bring them before me on Monday the 2nd day of June, 1902, at the hour of 10 a. m., then and there to show cause why they and each of them should not be punished for contempt as in said affidavit alleged, and that from the time of said arrest up to the 2nd day of June, 1902, at the hour of 10 a. m., said defendants be permitted to go on their own recognisance.

And it is ordered that a copy of said affidavit and of this order be served on the said Frank H. Richards and Joseph D. Jourden forthwith.

JAMES WICKERSHAM,
Judge U. S. District Court.

in utter disregard of his official duty, and in unlawful interferance with the process and proceedings of the court, and in furtherance of a conspiracy, combination and confederacy theretobefore entered into with Joseph D. Jourden and Joseph H. Wright and persons acting on his behalf, to defeat the ends of justice, and to unlawfully and corruptly procure trial particularly while the jury was being impanneled with the view and for the purpose of summoning them as jurors in said case, believing they would, if selected, render a verdict for the defendant, Joe. H. Wright.

Affiant further says that the defendant, Frank H. Richards, did then prepare and issue summonses for Geo. Shea, M. J. Sullivan and W. H.

Councilman Joseph D. Jourden Charged With Being a Fellow Conspirator and Arrested at Same Time.—Ugly Allegations.

SWEEPING DENIAL OF CHARGES

Both Men Claim That the Affidavit Filed Against Them is Without Foundation in Fact.

[illegible] seph H. Wright [illegible] ly and unlawfully [illegible] the due and lawful [illegible] and in furtherance of [illegible] tered into between [illegible] prior to the trial of [illegible] fully, wickedly and [illegible] behalf of said Joseph H. [illegible] and [illegible] was then and there [illegible] regular panel of trial jurors in attendance upon the court [illegible] said Joseph H. Wright [illegible] der a verdict for him [illegible] pending.

Affiant further says that [illegible] Sullivan, Gaffney, [illegible] did qualify as jurors in said cause, and did render a verdict in said cause of not guilty; [illegible] of said acts of Frank H. Richards and Joseph D. Jourden and [illegible] the conspiracy [illegible] federacy and agreement [illegible] said cause of the United States vs. Joseph H. Wright was defeated and [illegible] thereby.

The case of the United States vs. Joseph H. Wright was called April [illegible], and after the jury, in the selection of which it is alleged Marshal Richards and Joe Jourden took a hand for corrupt and illegal purposes, was qualified and sworn [illegible] the greater part of two days. After five hours deliberation the jury returned a verdict of not guilty. It was not known how the jury stood on the various ballots. The jury was made up of the following persons: W. A. Snyder, P. L. Eddy, J. C. Gaffney, [illegible] H. Murphy, C. M. Lambert, G. M. Shea, A. F. Long, W. T. Kames, John McDonald, M. J. Sullivan, Ed Jones, C. P. Vogel, five of whom, it is alleged in the complaint filed by Prosecutor McGinn, were tampered with by Richards and Jourden.

Best Carter's ink, 5 cents per bottle,

The arrest of Marshal Frank Richards and Joe Jourden under the orders of Judge Wickersham garnered a full front page of coverage.

McKenzie crowd, and from that moment he joined with Stevens in attacks upon me both in Nome and in Washington.*

Before the trouble arose over his false accounts Richards had officially informed me that a fund had been raised by certain interests to bribe the acting district attorney [John L. McGinn]. I had complete confidence in the integrity of the prosecuting attorney, and none in the marshal, but answered that if the statements could be verified by competent evidence it would be allowed to go to the grand jury. No such evidence was ever produced.

About the same time, reputable members of the bar complained that the marshal was engaged in fixing juries. When a jury was called in such cases, and the regular panel was exhausted, it was the practice under the law to issue an open venire to the marshal to summon a sufficient number of persons to complete the jury. The marshal, or one of his confidential deputies, would go out in town, more often to Joe Jourden's saloon nearby, and summon known partisans of the litigant he wished to help to fill up the jury.

Those men would know or be advised how to qualify when questioned. Once seated they could at least hang the jury. In one case particularly, when Acting District Attorney McGinn was prosecuting a defaulting postmaster [Joseph Wright], this scheme was carried out

---

* By the end of 1901, the battle of wills between Judge Wickersham and Marshal Richards had neared the breaking point, with the Judge determined to make Richards stop embezzling public funds through excess charges.

"The U.S. Marshal is very much exercised over a rule requiring him to call for competitive bids for all purchases supplies &c. He came to see me & said that in his opinion I had nothing to do but just to approve his accounts! That he had the power to purchase &c. &c. He is the last relic left of the old regime & he yields badly, but he will yield. I will not approve a dollar of his accounts except in compliance with the rule. Heretofore every petty official in this district seems to have been a law unto himself so far as expenses were concerned, and Judge Noyes was never known to refuse their exorbitant demands out of the goodness and weakness of his heart. When the Marshal falls into line, as he will, the court will then have full and entire charge of all expenditures in this district except for fixed salaries, fixed by law. As long as I remain here I intend to keep control, and no expenditure either in the clerk's or Marshal's office, or by any Commissioner or other official where I am required to audit the account will be allowed except such as are incurred under the rules and honestly. The auditing of such accounts, and the duty of dividing the funds between towns and school boards, and my general duty as financial agent for the government in all court and municipal matters give me more real trouble and annoyance than anything else I have to do. But so long as I have it to do I intend to control it" (December 21, 1901).

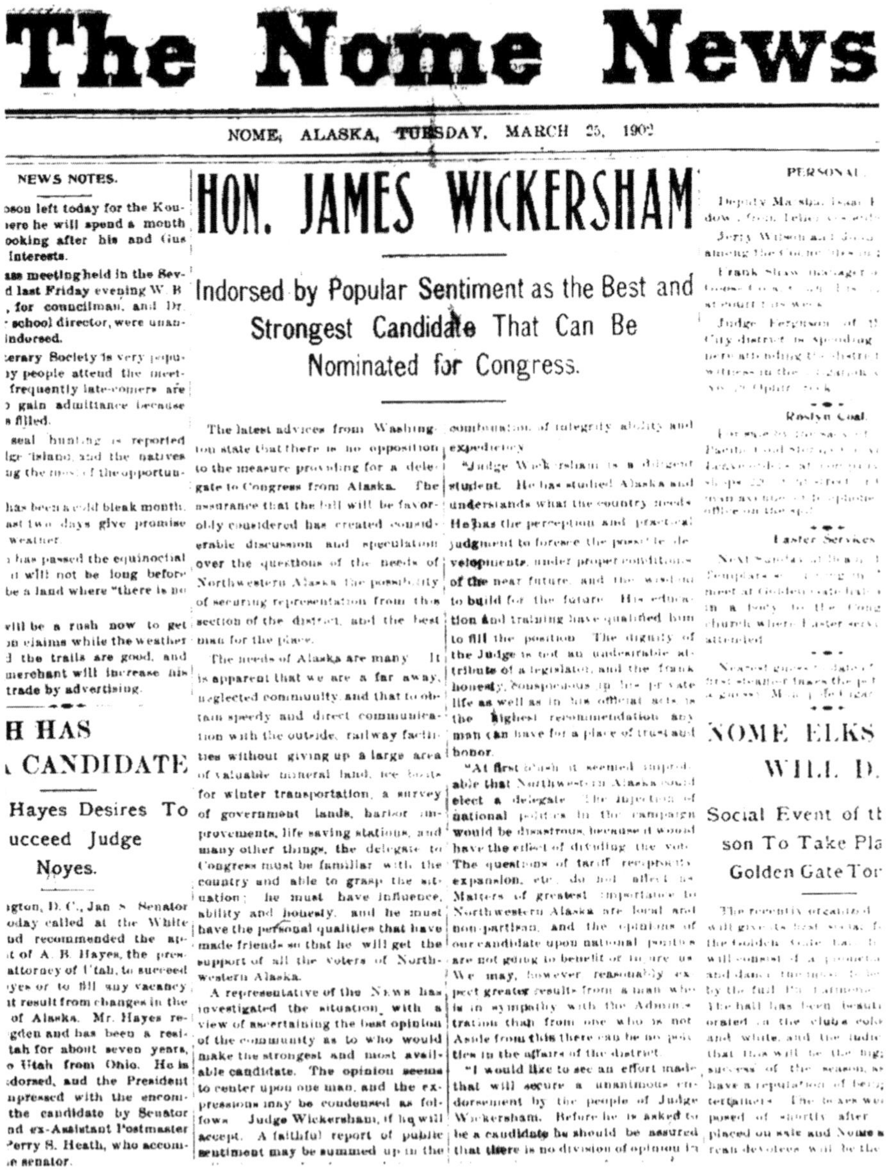

The Nome News

NOME, ALASKA, TUESDAY, MARCH 25, 1902

HON. JAMES WICKERSHAM

Indorsed by Popular Sentiment as the Best and Strongest Candidate That Can Be Nominated for Congress.

The latest advices from Washington state that there is no opposition to the measure providing for a delegate to Congress from Alaska. The assurance that the bill will be favorably considered has created considerable discussion and speculation over the questions of the needs of Northwestern Alaska the possibility of securing representation from this section of the district, and the best man for the place.

The needs of Alaska are many. It is apparent that we are a far away, neglected community, and that to obtain speedy and direct communication with the outside, railway facilities without giving up a large area of valuable mineral land, ice boats for winter transportation, a survey of government lands, harbor improvements, life saving stations, and many other things, the delegate to Congress must be familiar with the country and able to grasp the situation; he must have influence, ability and honesty, and he must have the personal qualities that have made friends so that he will get the support of all the voters of Northwestern Alaska.

A representative of the News has investigated the situation with a view of ascertaining the best opinion of the community as to who would make the strongest and most available candidate. The opinion seems to center upon one man, and the expressions may be condensed as follows: Judge Wickersham, if he will accept. A faithful report of public sentiment may be summed up in the combination of integrity ability and expediency.

"Judge Wickersham is a diligent student. He has studied Alaska and understands what the country needs. He has the perception and practical judgment to foresee the possible developments under proper conditions of the near future, and the wisdom to build for the future. His education and training have qualified him to fill the position. The dignity of the Judge is not an undesirable attribute of a legislator, and the frank honesty, conspicuous in his private life as well as in his official acts is the highest recommendation any man can have for a place of trust and honor.

"At first blush it seemed improbable that Northwestern Alaska could elect a delegate. The injection of national politics in the campaign would be disastrous, because it would have the effect of dividing the vote. The questions of tariff reciprocity, expansion, etc., do not affect us. Matters of greatest importance to Northwestern Alaska are local and non-partisan, and the opinions of our candidate upon national politics are not going to benefit or injure us. We may, however, reasonably expect greater results from a man who is in sympathy with the Administration than from one who is not. Aside from this there can be no politics in the affairs of the district.

"I would like to see an effort made that will secure a unanimous endorsement by the people of Judge Wickersham. Before he is asked to be a candidate he should be assured that there is no division of opinion in

For his diligent and courageous legal work in cleaning up the corruption in Nome, Wickersham earned wide admiration. As early as 1902, the Nome News *started boosting him as a candidate for delegate to Congress.*

successfully and the postal officer walked free. Furious at this miscarriage of justice, McGinn brought a proceeding for contempt of court against Marshal Richards and Jourden, the saloonkeeper who assisted in fixing the jury.

I presided at the nonjury trial that found both Richards and Jourden guilty and fined each of them the sum of three hundred dollars.* Jourden paid his fine, but the marshal—realizing the conviction would mean loss of office—moved for a new trial and attacked me savagely for prejudice.

A year later the appellate court did overrule my decision in the Richards case—on the grounds that the record did not contain sufficient evidence to sustain the verdict—but I think the Department of Justice eventually came to agree with my evaluation of Richards. When Assistant Attorney General Day came to Nome in 1904—in the investigation into my judicial conduct—on Day's recommendation Richards was finally removed from office because of the jury fixing scandal. Naturally the marshal then joined in the Stevens hue and cry against me, filing charges in Washington complaining about my conduct—but the filing of false accounts under oath against government funds, and the fixing of juries through the marshal's office, ceased.†

---

* "Instructed McGinn to procure the evidence & institute proceedings in jury fixing cases" (May 3, 1902). Since the jury-fixing trial pitted half of the Nome legal establishment against the other half, the hatred and rancor came through with every word of the proceedings. "Never in the judicial history of Nome," the *Nome Nugget* reported, "has a case been so bitterly prosecuted as this one." *Nugget* editor J. F. A. Strong, an old friend of the marshal, thought Wickersham was much too personally involved in this case in order to render a fair judgment. Strong claimed the "unseemly" language of Wickersham's final opinion, an angry diatribe that took him 45 minutes to read, revealed his animus towards the Marshal. "It is not an opinion that can be classified as dignified." According to Strong, the case against the marshal was "a gross miscarriage of justice and grave judicial error" and Wickersham had convicted him without "a scintilla of evidence" (*Nome Nugget*, June 18, 1902).

† The Marshal Richards jury-tampering case would prove to be one of the most important in Wickersham's career. Though the Ninth Circuit Court of Appeals overturned the conviction in 1903 due to a lack of evidence on the record, Wickersham remained convinced that there was more than enough evidence off the record proving Marshal Richards was a crook.

The Judge's uncompromising stance was one reason he would be denied the permanent position as Nome Judge in 1902; it would also be repeatedly used against him in his reconfirmation battle in Washington, D.C., from 1904 to

THE LAST BOAT OF the year en route to San Francisco left Nome on October 30, 1901, carrying away those who had remained as late as possible either as litigants or witnesses in completing the records in cases which had to be prepared for trial before they could leave. We then had time for the careful examination of the clerk's records and the orderly arrangement of the court's business for the winter's work. We began with the first case on the dockets and dismissed or set for hearing every case to the last one filed. About one hundred cases were dismissed for want of prosecution. Counsel voluntarily dismissed many others rather than go to trial without witnesses who were in the States.

The live cases were arranged in calendars for further action. We found about two hundred live cases pending, many on incomplete pleadings and arranged these as they were for action or trial by the court or a jury. We set a case a day for trial, and began trying them in order. Court convened at nine o'clock in the morning and, if necessary to conclude the case, continued until 10:30 at night. In this way we continued until January when the work began to slow up. The greater number of these cases had been on the court's dockets for several months, some for a year, and no previous attempt had been made to try them. Most of them were mining cases involving "jumpers" who had taken possession of claims. As the trials proceeded and the legal owners of claims were established by law, the business of the town and district began to respond to the settlement of titles and enabled us to try them with some speed and satisfaction.

IN JANUARY 1902, AFTER several months of active work in court, both day and night, and the final trial of most of the important mining cases, the court and members of the bar agreed on taking a month's vacation to enable the clerk to make a new list of cases for action and trial in the February term. I made a dog team trip to Cape Prince of Wales, the clerks made up new trial dockets, and the

---

1907. Wickersham was certain of the marshal's guilt and could not tolerate his perversion of justice, in spite of the threat Richards posed to him personally. As he wrote in his diary on June 9, 1902: "They are preparing to attack me, so I am told, upon the old trouble of 1888 [Sadie Brantner seduction case]. Well, I must meet it with fortitude and courage for it must come sooner or later—if I shrink from duty on account of that threat it proves that I am unworthy to be a judge" (see pp. xvi–xvii).

attorneys were busy preparing their cases. The spring term began on February 17th, and court was constantly in session thereafter until the summer boats came to Nome.

In the meantime Judge Noyes had been removed from office and Alfred A. Moore, of Pennsylvania, had been appointed in his place. Judge Moore arrived at Nome on July 13, 1902. On the next day it was my pleasure to introduce him to the attorneys, court officials, and other persons in Nome. My wife had reached Nome on one of the first boats in June, and two days after Judge Moore's arrival we left there for our home at Eagle City. Terms of court had previously been called to meet at Rampart and at Eagle on my arrival there, where it was necessary for me to begin trying the accumulated business in my own district after a year's absence. The evergreen forests along the Yukon looked like the flowery fringes of Paradise to me after a year's residence on the barren and treeless tundra at Nome.*

---

* Despite his claim that a year in Nome had made the Yukon forests look like the "flowery fringes of Paradise," Wickersham would have much preferred to stay on the tundra as the judge of the Second Division. In 1902 Nome was Alaska's largest and most important city, with the most exciting prospects for future development, and he hated the thought of being sent back to the small villages on the Yukon.

"Am to go back to Eagle—[big opposition against me] in Washington. I am disappointed only in one respect—that my friends have made a strong fight & have lost, and there is work to do here [in Nome] and little there [in Eagle]" (June 5, 1902).

Except for Marshal Richards and others who had come out on the losing side of battles in Wickersham's court, most Nome residents—including attorneys—were sorry to see him go. The *Nome News* said Wickersham had inherited from Judge Noyes a gavel "rapping the signals for loot and reprisal" and a legacy of "discord, enmity, dissension and soul-sickening scandal," but was in turn leaving behind a clean slate and a fresh start. Even editor Strong of the *Nome Nugget*, who would lambast the Judge's treatment of Marshal Richards, had nothing but praise for what Wickersham had done for Nome. "He has done much to restore a confidence that was lacking, and his single-minded efforts have taught most men that there is but one application of the laws of the land—that which guarantees equal rights to all and discrimination against none.... No breath of suspicion has ever been directed against his honesty and integrity of purpose, though, perhaps, in the discharge of his multifarious duties, he has made stout enemies as well as staunch friends. We regret that he is to leave us" (*Nome Nugget*, June 4, 1902).

11

SOCIAL LIFE AT NOME, 1901–1902

The Judge was a Christian and he played on the square,
But he figured the cards pretty close;
He could call out your hand every time to a pair—
And could lay down a full when he chose.
The Colonel, he played a more difficult game—
I don't mean to say he would cheat;
But he held the top cards when the big betting came,
And some hands that you never could beat.

—Jack Hines

IN 1899, HON. CHARLES S. Johnson, the U.S. district judge for Alaska, heard that a great gold strike had been made at the mouth of the Nome River. He advised the few men at Anvil City (Nome) to form a consent municipal government to prepare to receive and control the great number of people they expected to land on the Nome beach next summer. A committee of seven—Thomas D. Cashel, Edward R. Beeman, Arthur M. Pope, William M. Eddy, Edward P. Ingraham, Robt. Bruce Milroy, and A. E. Claflin—was appointed to serve until Congress should pass appropriate laws. This committee changed the name of the town from Anvil City to Nome and elected Cashel mayor, Eddy chief of police, Key Pittman city attorney, James P. Rudd treasurer, and Alonzo Rawson municipal judge.

IN THE SUMMER OF 1900, twenty thousand men and a few women, coming pell-mell from every quarter of America and from every race and walk in life, landed upon the tundra meadow at the mouth of Snake River. They gathered in great confusion, landing from a fleet of vessels anchored two miles off the shallow roadstead. They climbed from the gravelly beach to sink knee-deep into low and soggy tundra meadows.

The first thought of these twenty thousand people was to get a small spot on this wet tundra, as near to the center of the town as possible, upon which to erect a cabin or a tent. Crowding and pushing against one another, with no place to pile their luggage or to lay a bed, they unavoidably trespassed upon claims located by those preceding them; and here the wisdom of the ordinances of the consent government compelled a recognition of the prior rights of those in possession. The municipal court heard all these cases, and they were many; the court applied the evidence; the titles by prior possession were settled summarily, whereby peace was maintained. And that by a court having no statutory law behind its judgments, but only the common consent and good sense of American citizens.

The western cowboy, armed with an over-ready revolver, mounted on his fleet cattle pony, able to fly to safety across wide, dry plains, was wholly unknown to the Nome country. The adventuring and too often intoxicated and armed ruffian of the western mining camps was as rare on the shores of Bering Sea as he was common and dangerous in Colorado and California. Former members of the "Soapy" Smith gang of desperadoes from the Chilkoot Trail, and hundreds of other criminals—escaped and hunted convicts from the States and foreign countries—landed at Nome, took a good look at the conditions that confronted them—and became quiet, discreet, and sometimes hard-working and peaceable citizens. The saloons, gambling rooms, dance-halls, and houses of prostitution ran wide open, but under strict police protection; there was but little drunkenness, few hidden dens of vice, and no gunfighters or highwaymen in wild western style.

In the short summer season, one moved only by the river and sea routes, or very slowly, if at all, over tundra quagmires which extended for great distances overland. Steamers voyaged regularly from mid-June to mid-October between Nome, Seattle, and San Francisco, but criminals found little safety on their decks. From early fall till late spring, the sea route was closed by Bering Sea ice fields, and the only route of escape for the fleeing criminal was by dog team over the frozen Yukon River. A two-thousand-mile journey along its always dangerous, cold, and lonesome trail was a far greater deterrent to crime than the Nome jail or even a jury trial. Nome was, in its first three winters, the most orderly mining camp ever known in the Far West—thanks to natural climatic conditions and the common sense and courage of the people of Nome.

Self-interest, also, made a strong appeal to the saloonkeepers at Nome. They had brought their liquor and other supplies and paraphernalia to that far-away camp and fitted up their places of business at great expense. Generally their whole fortune was in the enterprise; money was plentiful, business was good, and consequently it was to their advantage and best interest to support law and order, rather than to engage in criminal pursuits. Tex Rickard, of the Northern saloon, and others of his kind, led in this wise course and made good advisers to the sporting class, their employees, and patrons.

Congress had recently authorized the sale of intoxicating liquor in Alaska saloons, fixed a license fee of one thousand dollars per annum, and placed the control of saloons under a modified form of local option, under control of the judges of the district court. Of the many saloons licensed in Nome before my arrival, or later by me, not one descended to the level of the criminal dives so common at one time in cities in the eastern States.

In a lesser measure all the sporting resorts at Nome followed the practical course of conduct adopted by the saloons, thereby greatly lessening crime and more certainly aiding in its punishment. My practical experience with the Nome saloons and their keepers led me to look upon them, managed and controlled as they were by self-interest and the law, as aids in basic social work in that distant frontier mining camp, for they afforded idle men a warm and cheerful meeting place, which they needed, and gave them fair protection from sharpers who were not permitted to rob them in or about the saloons.

Gambling? Yes, of course, in every saloon and cabin in Nome. Every real miner and prospector in the early-day goldfields in Alaska, or any other goldfield for that matter, was a gambler. Nature so mixed the clay in him that but one thing was needed to start him off—a game! The natural-born prospector, and there is no other kind, will hoist a mule-load pack on his back, tramp off alone into an Arctic wilderness, and bet his life, his family, his grubstake, and his best friend—his dog—that he will find the richest paystreak in America before he returns to town or camp. A thousand such characters spent

The Officers' Club at Fort Davis, which Wickersham called the center of Nome society.
(Alaska State Library, William E. Hunt Collection, ASL-P155-1-042)

a thousand years—all together—before they found the Forty-Mile, Circle, Klondike, and the Nome gold creeks.

Failure? They never failed, they merely renewed the bet the next winter, and the next, and continued to renew it every season until they crossed the last divide which led them to the bourne whence no prospector or gambler ever returned.

The frontier prospector had an uncontrollable desire to gamble. As the story goes, a friend warned one who was losing heavily at the faro table that the game was not on the square; that he was being swindled; that he had no chance to win. "Yes," he replied, "what you say is probably true, but it's the only game in town."

The first boat and the second dog team to reach a new Yukon gold strike always carried a woman of the bright lights, for these women struggled as valiantly as the men to be earliest in a new camp where they were classed as "warm storage" and deemed quite necessary to the comfort and permanence of the place. Nome, of course, had her dance halls and a restricted district both much patronized by the sporting crowd.

Coming into the camp in search of fortune and adventure—and sometimes a husband—these women lived under better conditions than usually prevailed in the more crowded resorts of that kind in the States. The sporting women were of a more robust class than usual among their kind, hence there were fewer cases of venereal and other diseases among them.* The women also were younger, more vigorous, and independent than those of the same class in the older and more crowded communities in the States, and for these reasons they were less addicted to criminal activities outside of those peculiar to their mode

---

* At the time Wickersham did not have such a rosy view of the prostitutes he encountered in the courtroom. For instance after one "Helen Wagner" was convicted of larceny in October 1901, a parade of her colleagues and customers came to perjure themselves to try to get her a new trial.

"The defense filed a lot of affidavits, including one by . . . the prosecuting witness, who retracted all the evidence [responsible for] the conviction of the defendant. She robbed him in the Gold Belt Saloon rooms while he occupied her bed with her. She is, of course, a prostitute and dance hall performer of the lowest type. All of her companions in infamy gathered to her aid and flooded the court with false affidavits on the motion for a new trial: I sent out the Marshal, rounded them up, put them on the witness stand, and sifted their stories to the bottom . . . and sentenced the woman to 3 years at the McNeil Island penitentiary. The only face that class of people recognize is the ability of the law to punish. . . . They live by violating the laws, and I am not going to be too lenient with them" (October 22, 1901).

of life. A goodly number of these women yielded to the persuasions of their favorite male customers, married them, quit the life of the dance hall or the bawdy house and calmly settled down to a quiet home life with their husbands. It quite frequently became my duty as judge to perform marriage ceremonies for persons of that class, and more often than not such marriages were successful.*

Fort Davis, situated two miles east of Nome on the sea beach, with its young army officers and their wives, was the center of the social life of the town. The Golden Gate hotel, the Elks and Arctic Brotherhood halls, and the Standard theater gave weekly balls, with extra dances when desired by any of the fraternal orders. The hotel, and the theater especially, had large and well-arranged ballrooms, provided good music, and were splendidly lighted by electric globes newly installed. Crowds of fashionably gowned women and well-dressed men filled these orderly and respectable places. The fraternal orders—the Masons, the Elks, and particularly the Arctic Brotherhood, a distinctly Alaskan order—kept social life busy during the winter months and especially during the holiday season.†

---

* One such marriage that Wickersham performed in 1902 was for Magnus Kjelsberg and Olga Riskin. The Judge initially met Olga at a party in December 1901 where she was introduced as Mrs. Kjelsberg. He was told at the time that "Magnus married her in S.F. where she was known in the highest demimonde society as 'Russian Rosa' & where she made a fortune as an adventuress" (December 21, 1901). The Judge was infatuated with the mysterious and "beautiful tigress":

"She is really a remarkable woman. She has tact, taste and great talents. Her power with men is astonishing. Highly educated—a linguist—a woman of great physical charms and strength, strong in her natural mental endowments, and skilled in the game of the world—she is such a woman as has in times gone by overturned thrones. Cleopatra—Sara Bernhardt—Delilah. These are the ingredients that enter into the composition of this Russian adventuress—who made a fortune in San Francisco as the keeper of an assignation house—and in a year—as the wife of one of the magnates of Anvil Creek, gets Nome society by the ears.... The Pioneer Min. Co. is composed of Lindblom, Byrnteson, Lindeberg and Kjelsberg—all Russian Finns—over whom this bold, black-eyed woman will rule like a barbarian queen. Is she in love with her great, strapping, silent husband—or is it only another 'graft'?" (December 26, 1901).

Three months later "Mrs. Kjelsberg" confessed that she and Kjelsberg were not married. The Judge quietly performed the ceremony for them in front of two witnesses on March 31, 1902.

† Nome's recently completed electric plant made the regular evening socials particularly pleasant in the long winter nights. However, the Judge was usually only a spectator. "The town is 'dance mad'—but I have escaped that disease" (January 1, 1901).

The churches vied to afford opportunities for social gatherings, and all of them provided open reading rooms and libraries for those who wished to enjoy them. Card parties, private dinners, and home dances and musicales were almost nightly forms of innocent pleasure. The most brilliant young lawyer at the bar of the court and one of the most vivacious and beautiful young women in town kept the gossips agog until one happy day they were joined in wedlock by the Episcopal parson at a splendid ceremony followed by a marriage feast.*

THREE LIVELY NOME NEWSPAPERS, though unaided by telegraphic dispatches from the outside world, kept their readers somewhat familiar with local gossip, mining matters, and such items of news as passed over the "grapevine" along the Yukon winter trail, via Skagway and Dawson. The *Nome News* was established by Major J. F. A. Strong and its first issue was that of October 9, 1899. He was an experienced man in every job on the paper and a brilliant writer. He had shipped his small outfit of machinery, type, and supplies from Dawson down the Yukon to Nome in 1899 on hearing the first whisper of the rumor of the Anvil Creek strike. The *Nome Gold Digger* began to set type only two weeks after the *News* had opened its shop, and the *Nome Nugget* began business on the opening of navigation in the spring of 1901.

A public school building was erected in 1900 from lumber shipped from Puget Sound, and its rooms were filled with children, who loved their dogs, sleds, and the snow trails better than they did their books. Dog racing had already been organized as a permanent Arctic sport, and races from Nome to Solomon River and return were run by contesting teams for a fair division of a public purse and side bets. Bering Sea was covered with a heavy coat of winter ice; pressure from the sea had driven the ice, many feet in thickness, high upon the shallow shores along the Nome front into huge rough ridges.

The great single electric light atop the Catholic church spire guided the Anvil Creek miners coming to town to enjoy the warmth and

* "Attended marriage of [attorney Albert] Fink & Miss [Laura] Meiggs yesterday afternoon at 4 o'clock.... The punch was composed of brandy, whisky, champagne & a little coloring matter—I only remained 10 minutes, got my small bit of wedding cake and left—but the occasion, I am informed today was worthy of the reputation that both of them have for hard drinking" (December 19, 1901).

comfort of the New Year's festival. The surrounding region—the ice fields of the sea, the wide frozen tundra, and the nearby rolling Arctic mountains—were covered with a mantle of snow. But not even a north-wind blizzard could cool the ardor of holiday cheer.*

* "This is the shortest day [December 21] of the year—exact mid-winter, and I am pleased to find that it has gone by so quickly.... So far the weather at Nome has been mild, and for a week now rather moist. But it blows very badly" (December 21, 1901). And while the Judge found Nome's weather to be relatively tolerable, he thought the gossip in the icebound community was beyond belief. "This is the meanest town for small talk I ever knew" (February 27, 1902).

12

THE DOG TRAIL FROM CIRCLE TO FAIRBANKS

It winds afar o'er hill and dale,
A ribbon fair on Nature's breast—
That breast in silken whiteness dressed—
A token sweet of love confessed—
The satin ribbon of the trail.

—Rev. S. Hall Young

I WAS FORTUNATE TO be at Circle City in the spring of 1903 when the first stampede was underway to the Tanana Valley. Originally I had planned to visit the Koyukuk mining district where there had been urgent requests for a court session to settle mining disputes, but the news from the diggings near Fairbanks changed my direction. Jim Eagle and Ben Bennett, two miners from the Tanana, had just arrived in Circle from that camp with a sled load of mining claims to record. They were careful not to say too much, but their very reticence added greater certainty to the richness of creeks where yet no shafts were dug to bedrock. The hushed rumor of a strike, a few whispered words and a quiet tongue, either because the silent one is ignorant or just naturally declines to lie, will often start a stampede.

Already the few remaining Circle sourdoughs were ready to rush over the divide to the Tanana, having heard it whispered that even I was going there on the morrow to establish a recorder's office and to see for himself. The very litigants so insistent a few weeks ago upon holding a term of court in the Koyukuk were now en route to the Tanana diggings. All urged the abandonment of the Koyukuk trip and suggested that we go together over the mountain trail to the new strike—and it was so ordered. We packed our sleds for the Tanana. Coldfoot and the Chandalar were neglected—Duty had changed her call to the Tanana.

April 2, 1903. With six big malamute dogs attached Indian style to a well-loaded sled, and with "Strongarm"* for guide and driver, we left Circle this forenoon for the Tanana. The blank recorder's books intended for Coldfoot are in our luggage and will serve at Fairbanks instead. The Twelve Mile roadhouse at the crossing of Birch Creek set us a good lunch after which we pushed on to the Jumpoff roadhouse for the night.

Pack-train men and prospectors filled every bed and the floor at the Jumpoff roadhouse. Met my old Tacoma friend, Ed Stier, here tonight. When I knew him in the States he was a fashionable jeweler, a dude who spent much time at pink teas and musicals. Ill health drove him into the open, and the lure of the mining camps to Alaska. Tonight he drove his flea-bitten mule, hitched to his Dawson double-ender sled loaded with a grubstake and camp equipment, into the Jumpoff barn lot, rubbed down his mule and slept on the kitchen floor in his blankets like a true stampeder. Prospecting and the mining life in the northland had filled him out and expanded his lungs. His skill as a miner and a mule skinner makes him a bully companion in the wilderness.

April 3. We had lunch today at the Central house near which is a remarkable hot spring, the waters of which were thought to have great curative properties. Tonight we reached Miller's roadhouse on Mammoth Creek, the trail rising nearly two thousand feet and landing us underneath Mastodon Dome. Those who had preceded us on the trail during the last week were camped in and around the roadhouse, stalled by a storm on the divide that made traveling over the pass dangerous. The best accommodation to be had was a bunk on the dining-room table, where I spread my blankets and slept peacefully

* "Strongarm" was the Judge's younger brother, Circle City Deputy U.S. Marshal Edgar Wickersham. For whatever reason, he never made it clear in *Old Yukon* that it was Edgar who drove the sled for him on his first trip to Fairbanks. Judge Wickersham had arranged to transfer Marshal Wickersham to the new mining camp in the Tanana Valley so that Edgar could accompany him as his dog driver and guide and provide law-enforcement assistance. The Judge said he had been "informed that crime is prevalent" in the new diggings, where a plentiful stock of raw material "for the manufacture of 'Hootch' or native whisky has already gone in" (March 16, 1903).

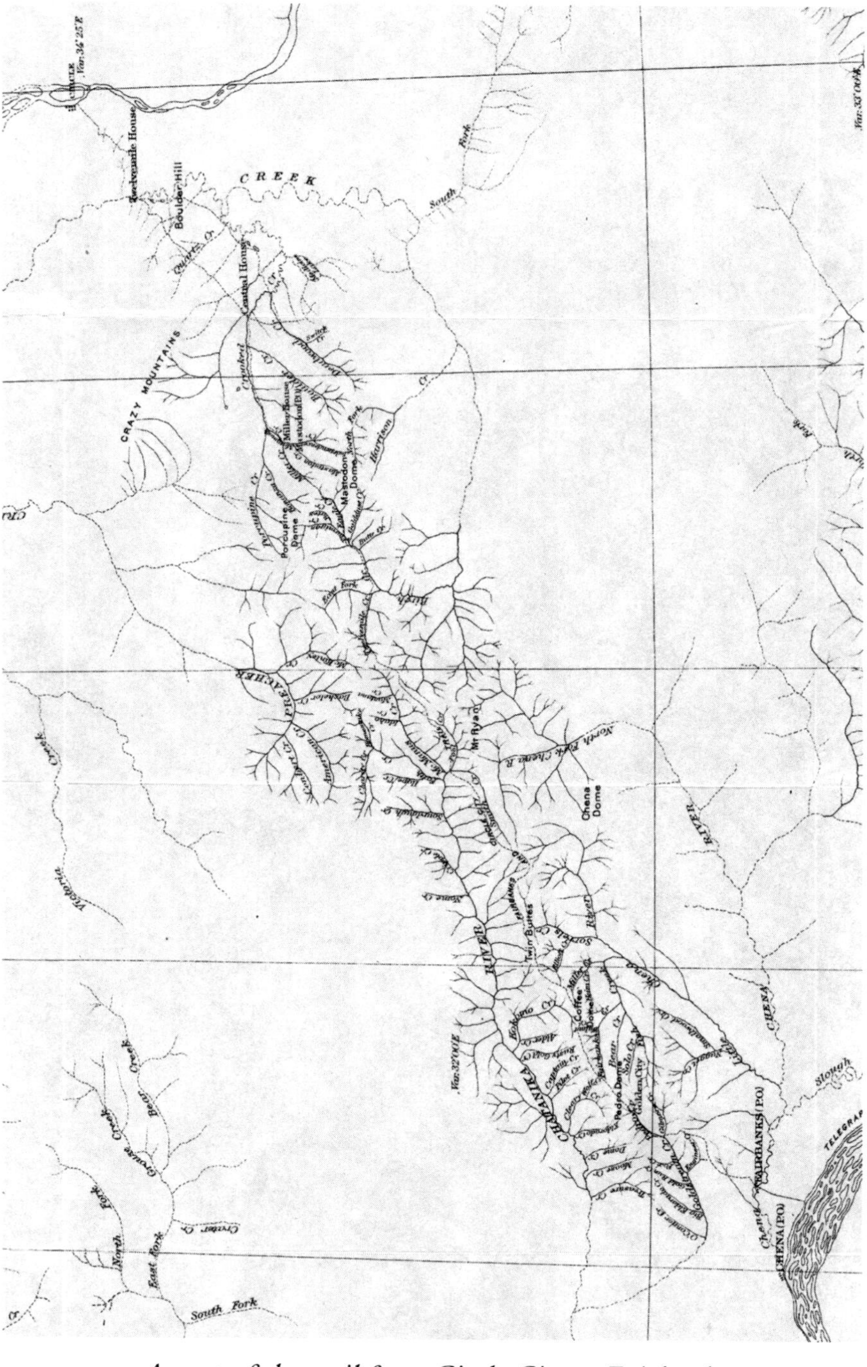

A map of the trail from Circle City to Fairbanks.

(Rare Maps Collection G4372-T353-1904-U51, Archives, Alaska and Polar Regions, University of Alaska Fairbanks) until the cook demanded possession for the five o'clock breakfast. The stampeders express great satisfaction at my action in joining them, since it gives assurance of the establishment of a recorder's office near the Tanana mines.

April 4. A beautiful winter-spring morning, clear and cold, with a few flying clouds. Big Dan went out to the gulchside early and returned with the story that it is yet blowing hard on the summit. Dan is a mule driver and intends to wait until other teams start on ahead, so he may follow in the trail they make through the soft snow drifts. There are tricks in all trades but mine, so I innocently caught on a light sled with a hardy traveler and off we started up Miller Creek toward the pass.*

Being light, our sled skimmed over the snow, while the dogs after a two days' rest in a cold yard were willing to run. The horse teams which started ahead were floundering in deep drifts as we passed them and came to the upper level of the pass ahead of the long struggling line which we could see coming after and far below us. Finally we rounded a bend in the gulch and came out on higher ground—and saw the pass ahead, snow-white and clear. My team caught up; we sent a cheering word back to the struggling teamsters and soon reached the wide flat on the summit to find the sun shining and the storm abated. The Porcupine and the Mastodon domes gilded by the rising sun towered above us on each side, and from the summit of the pass we could see far ahead down Eagle Creek.

A dozen or more caribou, easily mistaken for rather rangy Jersey cattle, with Santa Claus horns, came running round a little butte near us. And now we fairly flew down the long snowy slopes into Eagle

---

* In his diary that night the Judge admitted he had to force Edgar to keep moving and was quite angry that "Big Dan" Callahan and the others were too timid to head up the trail by Mastodon Dome (4,418 feet).

"Nice morning but out of the 35 men in the Miller house none seemed to want to make the start. Two or three of us insisted upon going across the divide. Callahan and others would look at the sky and then exclaim how bad the summit would be—that it would be blowing so hard that nothing could live on it &c.... I finally prevailed on two or three to start—made Edgar go—and I went on with the first sled—six miles brought us in sight of the summit—and it was clear! I... was the first to cross.... Sent back word how good it was at 10:30.... No one ahead of me. Men, horses, dog teams, sleds—everything in sight coming... looks like the Chilkoot" (April 4, 1903).

Creek. We passed Abe Spring, merchant and dog-driver, and his son Solly, going back to Miller divide for a sled load of merchandise for Fairbanks. They are double-tripping their outfit to the Twelve Mile divide, beyond which they have a downhill pull to the Tanana.

Late in the afternoon we reached the mouth of Twelve Mile Creek, where we spied a tent set well back in the evergreens. We approached and begged for a night's lodging. Our request was answered with a hearty welcome and we enjoyed all the comforts of a crowded tent and generous hospitality. Our three hosts for the night are Gus Miller, one of my Puget Sound friends, young Norton from California, and Bill Woodman, a grizzled frontiersman and a mighty hunter. What a fine batch of sourdough hot cakes old Bill made us for supper and breakfast! And how we enjoyed his hunting stories! May he live long and prosper!

AMONG THE "BAR" STORIES Bill told us while we smoked and talked after dinner this evening, was one which his old Juneau friend, Dick Willoughby, told tourists so often that, Bill said, Dick got so he believed it himself.

One day a group of Boston tourists were being entertained on the Juneau streets by Dick, who told them of certain great glacier bears he often saw round his cabin on an island in Glacier Bay. One of the tourists suggested that such gigantic animals must be slow in their movements, but Dick told them this story to illustrate the agility with which these great bears could turn around:

> I rolled out of my bunk one morning as the rays of the rising sun filled my cabin through the east window.... As I stood in my door filling my lungs with the morning air, I noticed a monster bear, probably fourteen feet long from tip to tip, approaching my house.... I reached above the door and took down my trusty buffalo gun.
>
> The bear's eyesight is not sharp and this one exhibited his surprise at seeing the house and me standing in the door by stopping about fifty yards away, raising his head, and opening his mouth. Just at that moment I...fired. The bullet struck the bear along the top of his tongue and went through his backbone. And that bear was so quick in turning around that...when the bullet came out, the other end of the bear was toward me, and the bullet came back and split the door jamb within three inches of my face.

I've always been thankful that the bear, probably by reason of his age, was just the fraction of a second slow in turning, else that bullet would certainly have hit me in the eye."*

April 5. This day brought us a long hard climb up Twelve Mile Creek toward the divide between Birch Creek and the McManus, or Chatanika River, which flows westward into the Tanana. Twelve Mile had no trail broken since the storm, the drifts obscured the old trail, but since the mountains on each hand confined us to the narrow valley, we could not get lost—yet that is just what happened. It was a day of bumps and accidents—one darn thing after another. First we came to the forks and "Strongarm" [Edgar] guessed wrong. He drew off up a fine-looking gulch on the south limit, where a good trail ought to have been, but was not. After hours of wrestling with the sled, abusing the dogs and wading deep, soft snowdrifts, about noon we found ourselves lost and the sled broken.

The Lord is said to care specially for idiots and drunken men, and while we were not intoxicated, it just happened that at that moment two caribou hunters came by and told us we had followed up the wrong gulch, so we turned back to Twelve Mile. With two other travelers to the Tanana, we holed up in an old tent in the dark spruce forest. The spruce bough feathers were soft and grateful to tired limbs that night.†

April 6. When we awoke this morning we found the air full of fine snow, and we could see on the high summits that a heavy wind

---

* The Judge so enjoyed this fanciful story of Willoughby's nimble bear that he sent it to the 1935 Sourdough Reunion, which they acknowledged as follows: "Judge James Wickersham of Juneau sent a 'bar' story to the recent reunion to be read at the Prevaricators' Luncheon which bears retelling.... He said he stole it the same as the old Yukon liars do most of the yarns they repeat to open-mouthed Sourdoughs and Sourdoughesses. The story has been told to him by old Bill Woodman...who had taken his oath many times, between drinks, that the incident happened" (July 10, 1935).

† Grateful as the Judge claimed to be, that was only in retrospect. At the time he was thoroughly fed up with Edgar's errant sense of direction and foul mouth. "Edgar thought it was right road—we went two miles—into snow waist deep—raw labor—struggles—profanity.... Finally found we were on wrong trail and turned back—broke handle bar off sled.... At one o'clock we turned up the right road—tired and worn out.... Camped in an empty tent just below the summit. Condon & Stevens were ahead of us & the four of us camped together...unable to sleep, too tired. Am dreadful tired of Edgar's extreme profanity" (April 5, 1903).

storm was raging. However, we hitched up our dogs and began the ascent. After a long hard struggle, the dogs pulling and we pushing, we reached the upper fringe of the spruce timberline to find a howling gale blowing in our faces, from over the divide, which almost blew us off the mountain. Heavy drifts, clouds of flying snow, and no trail. We could not even see our dogs, but we hung to the gee-pole and handlebars and urged them into the wind with near profanity and a long whip. Soon the sled ran more easily—we were on the summit! Then we ran into a cut stake and found that our leader, with dog sense, was on the trail.

At the mouth of Faith Creek we found a good cabin roadhouse, for Faith, Hope, and Charity creeks, whose waters unite here with the McManus to form the Chatanika, were stampeded two years ago by prospectors from Birch Creek and this cabin is the sole remaining beneficial result. Oscar Smith, a sourdough miner, fried hot cakes for supper, which we ate with caribou steaks and brown gravy. Eight weary, but happy Tanana stampeders slept in the twelve-by-twelve shack while the forest round about was vocal with dogs, each chained to a separate tree. With more respect for the judiciary than Webber exhibited, they gave me the pole bunk for a bed, while the slumbering seven reposed on spruce boughs on the gravel floor.

April 7. From Faith Creek the trail leads down the narrow valley of the Chatanika, deep sheltered in the mountains which rise on either side. The storm has blown itself away. The sun fills the valley and we are delighted to be over the divide. It is a beautiful sunny day and a dry trail and I am feeling physically fit so I walked all day in preference to running at the handlebars.

Tonight we camped in an empty tent. Probably belongs to some stampeder who is double-tripping his outfit to the Tanana and using it as a way station. The tent had an inviting appearance to homeless travelers and we entered in peace for the door flap was open. Here we met the first disappointed prospector tramping back to Birch Creek, hurling anathemas at the Tanana. His name is Joe Cascade and he readily accepted our invitation to dinner which we cooked in front of our borrowed home. We had "nothing" to eat but juicy moose and caribou steaks, fried grouse and ptarmigan shot along the trail, bacon fried crisp and laid on fat chicken breasts, cans of California peaches, coffee well sugared and tinted golden with canned cream.

After all this had been disposed of, the fire replenished and the dogs fed, we lighted fat cigars and told our life histories. A little later we rolled into our spruce bough beds—and it was morning.

April 8. Down the valley the trees increase in size and the forests widen. Our dogs are well fed and we are making good time. About noon we came to an Indian camp by the trailside, and ate a lunch of moose steak and grouse cooked by a native. He is a Tanana Apache, tall and straight, slender and active, but not a good cook.

Toward evening the trail came into Cleary Creek valley, one of the streams on which Pedro located placer claims. We followed up the valley to Jesse Noble's cabin on No. 2, below Discovery, the only house on the creek.*

Besides Noble, three other miners occupy this cabin and sleep on new shavings and spruce boughs in the corner—Al Hilty, Pete Kling, and young Dan McCarty. We were invited to stay all night, for it was too late to cross the divide to the next creek, and we occupied our share of the spruce beds. They talked to us until a late hour about locations, new strikes, prospecting trips, and the coming of an army of stampeders into the wilderness of the Tanana. They seem sanguine of the presence of gold on this creek, but why is not apparent, for the only hole to bed rock on the creek which carries a prospect, is the shaft on Pedro's claim at Discovery.

April 9. We left Noble's cabin this morning early, for we want an hour on the summit, and it is twenty miles or more to Fairbanks. The trail is only a blazed line through the forest of spruce. We followed its marks upstream to the toe of a long medial ridge, coming down to a point at the junction of the largest of the upper tributaries of Cleary Creek, whence we mounted the hogback to the summit of

---

* Like Wickersham, Jesse Noble had come from Pierce County, Washington, and he would become one of the most prominent mining men in early Fairbanks. In 1907 Noble married Helen "Nellie" Mulrooney, the sister of Belinda and Margaret Mulrooney, with whom Noble founded the Dome City Bank on Dome Creek north of Fairbanks. Noble hired Wickersham when he retired as Judge to be the bank's attorney, and it would prove to be a thankless assignment.

"Trouble is brewing at the Dome City Bank," Wickersham wrote in March 1908. "Jesse Noble is drinking & making a fool of himself generally, but particularly in fighting with his wife's sisters who have the money in the bank. Margaret Mulrooney...told me today that he drank 10 bottles of champagne last night—which is going some for even a 'rough-neck' miner" (March 18, 1908).

the pass. From this summit which constitutes the divide between the two mining streams respectively called Cleary and Pedro, we had our first sight over the surrounding region.

It was a bright clear day, and back down Cleary Creek and across the Chatanika we had a glorious view of the Beaver range through which we had passed. The high snow-covered domes to the northward gleamed crimson in the morning sun, while beyond them we could trace the void in which the Yukon flows westward.

But it is the view across the fifty-mile valley of the Tanana which makes the blood race in one's veins. To the east and west, as far as the eye can reach, and to the base of the snowy range along its southern bounds, the valley is carpeted with evergreen. Beyond this low valley of the Ohio-of-the-north rises the colossal Alaska Range and several sharp and symmetrical peaks: Mount Hayes, Mount Deborah,* and Mount Hess. To the westward the range rises, mountain upon mountain, to the greatest of all, Mount McKinley. This mountain is to the Tena, what it must always remain to all tribes of men in this region, Denali, the high one.

ROUGH-LOCKING OUR SLEDS WITH dog chains we plunged down the ridge between twin creeks, and through the forest, following the blazed trees until we reached a little clearing at Costa's cabin on Pedro Creek. As we stopped our husky team before his cabin, big Jack Costa came up the ladder out of a prospecting shaft near the doorway. His chubby round face was distorted and wrinkled with excitement and deep feeling, and, without knowing or caring who the stranger was standing by his shaft, he cried out, his rough bull voice vibrating with excessive joy:

"Oh, by Godda, I gotta de gold!"

He had just struck pay in his shaft, the first to be found on this part of the creek, and was fairly overcome with his sudden fortune. He had dug holes on Forty Mile, Birch, Faith, Hope, Charity, and a hundred unnamed creeks in the Tanana hills, but just now, after years of labor and failure, Fortune smiled! Visions of Italy, the old home and the old mother, the girl he left behind when he came to America, a vineyard and a wine press, wife and children—big Jack cried as he babbled to us of these and the gold in the pit at his door.

* Named by Wickersham for his wife.

Felix Pedro, the discoverer of gold in Fairbanks.
(Historical Photograph Collection UAF-65-20, Archives, Alaska and Polar Regions, University of Alaska Fairbanks)

A cabin at Golden City on Pedro Creek, the stream where Felix Pedro made his first strike.
(Terrence Cole)

We had lunch with Costa, and then raced on down the narrow valley to the cabin of the discoverer of gold in the Tanana—Felix Pedro. He, too, is an Italian and a typical prospector. He is slender, alert, erect, clear-eyed, and at home in wilderness or mining camp. We sat beside his little gravel dump while he washed a pan of gravel to show us he had gold on his claim. He told us the story of his long search for gold on the Tanana slope. Once before he had found pay on a creek flowing into the Tanana up Goodpaster way. His grub gave out and he was forced to cross the range to Circle to get more. He hung his vest on a prominent peeled tree and set his shovel blade upright on the summit of a nearby hill, but he could never find them again though he had searched the region carefully many times on his return from Circle.*

Down Pedro and Goldstream we went to Dan McCarty's dump, where we found Dan in an old tent on a very small gravel area but talking about millions—which later did come out of the gravel beneath him.† The trail then led us across the valley of Goldstream over a long flat point and across another moose pasture to the last and lowest of the Tanana bluffs. Below us, far and wide, lay the glorious valley we had come to help settle. We sped down the long southern slope, through a beautiful forest of silver birch, out upon a flat plain, over a slough, across an island, through a heavy forest of spruce, and, from the north bank of the Chena River,** the new Metropolis of the Tanana came into view on the opposite shore.

---

* It is not clear when Wickersham first met Felix Pedro, the original discoverer of gold in the Fairbanks mining district in 1902. The Judge does not mention seeing him in his diary until four days after he mushed down Pedro Creek. At that time Pedro promised to give the Judge the gold pan he used to make his initial discovery—which Wickersham would send to Senator Charles W. Fairbanks. The Judge also gave his power-of-attorney to Pedro, and several other local miners, to stake claims for him when they found promising ground (April 13–14, 1903).

† A year later Dan McCarty would be killed, Wickersham said, "with his boots on," in a fight over a mining claim with a man named Francis Ledger. Though the Judge thought it a case of "ruthless and premeditated" murder, the jury returned a verdict of manslaughter. He sentenced Ledger to twenty years (July 8, 1904).

** Wickersham notes: "The Chena River discharges its waters into the Tanana River slough about five miles above the site of Fairbanks; at that point it circles a pinnacle rock which thrusts its head above the valley floor; this peculiar rock, in mid-valley, at an ancient fish and hunting camp, evidently suggested to the natives the Tena name for the incoming stream, 'Che,' meaning rock in the Indian language, and 'Na,' the generic name for a river, or Rock River."

Across the river we saw a half-dozen new log cabins, a few tents, and a rough log structure with spread-eagle wings that looked like a disreputable pigsty, but was in fact, Barnette's trading post. That was Fairbanks as I first saw it at five o'clock in the afternoon on April 9, 1903.

MY FIRST OFFICIAL ACT on the date of my arrival was to appoint J. Tod Cowles a deputy for Fairbanks under the Circle City recorder and deliver to him the blank record books intended for the Koyukuk—and thus Fairbanks and civilization in the wilderness!*

---

* James Tod Cowles, twenty-seven, the U.S. commissioner appointed on Wickersham's first day in Fairbanks, was the brother-in-law of Charles E. Claypool, the U.S. commissioner at Circle City who had served in the Washington legislature in the 1890s. Judge Cowles' tenure as Fairbanks' first magistrate was not long or distinguished and by 1904 Wickersham would force him out of office.

"Have just had a talk with J. Tod Cowles, Comr. for this precinct. Told him that complaint had been made about his conduct—that I was informed that he had been consorting openly in broad daytime with prostitutes and had often been drunk, had visited the vicious low dance halls & had danced there, &c. &c. He admitted the truth of the complaints. I then told him about the friendship I had for his father—of Mrs. Wickersham's for Mrs. Claypool his sister [Helen Cowles], &c. and appealed to him to quit his bad practices.... I hope this talk and arrangement will bring him up, and that hard work will keep him away from the evil road down which he is galloping. His conduct has been so bad that the decent women in the camp refuse to associate with him. But I cannot bring myself to dismiss him on account of his youth, his family and my hope that he will stand up and do better now" (April 23, 1904).

"Since talking to [Cowles] on April 25th [*sic*] his conduct has grown steadily worse, until now he stands in the saloons night after night playing games, and openly consorting with whores. One of these—the 'Sheeny' whore, a Jewess—has him completely under her control and she sleeps at his house openly and notoriously. He hugs and kisses her in public, standing drunk at the bar &c. Many complaints are made to me and I feel that I can no longer fail to act.... At my suggestion [District Attorney Luther] Hess went over & told Cowles that unless he resigned at once he would file official charges against him, and make the matter public.... I regret the matter very much for Claypool alone is to blame for destroying this young man's prospects. I saw Claypool going to dinner today at noon, down the public street with a sore faced whore known as 'Birdie,' whom he keeps. He and Tod have two beds in one room and each keeps a whore, both in the same room. They are out every night, drunk with their whores, it is open, notorious, bad! and I intend to put a stop to it at once.

"Cowles has just resigned & he and Claypool both write me nice letters thanking me for my confidence & friendship. I hope this unhappy chapter is now finally ended" (May 28, 1904).

Katherine and Jack Claypool in front of the Circle City law office of J. Tod Cowles. On his first day in Fairbanks, April 9, 1903, Wickersham appointed Cowles as the first Fairbanks magistrate.

(Charles E. Claypool 1861–1944, Alaska Historical Society Collection, UAA-HMC-1023-45)

E. T. Barnette.

(Historical Photograph Collection UAF-1989-12-102, Archives, Alaska and Polar Regions, University of Alaska Fairbanks)

13

FAIRBANKS AND THE TANANA MINES

So while others sing of the chosen few
who o'er the fates prevail,
I will sing of the many, staunch and true,
whose brave hearts never quail—
Who with the dauntless spirit of pioneers
a State are building for the coming years
Their sole reward their loved one's tears—
the men who Blazed the Trail.

—Sam C. Dunham

I FIRST MET E. T. BARNETTE at the mouth of the Tanana River in the summer of 1901 when I was on my way down the Yukon on the steamer *Leah*. Our vessel tied up alongside the *Lavelle Young*, the sternwheeler loaded with Barnette's trade goods, waiting for high water to enter the Tanana.

The trader told me of his purpose to get his cargo of Indian trading goods up to where the main Indian trail from the Copper River crossed the Tanana, the point where rumor then fixed the crossing of the all-American trail from Valdez to Eagle. There he intended to establish a post for trading with Indians and a supply point for travelers over the Valdez-Eagle route.

Upon my return from Nome in July, 1902, I found Barnette at St. Michael building a small, high-power, flat-bottomed boat, and sat with him on a log on the beach by his ways, while he told me of his failure of the previous summer. He had found it impossible to get the *Lavelle Young* over the Bates Rapids above the Chena bluffs, and was obliged to bring the cargo back into the Chena River, where he had cached it on the bank.

He now intended, so he told me, to reload it into his new boat, the *Isabelle*, which being flat-bottomed and light of draft, could, he hoped, cross the miles of bars and shallow waters, and thus finally reach his intended location at Tanana Crossing.

The duty of establishing recorders' offices and mining districts in that immense northern half of Alaska was upon my shoulders, so I gave him encouragement and promised to establish a recorder's office at the Crossing when he should have located his trading post there and found the country had mining prospects to justify it. We talked of the All-American route to Eagle and the Klondike; of the coming of prospectors who would search the Nabesna and the other upper tributaries of the Tanana for mineral treasures; of its proximity to Forty Mile, and generally of the peopling of the great upper Tanana country with Americans. At my request, he agreed to name his new post in the wilderness, wherever he finally settled, "Fairbanks" after Charles W. Fairbanks, U.S. senator from Indiana.*

WHILE BARNETTE AND I sat droning on the drift log on the St. Michael beach—dreaming and proposing—prospector Pedro, in the creeks near Barnette's cache on the Chena, was prospecting and disposing, for nine days before our talk at St. Michael, Pedro had quietly come into the log cabin cache on the Chena and confided to Barnette's brother-in-law Frank Cleary, who was in charge as watchman while Barnette was at St. Michael building the *Isabelle*, that he had found gold on two creeks in the nearby hills and had located a discovery claim on each. Pedro was a good miner, as active and earnest as a crusader, and that night Frank Cleary, Jim Eagle, and one or two others then at the cache struck out through the forest in company with the discoverer and made locations on adjoining claims. They named one of the streams Cleary Creek and the other Pedro Creek.

* When Barnette agreed to adopt the name "Fairbanks" for his future camp somewhere in the Tanana Valley, Wickersham promised in return to "assist him all I can" (July 19, 1902). Indiana Senator Charles W. Fairbanks, a member of the 1898 commission working to settle the Alaska-Canada boundary dispute, ensured Wickersham could land the judgeship in 1900 by generously withdrawing his favored candidate for the Alaska position and endorsing Wickersham instead (January 22, 1900). Ever after Wickersham considered Senator Fairbanks a trusted mentor. When Charles Fairbanks was nominated to be President Theodore Roosevelt's vice presidential running mate in 1904, Wickersham wired: "Fairbanks Alaska congratulates Fairbanks of Indiana" (June 24, 1904).

"Downtown" Fairbanks as Wickersham first saw it in April 1903.
(Alaska State Library, Wickersham State Historic Sites Photograph Collection, ASL-PCA-277-11-3)

Washington Congressman Francis W. Cushman and his wife in Valdez in 1903. Wickersham named the main street of Fairbanks in honor of Rep. Cushman.

(Alaska State Library, Wickersham State Historic Sites Photograph Collection, ASL-PCA-277-007-102)

When Barnette arrived at his Chena cache a few weeks later, on board his new boat, the *Isabelle*, ready to load his trading goods and ascend the rapids of the Tanana two hundred miles to the Crossing, he was amazed and delighted to find an active mining stampede. He wisely changed his plans and established his camp as its business center. Barnette's cache was now to become "Fairbanks."

THE STAMPEDERS WHOM WE had passed on the mountain trails were coming in every hour. Luther C. Hess, the slender assistant district attorney, accompanied by the court stenographer, George Jeffery, led the column. Dog sleds, double-enders dragged by mules or horses, Yukon sleds guided by gee-poles and pulled by dog teams, single sleds dragged wearily along by ropes over prospectors' shoulders, and troops of prospectors loaded like pack-train mules, were hurrying in and locating.

Four lawyers assisted the frontier judge and the deputy marshal to stake the courthouse lot. A plan for a log jail was approved, a contract for its construction was let, and, before night, the logs were cut in the overtopping forest for the Fairbanks jail, the first public building in the Tanana Valley.* An iron bar off the *Isabelle* was driven deep into sandy loam at the southeast corner of the official lot, and all measurements for town-lot locations were made from its center. Every

* As proud as a parent of bestowing the name of "Fairbanks," the Judge did all that was possible to ensure the community's survival. Most important, he would place the courthouse in Barnette's town.

"I find a conflict of interest and some feeling between this place & 'Chena' at the mouth of the slough & junction with Tanana. Mr. & Mrs. Wissel of Chena came in to see me today & presented a letter from citizens of Chena asking me to come & see that place with a view of locating recorder's offices &c. there. Agreed to go down Monday." But meanwhile before the Judge ever saw Chena, Barnette's brother-in-law Frank Cleary had offered the government a central corner lot in Fairbanks for a jail, and in addition gave the Judge himself the choicest piece of commercial property in Fairbanks, almost adjacent to Barnette's store. Furthermore on Wickersham's suggestion two of the main Fairbanks streets were named in honor of a pair of congressional powerbrokers friendly to the Judge: Cushman Street and Lacey Street for Francis W. Cushman of Washington and John F. Lacey of Iowa (April 10, 1903).

Though local lore would later claim the Chena folks were rude and dismissive, in fact he found the roughly three hundred people building cabins in Chena to be hospitable and welcoming. He realized with some dismay that Chena "has some advantages—or at least one: it is on the main river!" But Fairbanks was closer to the mines and it held the high card—the name "Fairbanks"—so the Judge rapidly new arrival staked a town lot, and streets were hourly stretching in all directions from the official crowbar.

A hundred men were felling trees and whip-sawing lumber. Stampeders from Valdez and the Klondike were coming down the Tanana, others from Koyukuk and Rampart across country, and new trails from all directions were converging on the central point. A newcomer with a pack on his back broke through the forest, blazing trees as he walked, and before he could erect his tent in Fairbanks, an almost endless line of prospectors followed his blazes into camp. Frank Cleary was elected town recorder at a mass meeting and was busy making a rough map, extending and naming the streets, and penciling locators' names on stakes and on the map. The music of the saw and hammer was never stilled, and within a month more than two hundred cabins were constructed.*

THERE WERE INDIAN CAMPS along the river, but not a wagon road, not a schoolhouse, nor a white child; not a church, nor a solitary farmhouse in the great valley; not even a grave occupied by a white man added the suggestion of permanence. What the land contained in mineral or agricultural values, no one yet knew. It was truly a virgin wilderness, but with what wonderful possibilities!

---

dismissed any thought of locating the courthouse anywhere else, planting his flag at the corner of Second and Cushman, where the courthouse would be built in 1904, one block from his own commercial lot at the corner of First and Cushman. In years to come Wickersham's enemies would claim the commercial property Barnette gave him in the center of Fairbanks was akin to bribery, as within a year the lot would earn him an estimated $3,600 a year in rental income, or more than twice his annual salary from the Department of Justice (June 6, 1904).

When Wickersham stepped down as Judge in 1907, his ties with Barnette were a major issue. "Millions of dollars in value have gone through my hands—actually and in litigation—but no one has yet accused me of a graver crime in connection with decisions than favoring Barnette!! A silly charge—easily made, hard to prove & still harder to disprove! So I'll not try it" (December 31, 1907).

* "At this time there are three streets roughly staked out through the woods, parallel to the river.... The town is just now in its formation period—town lots are at a premium—jumping, staking, recording, building! It is a motley crowd too. Miners ["sourdoughs," "chechacos"] gamblers, Indians [Negroes], Japanese, dogs, prostitutes, music, drinking!" (April 20, 1903).

Though without a church, in April 1903 Fairbanks had four saloons—the Fairbanks, Pioneer, Northern, and Tanana—and four women of "easy life." "'Chee-Chaco Lil' has reached town from Dawson and has purchased a small establishment on 2nd Ave. There are three others of her kind here including a negress" (April 24, 1903).

Thanks to a gift from E. T. Barnette, James Wickersham owned one of the most valuable pieces of commercial property in the center of Fairbanks. The two-story Apple Building on Wickersham's lot, housing the Horseshoe Saloon, was immediately to the right of the Cushman Street Bridge.
(Anchorage Museum of History and Art, John Urban Collection, AMRC-B64-1-67)

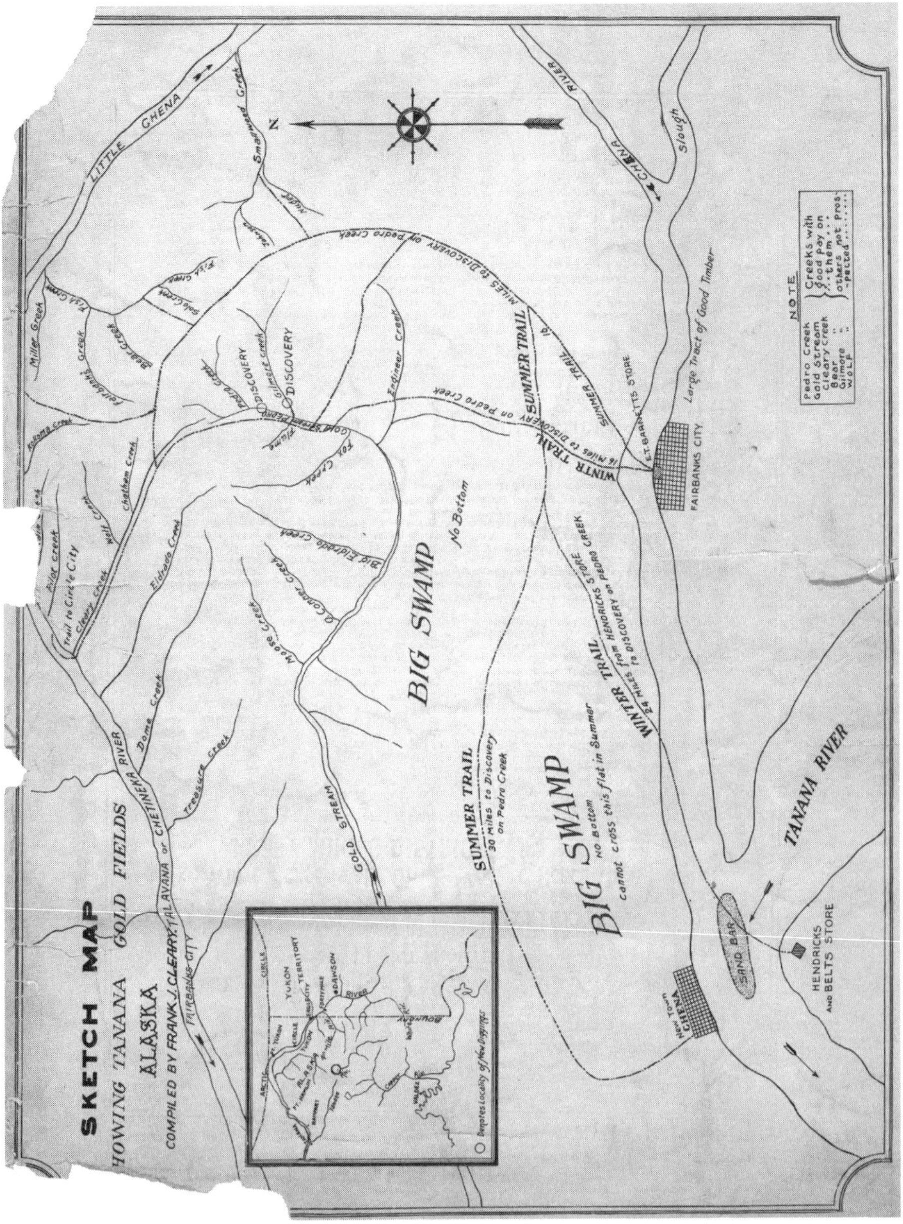

The first relatively accurate map of the Fairbanks mining district, Frank J. Cleary's sketch map of the Tanana gold fields, including the towns of Fairbanks and Chena.

(From *The Tanana Gold Fields*, Fairbanks, AK: Mason & Hill, Publishers, 1904. Alaska and Polar Regions Collections, Rasmuson Library, University of Alaska Fairbanks)

My humble part in organizing civil government in the Tanana had been a labor of love. It had given me the liveliest sense of satisfaction, notwithstanding the imperfect and pioneer style of the work. My vision of the future comforted me for all our shortcomings, for it was to be a land of mines, farms, and factories; of towns and cities; of roads and railways; of schools, churches, and colleges—the foundation of a sovereign state in the American Union. To have been able to assist in laying the foundation for such a land was ample compensation for any hardships.*

AN EPISCOPAL EVANGELIST AND a Presbyterian preacher followed the line of march into the churchless camp, and both held Sunday services in Marston's saloon, christened publicly the night before after license was issued by the court. The proprietor declared he was sport enough to give the preachers a fair deal, and courteously spread his only white sheet over the glasses and decanters, while the Rev. C.E. Rice and Rev. C.F. Ensign conducted the first church services before the entire population of the new town.

Later a highwayman, known by his disguise as the "Blue Parka Man," engaged for a time in holding up travelers on this trail. With his parka pulled well over his face and a Winchester rifle held in a steady hand he would command the unfortunate ones to line up and lay their pokes of gold dust, watches, etc., in the trail and then move on. It is said that Bishop Rowe was in one of these groups and, after placing his little wad of money on the heap, he began with his winning smile and gentle voice to expostulate with the highwayman for robbing a minister of the gospel. The highwayman asked if he were a minister.

"Yes," was the reply, "I am Bishop Rowe, of the Episcopal Church."

"Oh," the highwayman said in evident surprise, "you are Bishop Rowe, are you? Well, I'm pleased to meet you, Bishop. Of course I

---

* "I arrived in Fairbanks 36 days ago and it is beyond belief what has been accomplished here since then. The fact that the public offices were established here determined most people in the belief that this would be the important town in the district. All the lawyers located here to be with the courts. I am told by one who says he has counted them that 387 houses are now erected or in process—yet there is not a white child here—nor in the Tanana Valley!! Whole blocks of cabins have been built since I came—yet there is no saw mill in the Tanana—all the lumber is whip sawed. There is yet no church—but 6 saloons—no school house for no children" (May 15, 1903).

won't rob you; take your poke off the heap in the road, Bishop, and take that poke with the shoestring on it too. Why, damn it all, Bishop, I'm a member of your church."

When they finally caught the highwayman and the court sentenced him to a long term of imprisonment in the United States penitentiary at McNeil Island on Puget Sound, the evidence clearly disclosed that he really was a constant visitor, when in town, at the Episcopal Church library, where he was well known as a reader of good books. Anyway the dear old Bishop always enjoyed the joke which was often told in his presence.*

BARNETTE'S CACHE WAS ABOUT out of provisions, and to get a sack of flour the purchaser was required to take as part of his outfit, a case of canned turnips, the cache being long on turnips which

* At the time the notorious bandit in blue was terrorizing travelers on the trails outside Fairbanks in summer of 1905, the Judge found nothing amusing about the situation.

"Bandit holding people up on the trail daily," Wickersham wrote on June 25, 1905. "Perry seems to be paralyzed." The following day Marshal Perry claimed there was nothing he could do about the hold-up man. "Perry is quoted in evening paper as saying that he has no authority to attempt to capture highwayman. He . . . is incorrect from a legal point. Much criticism has been aroused by Perry's failure to do something to protect the public" (June 26, 1905). Wickersham wanted the marshals to round up a posse of twenty men to apprehend the fugitive.

When finally captured a few weeks later, the Blue Parka Bandit was identified as Charles Hendrickson. Hendrickson was "viciously guilty" of the 1905 crime spree in Fairbanks, the Judge concluded, but the trial resulted in a "radically bad verdict" because the "soft headed and soft hearted jurors" voted for acquittal. Before the verdict, however, the career criminal made the mistake of breaking out of the Fairbanks jail by sawing a hole in the log wall; the Judge thought a smarter or more patient man would have simply trusted his fate to the fools on the jury! (August 13, 1905).

Though soon recaptured, Hendrickson broke out for the second time in January 1906 with a local crook named Thomas Thornton. Once the fugitives were trapped they remained locked up until the summer of 1906, when they were both tried, convicted, and sentenced by Judge Wickersham to fifteen years at the federal penitentiary at McNeil Island. While being transported up the Yukon River by sternwheeler to the penitentiary, Hendrickson, accompanied by Thornton, escaped for the third time. The Judge confessed he was "much disturbed for 3 or 4 days" until the "two bad men" were caught (October 12, 1906).

In December 1906 Hendrickson yet again briefly broke out of the penitentiary and as a result was transferred to the maximum security prison at Fort Leavenworth, Kansas. Even there he made two unsuccessful breaks, the last in 1916. "Hendrickson was released from Leavenworth on February 11, 1920," wrote his biographer H.C. Landru, "and was never heard of again."

P.S.HUNT
E 366.
PASSENGERS AND 2800.LBS GOLD DUST FROM FAIRBANKS BY KENNEDY'S STAGE.

E. T. Barnette (far right) and the other bankers of Fairbanks, guarding a shipment of more than a ton of gold.

(Lulu Fairbanks Collection UAF-1968-69-1547, Archives, Alaska and Polar Regions, University of Alaska Fairbanks) were so bad that no one thought of sledding them farther than the riverbank, but it increased trade and was the only way to get a sack of flour. The price of supplies was rising, of course, as the quantity decreased and the demand increased. There were neither boots nor shoes in the cache, nor for that matter in the country. One day I saw my friend Nestor of the bar, sitting on the pole counter in Barnette's cache, shod in an ancient pair of dripping rubber boots, minus tops, and full of holes. I expressed my sympathy and asked why he did not take better care of his precious health.

"How can I?" he answered. "I have no shoes and there will be none in the camp until the boats come up the river in June."

I answered; "Well, that's too bad. I have an extra pair that I carried in my bag from Seattle. If you cannot get a pair at the store, let me divide, for I cannot bear to see you go with wet feet."

He thanked me and begged to have them at once. He paid me seven dollars—what I had paid for them in Seattle—and carried them away with overflowing thankfulness. The next day I saw him again sitting on the same counter with the same old rubbers on his feet; the ice water dripping from each wet and muddy sock, and I exclaimed in astonishment:

"Why are you not wearing the shoes I gave you yesterday?"

"Oh," he replied, "I can't afford to wear such shoes. They are too expensive; I'll have to wear these rubbers till the boats come in."

"But," I said, "they were not expensive. I let you have them for seven dollars."

"Yes, I know," he replied, "but they are expensive here, and I could not afford to keep them. I sold them last night to Al Hilty for twenty-eight dollars!"

Footwear is much more necessary to comfort and the preservation of health in far northern Alaska than in a more genial climate. Its absence naturally attracts more attention here, and especially from the Koyukuk natives, who are never seen without such protection. A merchant from a northern camp, who had recently come to the Tanana stampede, told me this story to indicate the Indian idea of a shoeless man.

These Indians are deeply interested in the large colored-picture advertisements coming to the stores and will examine them long and carefully and discuss them in the Indian tongue as they might a circus poster. They had so often heard about Uncle Sam as the big chief of the white people, that they seemed to believe him to be a veritable chieftain in the flesh and to reside in a great house in Washington. One of these large and flaming poster advertisements which caricatured Uncle Sam as a barefoot man particularly attracted these natives, who discussed it solemnly at great length. After long study the chief of the Koyukuks said to the merchant, in sympathetic concern, "What's matter, Uncle Sam got no shoes ?"

"Oh," the trader carelessly replied, "he pretty poor this summer."

"Too bad," the Indian said as he walked away, "Uncle Sam got no shoes."

Two weeks later the Koyukuk chief returned to the store and laid on the merchant's counter two pairs of the finest moose-hide moccasins the Indian women could make, and said; "Too bad Uncle Sam got no shoes. My wife make this shoes for Uncle Sam, you send 'um tell Uncle Sam Koyukuk chief his friend, send 'um shoes, Uncle Sam." The merchant had not expected this result of his careless statement, but accepted the moccasins and promised to send them to Uncle Sam for his winter use as a present from his friend the Koyukuk chief.

What he did was to send them out with his summer shipment of furs and sell them to a trader in Seattle, but that winter when the old Koyukuk chieftain and his family were at the usual point of starvation, he was greatly pleased to be told by the merchant that he had just received a letter from Uncle Sam in Washington, thanking his brother the Koyukuk chief, for the moccasins and ordering the merchant to present to the chief a sack of flour and other provisions sufficient to keep him and his family in food until the time for the spring moose hunting arrived. The value of these supplies just about equalled the price received by the merchant for the moccasins. The old chief was greatly pleased with this exchange of presents with Uncle Sam, and told his people about it with much pride.

As it was at Eagle City, so here in Fairbanks the first case to engage my judicial attention was one brought to me by an Indian. Unlike Chief Charley at Eagle, this native of the Tanana forests came in fear and trembling. He called at the cabin where I had my temporary abode, and in halting English intermixed with trade jargon and Indian, he made it known that he wished to talk to me privately. When the door to the cabin was closed and he was sure there was no other ear to hear his confession he told me a story about a hunting trip he had made three days before out towards the Tanana bluffs, east of town where he hoped to find a moose. In a small glade he saw his target. Creeping cautiously nearer he reached a place where he got a good shot, fired, and the moose fell dead. When he reached the carcass of the animal he was amazed at its queer appearance. It had the ears of a moose, the color, and the size—but, he explained to me—it did not have the cloven hoof of a moose—but solid round feet and an iron shoe on the bottom of each round foot! It was a "white man's moose"—a mule! His fear that the owner of the animal might attack him for his unfortunate act, and his full confession of the facts gave me entire confidence in his innocence of any intent to do malicious mischief by killing the mule.

I considered the matter a moment and then asked whether he had told anyone else about the matter. He said he had not, that he was afraid to do so; and only came to tell me because he knew I was the man who might punish him if it was found out. I then advised him not to tell anyone about the mishap, and told him if it became necessary to do anything about it I would send for him, but not to fear for it was not a serious matter.

After a day or two rumors about the killing of the mule became known, and the owner was seeking evidence to show that one of the packers in opposition to him had slain the animal, but the accused had a perfect alibi. For some time the matter was talked about among packers and idlers on the street, and then it ceased to attract any further attention. The Indian often saw me, but never spoke about the incident again, and that ended the first case in the Tanana.*

THE FIRST BANQUET EVER held in the Tanana country was given one night in true frontier style in the Tokio restaurant on Second

* The first official "criminal proceeding—or civil either—ever held in the Tanana Valley" was a trial of William Duenkel on April 14, 1903, before Justice of the Peace J. Tod Cowles, with J.C. Kellum appearing for the defense; Duenkel [Dunkel], Cowles, and Kellum all have Fairbanks streets named after them (April 14, 1903). At the time Kellum was not a member of the Bar. He had been disbarred by Wickersham in 1902 for alleged perjury on behalf of a defendant in an adultery case. The Judge officially reinstated Kellum in May 1904, when all the lawyers in Fairbanks signed a petition in his support. "I will grant it," Wickersham wrote, "as I think the good sought to be done has been fully accomplished" (April 29, 1904).

Felix Pedro.

(Historical Photograph Collection UAF-1966-9-7, Archives, Alaska and Polar Regions, University of Alaska Fairbanks)

Avenue. The Tokio in outward appearance lacked Japanese architectural style, for it was a ten-by-twelve Seattle tent with a red-hot Yukon stove in a lean-to at the rear, for a kitchen. All seven lawyers in Fairbanks were bidden to attend, as were four prospective clients, prospectors made suddenly rich from wildcat mining claims.

The table of whip-sawed spruce boards was covered with flour sacks carrying the name of the mill and the weight and brand of the contents; nail kegs served as dining-room chairs; and the viands and liquors were the best the country could produce. Roast moose, caribou cutlets, grilled grouse, baked white fish, evaporated spuds, canned goods (turnips barred), coffee, cigars, and cultus wa-wa [big talk]. The wine list included Hootch Albert's Best Brew, served in tin cups (no glasses in camp). Pedro's old gold pan was used as a tray; the menu was done by the official scrivener, George Jeffery, in his best letter press on birch bark. Pedro presented his battered, long-carried discovery gold pan, and the first ounce of gold dust off his first Tanana claim, to be forwarded as a present from Tanana miners to the Camp's godfather, Senator Fairbanks of Indiana. What we lacked in style at that historic banquet we made up in good cheer.*

EVERY SPOT ON THE earth's surface, in the course of the solar year, has the same number of hours of night and of day. Fairbanks is on latitude 65 north, and on December 21 the low southern sun (shining then in mid-summer splendor over Argentina) skirts the Tanana horizon for about two hours and slowly sinks into the western

* When the Judge hosted the first "Bar Banquet" on April 28, 1903, the seven lawyers in Fairbanks who attended were Luther C. Hess, Edward B. Condon, Abe Spring, H. J. Miller, Bion A. Dodge, James Tod Cowles, and Allen R. Joy. The prospectors present were Felix Pedro, Jesse Noble, Frank Cleary and Dan McCarty. The main course was "Roast Moose, Prospector Style," and all made short toasts, but Pedro's "plain, honest, straightforward story of his hardships & discovery" was the centerpiece of the evening's entertainment (May 8, 1903). At the time Fairbanks had twice as many lawyers as doctors, though the medical establishment did include one "lady physician" a "Mrs. Dr. Fugard" who came over the trail from Circle City shortly after the Judge (April 12, 1903).

The attorneys of Fairbanks repaid Judge Wickersham's hospitality in kind on May 12, 1903, with the first banquet of the Tanana Bar Association dedicated in his honor. "In response to my toast I spoke of the courage and honesty of lawyers and defended them from the prevalent slander of trickery and dishonesty. The music was the feature of the evening. Morgan plays the violin like a master, and Dr. Whitney sang well. I wore my full dress suit—the first ever worn in the Tanana Valley—the only one present, too" (May 12, 1903).

Farming the fields of Fairbanks.
(Terrence Cole)

nightfall. But after December 22, it begins to rise, and from day to day, its course across the southern heavens is higher until on March 21, the day and night are of equal length. But it now compensates for its long absence during the winter months, and continues to rise in its flight across the heavens until on June 21 its culmination is reached, and the Tanana Valley is ablaze with twenty-two hours' sunshine and heat.

Not only does nature thus compensate the northland for the hours of sunshine lost in winter, but forces vigor and activity of growth into plant life in equal measure. Plant life there has the same number of sunlit hours for growth that crops have in more southern lands, though in fewer days. In a hundred days, between May 20 and September 1, the growing season in the Tanana Valley, the sun shines eighteen hundred hours, whereas during the same hundred-day period in sunny California it shines but fifteen hours, or one-fifth less sunshine than in the Tanana.

IN APRIL THE SOUTH wind and the warmth of advancing spring have turned the snow banks into flowing waters. Small rivulets trickle over frozen surfaces, cut channels into wintry ice sheets, and increase to torrential flow as the accumulated waters tumble tumultuously into river channels. Slowly the heavy river ice sheet rises with the flooding waters. The larger tributaries discharge the winter's accumulation of snow in the form of water from the great Tanana watershed into the river; the ice begins heaving, grinding, and floating—at last it is free!

"The ice is moving—there she goes!"

This cry on May 7th brought every inhabitant to the river's bank. At that hour every "chechaco"—every newcomer—was willy-nilly naturalized a "sourdough"—an accepted citizen of the great northland. The long looked-for ice-break had come.

For weeks the sporty ones had been dropping cash into the "pot," to be claimed by him who had guessed nearest to the moment when the break should come and the ice should move out; and now the lucky gambler cashed in, proudly boasting of his hydrographic wisdom. The river was bank-full and the ice moved, at first slowly and majestically.

Soon a great cake four feet thick, reaching from bank to bank, carrying on its surface a section of the trail across the ice, and the winter's garbage dumps, attempted to round a bend. The downstream end was pushed out upon a sloping bank, the pressure behind was irresistible, and the great ice sheet started overland through the forest. It slid higher on bushes and trees, tearing and rending, crushing and breaking, until the pressure and weight of the suspended mass broke the great sheet into fragments; those in the river floated away leaving large masses piled high on the riverbank.

A thick blue slab, worn circular from grinding along the bank and swirling in the eddy, suddenly turned on edge and rolled in the current like a mammoth wheel. The tremendous ice blocks rode and slid, rolled and dived, tore and rended and roared, and continually pressed downstream—for a day. And then the waters moved freely, unfettered by jam or ice clog, and the flood receded. The steady run of broken and disintegrating ice masses would go on for a few days when the break-up would end; the spring debacle—the stupendous rush of river ice—would be over for a season.

"STEAMBOAT!" THIS FAMILIAR SUMMER Yukon yell drew the town to the riverbank on May 10, 1903. There were no bells to ring, no whistles to blow, no flags to wave, but five hundred miners and a thousand malamute dogs joined in a grand chorus of welcome to the first boat of the season as the *Isabelle*, freed from her berth in the ice on a side slough below town, came puffing up the river, with her flags flying and her whistle blowing a welcome. Winter was finally gone!

14

THE MOUNT MCKINLEY EXPEDITION

Show me the trails that wind ahead,
where few men's feet have trod,
A campfire bright and a spruce bough bed,
and faith in the ways of God.
Give me the urge that will carry me on
till it comes my time to die,
And I will never dispute the Law
of the How, or the When, or the Why.

—Frank B. Camp

ONCE THE WORK OF organizing the courts and establishing the necessary public offices in the Tanana was done, there was time in the early spring of 1903 to look round and consider what to do next. To me the most interesting object on the horizon was the massive dome that dominates the valleys of the Tanana, the Yukon, and the Kuskokwim—the monarch of North American mountains—Mount McKinley. From the bluff point at Chena, one gets a superb view of its massive, snow-capped height, rising far above all surrounding peaks. The oftener one gazes upon its stupendous mass, the stronger becomes the inclination to visit its base and spy out the surroundings. From the moment we reached the Tanana Valley the longing to approach it had been in my mind; now the opportunity was at hand. Could we blaze a new trail into a distant and unknown wilderness of forest and mountain, extend geographic knowledge, and possibly aid in the development of a new mining camp? After much cogitation, I began to organize a party for the trip.

Many adventurous persons offered to go, but only the young and vigorous were accepted—men who were physically sound and would go from love of adventure and pay their share of the expense.* George Jeffery, court stenographer and a good amateur photographer, his friend, Mort Stevens, six feet tall and an all-round athlete, and Charlie Webb, packer and woodsman, were accepted.†

They chose the fourth and last man, John McLeod, the interpreter for Da-yin-nun, the medicine man of Too-whun-na. McLeod was the son of a Hudson Bay Company trader and was born on the Liard River in British America. He had spent the greater part of his life on the lower Mackenzie River, principally at Fort McPherson, from which point he crossed Rat portage and thence down the Porcupine to Fort Yukon the previous year. He spoke the Tena languages—all the northern Tena dialects. He was a hunter, canoeman, and trapper and knew the wilderness as well as his foster-brothers, the Indians. He, too, wished to go to the great mountain and we accepted him.

---

* The most notable character who volunteered to accompany Wickersham's Mount McKinley expedition was "Jujiro" Wada, a Japanese adventurer and son of a samurai, who worked for Barnette. Wada originally came to Alaska on a whaling ship in the 1890s, and during the gold rush had kicked around the Klondike and Nome before hiring on with Barnette as a cook and a clerk. More than anyone else it was Wada who started the gold rush to Fairbanks: On January 17, 1903, a front-page interview with Wada in a Dawson City newspaper detailed the "wonderful riches" of the Tanana, and by the following day the stampede was on.

During his first days in Fairbanks, Wickersham slept in a side room of Barnette's store and ate his meals in Wada's Tokio restaurant. When Wada had asked to join the McKinley party, Wickersham readily agreed, as Wada was an accomplished cook and dog driver and appeared to be a remarkable athlete. Within a few days, however, Wada backed out, supposedly for health reasons. "Wada has now concluded not to go with us on account of heart troubles," Wickersham wrote, "we cannot run the risk of his life, and of spoiling our trip" (May 10, 1903). Wada's heart would apparently make a full recovery, as he endured many long-distance treks in later years and garnered fame in the North as a championship long-distance marathon runner, winning a fifty-mile race in Nome in 1907 in 7 hours, 49 minutes, and 10 seconds. Wada Shigezirou died in San Diego in 1937 and is today revered and remembered by descendants and admirers on both sides of the Pacific for his remarkable adventures.

† Wickersham was particularly delighted to recruit Webb, even though it meant he had to promise him a job upon their return from the mountain.

"Yesterday I persuaded Charley Webb, an Eagle man and a splendid good hunter and packer to go to the mountain with us. He adds very much to the strength of my party and I am very much pleased over his determination to go. I shall undertake to provide him an appointment as guard in one of the jails when we get back" (May 14, 1903).

John McLeod, a crucial member of the McKinley expedition. Wickersham called McLeod the expedition "philologer" for his proficiency in the Athabaskan languages.

(Charles Sheldon Collection, Box 5, Folder 3, Archives, Alaska and Polar Regions, University of Alaska Fairbanks)

The two other members of the party were Mark and Hannah, so named in honor of Hon. Marcus Alonzo Hanna of Ohio, the friend of President McKinley, after whom Dickey had named the mountain. Billie Robertson had driven Mark at the head of his double-ender sled from Dawson to Fairbanks that spring, and Hannah, too, had hauled a grubstake load over the same trail. They were thoroughbred Kentucky mules, young and strong, yet learned in the ways of pack saddles and mountain trails, and their owners, in their enthusiasm, had offered them as transporters and carriers of packs. They were the only mules to be had in the Tanana Valley and were, of course, gladly accepted. The personnel of our party was thus completed!

NATHAN HENDRICKS AND GEORGE Belt were merchants and traders at Chena. Frank Cleary had no supplies for mountaineers in his log cache at Fairbanks, so the Chena merchants had held out a grubstake for our party. As soon as the ice was out of the Tanana and it was safe to send their mail steamer, the *Tanana Chief*, for supplies to Weare (Fort Gibbon), at the mouth of the Tanana River, the boat would make the trip. We had engaged passage on her to the mouth of a small river called "Dugan," whose valley comes down from Mount McKinley. This river comes into the Tanana about thirty miles above Baker Creek; whether it came from Mount McKinley we did not know, but were certain that its source was near there, and we intended to make it our valley of ascent. The Indians called it Kantishna, and told us it rose near the great mountain.

In April 1903, while we were organizing our Mount McKinley expedition, I learned that a band of Indians were camped below Fairbanks on the riverbank, and went down to visit them. It was a band of lower Tanana natives under old Koonah, the blind Kantishna chief, whom we met later on the Kantishna River. I held a long talk with Koonah and his hunters, with the assistance of a woman, Chotoadinneg, one of his tribe, who spoke English.*

They told me they went to this river each year early in the winter, but this season they first came up to Fairbanks to see the sights,

* "Old Koonah, the Tanana shaman, again visited me, with 'Ellen' as his interpreter. Ellen's Indian name is Chō-tā-ā-din-nah, and though young she is living with her 5th husband having procured her freedom from marital ties by walking off from her former encumbrances. Completed a good vocabulary of the Tanana dialect of the Athapascan tongue" (April 24, 1903).

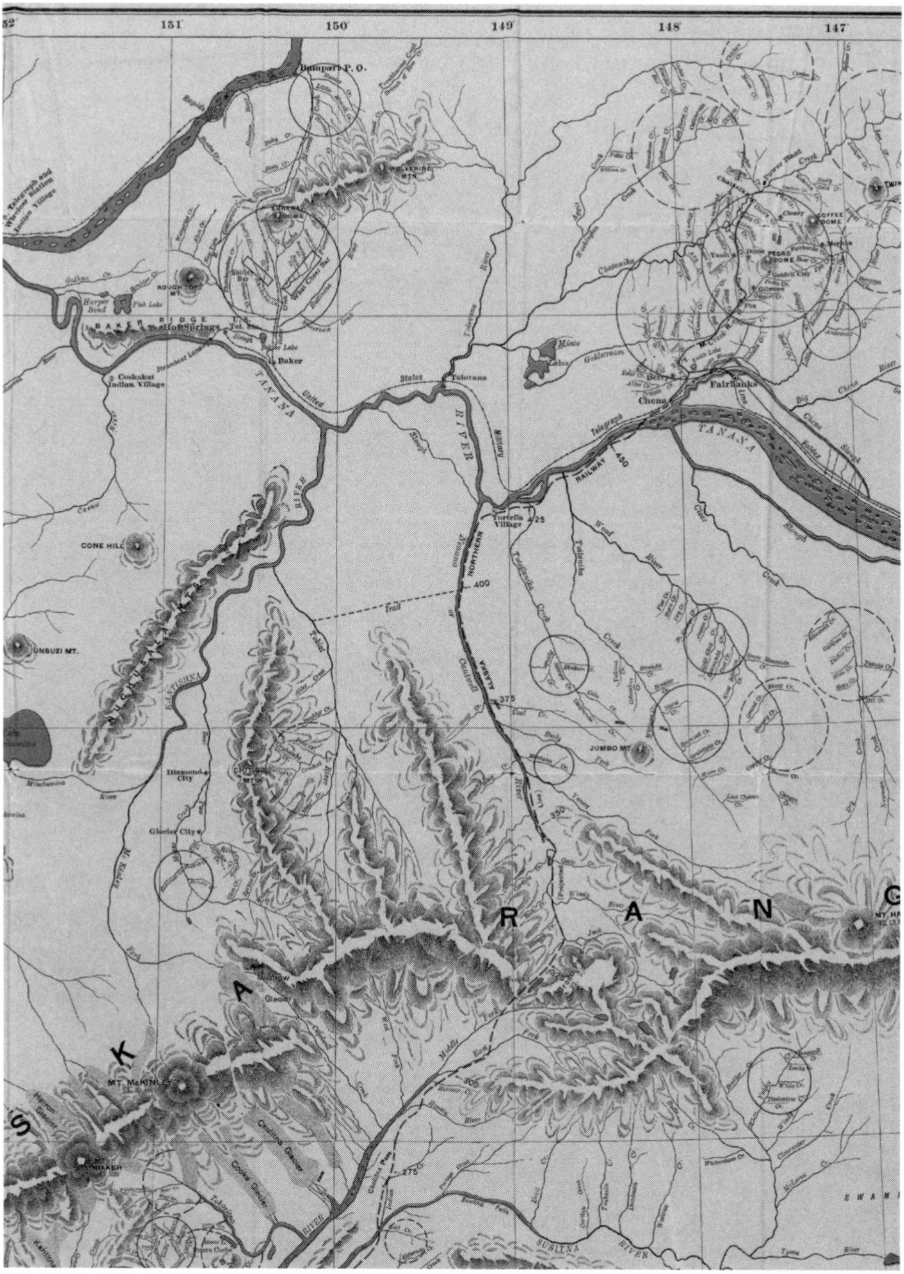

Part of Sleem's map of central Alaska. Wickersham's party ascended the Kantishna Valley (left) from the Tanana to the foothills of the Alaska Range.

(Rare Maps Collection G4370 1910 S53 c2, Archives, Alaska and Polar Regions, University of Alaska Fairbanks) intending to go on to the Kantishna across country on a cut-off trail. They drew for me a rough map of the Kantishna River, and the route to Denali, and gave me much information about distances and the character of the country. From them we learned that one branch of the river came down from Mount McKinley, the other from Minchumina the big lake over toward the Kuskokwim; and that the Kantishna was the stream that entered the Tanana at the place marked on the maps as the "Dugan River."

Captain Hendricks had said that if the lower Tanana should be filled with ice and there was yet ice in the Yukon, he would take us one day's journey up the Kantishna in his steamer, because he was curious to learn whether it was navigable for small boats. His assistance had been of great advantage to us, for without it we should probably have failed even to start on our trip for want of supplies and transportation.

THE PRIME NECESSITY IN every prospecting trip in Alaska is the "grubpile." It was Napoleon, or some other wise man, who said that an army travels on its belly, and that saying applies with equal force to a mountaineering party. I had a few dollars left in my pocket though but little credit in the bankless camp. My assistant mountain climbers had youth, hope, and mountain climbing excellence, but no money. It was finally suggested by one of their friends that they issue a newspaper, the first in the Tanana region, filled with camp news from the creeks and advertisements. There was no printing press in the country, no printing material or printers, no editor or reporter, which left the field open to anyone who wished to enter. Two of the boys had had some limited experience in newspaper work as newsboys, and the idea filled them with joy. Another was a skilled typist, and his machine would do the presswork. The athlete had (for a week) once solicited advertisements for a Dawson paper. The mule-skinner had a wide acquaintance; and the entire community were interested in the possibility of the discovery of new gold creeks.

Subscriptions and advertisements swamped the enthusiastic but inexperienced promoters, who were, however, slick enough to finagle me into doing their editorial work gratis. Finally there appeared in the camp the *Fairbanks Miner*, Vol. 1, No. 1, May, 1903, eight pages, double column—the first paper ever issued in the Tanana Valley—done on the first printing press ever brought to the valley—a typewriter.

This pioneer paper of the Tanana Valley mentioned every business interest in Fairbanks, and afforded a good view of the mining development of the camp to the date of our departure from Fairbanks on May 16, 1903, for Mount McKinley. Most of it is included in these pages for its historical value, if any.*

* "We completed the *Fairbanks Miner* today. I wrote every word of it except the poem, and arranged it. George A. Jeffery my stenographer did the type writing. We completed seven copies only. I gave one to Mr. Hess, one to E. B. Condon and one to Frank J. Cleary. Condon will read his to the multitude in the saloons. I will send one to Senator Fairbanks and keep one. Will also give Stevens one" (May 8, 1903). As far as is known, of the seven original copies of this first newspaper in Fairbanks, the only one that has survived is in the Wickersham Collection at the Alaska State Library in Juneau.

THE FAIRBANKS MINER.

Vol. 1. Fairbanks, Alaska, May, 1903. No. 1

Telegraphic.

ALASKA LAND LAW.

Washington, Mch. 5. (Special dispatch to the Miner.) Congress passed the Hoggatt donation land law for Alaska. This act permits the settler to take 320 acres of land under the general provisions of the homestead law, with these liberal changes: The act applies only to Alaska: it permits the squatter to take 320 acres of unsurveyed land and to stake it off as he would a placer mining location. After staking it out, and building his residence the settler must reside on the land four years when he acquires the right to a patent. The bill was prepared by Hon. Volney T. Hoggatt, late city attorney at Nome, now of Valdez, and was patterned after the old Oregon donation law.

AMENDMENTS TO ALASKA CODE.

Washington, Mch. 5. (Special dispatch to the Miner.) Several important amendments to the Alaska civil code were passed by Congress and approved by the President. One of these reduces the time of residence in divorce cases in Alaska from three to two years. The most important one widely extends the powers of towns and town councils. It also authorizes towns to elect a police magistrate, pass local criminal laws, and generally provides for wider self government. It also gives all saloon and other licenses paid in towns to the town for municipal uses—fifty per cent to the town, and twenty-five per cent to the school board, and the remaining twenty-five per cent to be divided as the court shall order. A new act provides for the formation of private corporations in Alaska.

DELEGATE BILL FAILED.

Washington, Mch. 5. (Special Dispatch to the Miner.) The bill providing for the election of a delegate from Alaska failed to pass Congress.

Local.

THE FAIRBANKS MINES.
NOME AND DAWSON RIVALLED.
DISCOVERY AND VALUE.

Felix Pedro discovered the Fairbanks placer mines in July, 1902, only nine months ago. Pedro is an Italian, forty-two years old. He was for many years a coal miner at Carbonado, Washington, and had been prospecting for three years in the Tanana hills before he made his rich discoveries on Pedro and Cleary creeks. His adventures in the Ketchemstock range, his long summer tours afoot, his dangers from the bald faced grizzly, the bull moose and other animals, how he was eaten by mosquitoes and how he ate his dogs, his travels through deep wooded valleys, across snow swept plains and over the high peaks of the Alaskan range, ever in search of the yellow metal—these would fill a volume and equal the richest book of travels in interest. His modesty and candor in relating the stories of his wanderings, hair breadth escapes and final success are indicative of the man's character. He has found a fortune and has the good sense to appreciate its value and he will save and lay aside enough for his old age.

In the summer of 1900 Pedro and Frank Costa prospected Fish creek and found colors on Fairbanks and other tributaries. In August, 1901, Barnette and Smith were trying in vain to push the steamer Lavelle Young through Bates rapids, intending to establish a trading post high up the Tanana. From his lookout on the dome at the head of Cleary and Pedro creeks, Pedro first saw a smoke far across the Tanana valley—a close examination with his field glass disclosed that it was rising from a steamer on the distant river. He watched it descend to the mouth of the Chena and enter that river, which Pedro had fully explored the year before. Hastily informing his companion of the the locality of the steamer, they descended from the hills crossed the valley to the Chena and that night came to the boat tied to the bank where the town of Fairbanks now grows. The merchant and the

ALASKA BOUNDARY TREATY

Washington, Mch. 6. (Special dispatch to the Miner.) The President has appointed Secretary Root, Senator Lodge and ex-senator George Turner of Washington as the American representatives upon the Alaskan boundary commission. England will appoint one commissioner from Canada and two from England, and the commission will undertake to determine the contentions raised by Canada over the Alaskan boundary. The Commission will meet at once in London.

THE FAIRBANKS MINER.

Published occasionally at Fairbanks, Alaska, by a stampeder who is waiting for the snow to melt and the ice to go out of the rivers. The paper will be mailed as soon as the Postmaster General establishes the first Post Office in the Tanana valley, to our living subscribers at the regular subscription price of an ounce. Single copies $5.00 chee-chaco money. No more advertisements wanted;—public notices refused—rate too low. If you don't like our style, fly your kite and produce your 30-30.

EDITORIAL.

The game law of Alaska ought to be more strictly enforced. Its liberal provisions permit travelers and prospectors to kill game needed for their own use, but this will not justify the promiscuous killing of moose for sale. Nor will it make it less brutal for men to run poor heavily laden moose cows down in the deep snow and slaughter them and their unborn young for dog feed as is too often done. Do not forget that there will be travelers and prospectors in the Tanana valley next winter.

Fairbanks was so named in honor of Senator Fairbanks, of Indiana, chairman of the Joint High Commission for the settlement of the Alaska boundary question.

miner—the only representatives of their classes then in the splendid Tanana valley passed a pleasant evening aboard the boat. Barnette informed Pedro of his inability to get over the rapids and of his intention to establish a trading post on the Chena. Pedro quietly informed the merchant that he had found "prospects" on several near by creeks, and then and there it was agreed to establish a post on the bank where the steamer was tied up. The next day Pedro and Gilmore renewed their packs from the ample supplies on the steamer and again disappeared in the wilderness.

The next day Barnette and Smith began to unload their goods. A small house was erected for the use of Captain and Mrs. Barnette, tents were put up as warehouses and assisted by Jim Eagle, Dan McCarty, Ben Atwater and John Johnson they soon built a log store and other log buildings and Barnette's trading post was the beginning of civilization on the Tanana. The first year at the Post was uneventful—a stampede to the Goodpastuer river and a good trade with the Tinneh for marten skins. That winter Dan McCarty went out to Valdez and met Frank J. Cleary, Mrs. Barnette's brother, and these two young men crossed the mighty Alaskan range in midwinter, came down the Delta river and amid hardships and suffering they reached the Post on February 20, 1902, traveling the last four days without food. On March 10, Captain and Mrs. Barnette left the Post for Valdez with dog teams loaded with the rich furs purchased during the winter. They went across the Tanana valley, up the Delta and climbed through the Alpine passes of the St. Elias range, and though often in water and snow reached Valdez in safety and thence went to Puget Sound for the next summer's outfit for the Post.

In April Pedro, accompanied by Gilmore came into the Post and renewed his prospecting outfit. They had one hundred dollars, only, but Cleary, though instructed to sell only for cash, gave them a full outfit and charged the balance to his own account. Early in July Pedro came back to the Post and reported that Gilmore had gone

FAIRBANKS.

Fairbanks now has a population of more than 1000 inhabitants and 387 houses by actual count. When the river opens and the boats arrive the population will be greatly increased. An application has been made to the District Court for town organization though this can not be acted upon until the July term at Rampart. In the mean time the MINER advises the citizens to perfect a consent government by the election of a mayor, a council of seven and a chief of police to enforce local rules and regulations for sanitary purposes and fire protection.

CHENA.

Chena is the name of our neighboring town at the junction of the Chena and the Tanana. It was started this winter and the influx of mushers from Rampart especially has rapidly built a generous rival to Fairbanks. Hendricks & Belt have moved their post across the Tanana to Chena, other business houses are being erected and the restless American is building a town there worthy of its name. They are also making active preparations to incorporate. Welcome to our sister town—but won't we scratch you for the trade.

As we go to press, May 7th, the Chena river in front of Fairbanks is breaking up and the ice must go out in a few hours.

Later: The ice went out at five o'clock P. M.

to Circle City. He was sick and got both medicines and provisions and returned to the mountains. On the 28th he again came into the store, very much elated and announced very secretly to Cleary that he had "STRUCK IT." He had found rich prospects on Pedro creek but in his nervous and weak condition had been unable to sink to bed rock—though he had gold to show as evidence of his success.

Pedro was known to many to be a careful and competent miner and prospector. He had been followed so often by others who sought to get the advantage of his well known superior information and knowledge of the creeks, that when his prospects on Pedro and Cleary grew to be a certainty he was nervously afraid these camp followers would descend upon him and stake the creeks before he could get his friends located. To avoid them he camped over on Fish creek and came quietly across the divide and prospected even without building fires to attract their attention. He succeeded in locating the best known claims for himself and friends—to which he was certainly entitled by reason of his arduous labors and great success. His report at the Post was quietly made known, and Costa, Cleary and his other friends stampeded off and staked. Pedro staked both discovery on Pedro and Cleary creeks, and the splendid dome between these golden creeks is his monument—Pedro's Dome. From its summit one overlooks the splendid Tanana valley framed on its southern limit by the giant peaks of the Alaskan range,—Mt. McKinley, at its western flank, the royalist of them all.

Accompanied by Ed. Quinn and Smallwood, Pedro set out by night and taking with them plenty of supplies. They sank a hole to bed rock, and there lay the glittering gold—seven feet of pay dirt. Other holes were sunk, and pay was located on Pedro, Cleary and Gold Stream. Locations were made, notices prepared and again Cleary and McCarty took their way through the wilderness—this time to Circle City to record a large number of claims. Pedro's claims have been carefully prospected and he now seems to be sure of Fortune's smile.

Telegraphic. | Local.

A TANANA TALE.

"Whoo-o" Windy Jim filled his cheeks with hot air and every body knew he was going to beat the king. "That nothing. In '98 I left Forty Mile to go over to the head of the Tanana with a sled and my dog Doughnuts to stake the copper mines that I afterwards sold to Patsy Clark. Whoo-o." Jim looked solemnly around and then proceeded. "The thermometer was froze up when I left Forty Mile but after I crossed the Ketchumstock hills it was much warmer, and the Tanana was wide open. I built a raft and put Doughnuts and my outfit on it and started down stream. We went fine for a while but in the afternoon we came round a sharp bend and into a big log jam. My raft tipped, sank and went under the drift. I jumped for the jam but missed my hold and I went under too. I swam a hundred yards or more under that drift holding to Doughnut's tail, and came out below and swam ashore. Whoo-o." And Jim puffed out his cheeks and looked as honest as God.

"And there we were, Doughnuts and me, five hundred miles from supper, for I had lost my entire outfit, gun, provisions, blankets and all. We started back to Forty Mile. Not a thing could we find to eat and the thermometer seventy below. Even rabbits had gone south and I could not even catch a cold. For twenty days we mushed across the hills, siwashing it at night, until we were starved. I couldn't kill Doughnuts," and Jim's eyes were filled with tears, "but we just had to have something to eat, so I cut off his tail—you know what a big long tail he had Frank," and Cleary solemnly nodded his head. "Well I cut off his tail and made soup of it, and it saved my life, for I came into camp four days later. Whoo-o." The other able liar ran his fore finger down his coat collar and scratched.

"Well I should say I did. I would divide my last meal with Doughnuts. Yes siree. I gave Doughnuts the bone out of his tail and after gnawing it a while he came on into Forty Mile with me. That tail saved us both and I could prove it by Charley Hall if he was here. Whoo-o." The ex-champion quit whittling, slipped off the counter and went out.

The writer made a personal inspection of the mines on Gold Stream, Pedro and Cleary creeks. A dozen pans from the top of the dump on Pedro's discovery claim on Cleary creek yielded an average of over seven cents to the pan. Noble brought five pans from the face of the drift in the shaft and they yielded twenty-five cents to the pan. The pay streak is located for more than 100 feet in width and 800 feet long on this claim and is at least six feet thick. On No. 2 above on Pedro creek Jack Costa's claim, the dump yielded eight cents to the pan, and Costa informed us that his pay streak had been located 150 feet wide, six feet deep and the length of his claim. A rough calculation shows that if his statement is correct there is about half a million dollars in his claim. Discovery on Pedro panned as well as Costa's. On Gold Stream Dan McCarty's claim panned an average of eight cents and Willig's but little less.

Pay has been located for six miles or more on Pedro and Gold Stream into which Pedro empties. Cleary creek heads just over the low divide from Pedro and extends the placer ground that much farther north. Coarse shot gold has been located on Fairbanks creek, and prospecting is being pushed on a number of other tributaries of Gold Stream and Fish Creek. Rich pay is known to exist on at least three creeks—Pedro, Cleary and Gold Stream, and the future of the camp is beyond doubt. Other creeks are prospecting high and the prospectors are confident. What the creeks need is systematic and careful prospecting.

BUSINESS CARDS.

BANQUET AT THE FAIRBANKS.

Mine host Marston of the Hotel Fairbanks entertained a few of his numerous friends at a dinner on the evening before May day. The dining room was handsomely festooned with evergreens surrounding the Stars and Stripes and the table was bountifully supplied. Among those present were Judge Wickersham, the lawyers and court officials, and many of the most prominent business men of the town. Harry West's orchestra made music and the guests remained long after dinner singing college songs and national airs. It was an enjoyable evening and will long be remembered by those present.

Within a week a party consisting of Judge Wickersham, M. I. Stevens, George A. Jeffery and Johnnie McLeod will leave Chena on the Tanana Chief for the Kantishna river on a trip to Mt. McKinley.

The Fairbanks hotel is being enlarged by the addition of a two story building in front and by raising the rest of the building to two stories.

A BAR BANQUET.

The first banquet in the Tanana valley was tendered to the members of the bar of his court by Judge Wickersham on the evening of April 28th, at the Tokio restaurant. The bill of fare may be of interest to prove that even in winter the Tanana is not without food.

"Hiyu-Muck-a-Muck.

Hooch—Chena Cocktails.
Consomme, a la Tawtilla.
Olives.
Chicken Mayonaise, Oyster Paties.
Sauterne.
Wine Jelly, Cream Sauce.
Roast Moose, Prospector Style.
Mashed Potatoes, Green Peas.
Ice Cream—Yuma Canned.
Jelly Cake.
Nuts, Raisins, Cheese, Coffee,
Cigars."

After the feast smoking and speaking entertained the company until a late hour. Mr. Allen R. Joy, from Koyukuk, came in at a late hour but was made welcome and spoke for the Koyukuk. The Gentlemen responded to the following toasts:

James Wickersham—Fairbanks.
H. J. Miller—Mushing with a Minister.
Jesse Noble—Cleary Creek.
Abe Spring—The First Sign-Board.
Felix Pedro—Prospecting.
L. C. Hess—The President.
Dan McCarty—The Moose Pasture.
E. B. Condon—Dawson.
Frank J. Cleary—Barnette's Trading Post.
J. Tod Cowles—The First Court in the Tanana Valley.
Bion A. Dodge—The Ladies.

Mr. Pedro brought the old gold pan in which he first discovered gold on the Fairbanks creeks, and Judge Wickersham informed the company that he intended to send it, with a bottle of Pedro dust to Senator Fairbanks of Indiana.

FAIRBANKS OFFICIAL DIRECTORY.

J. Tod Cowles, Esq., Justice of the Peace and Deputy Recorder.

L. C. Hess, Assistant U. S. District Attorney.

Edgar Wickersham, Deputy U. S. Marshal.

DAWSON—FAIRBANKS STEAMERS.

The Steamers "Isabella," "Gold Star" and "Lavelle Young" will connect with the "Robert Kerr" and other steamers from Dawson at Tanana, during the summer.

FREIGHT AND PASSENGERS.

E. T. Barnette, Agt.
Fairbanks. Alaska.

The members of the Arctic Brotherhood at Fairbanks organized recently, and applied to the grand lodge for a charter. They have also let the contract for the first hall for the order in the Tanana country.

It is to be a fine structure and is being built on Second Avenue. Messrs. Badger, Hess and Cleary comprise the committee in charge of the work.

THE PIONEER SALOON.
Whisky and Cigars.
First Ave. Dave Petree, Prop.

THE FAIRBANKS BAKERY.
Bread, Pies and Cake.
First Ave. Clark & Kiemberg.

The contract for building the U. S. jail was let to Laughery, the contractor, who now has it well under way. It is situated at the corner of Cushman street and Third Avenue.

THE CITY LAUNDRY.
Good Work Guaranteed.
Fairbanks, Harry & Saito

THE "MINOOK."
Good Whisky, Wines and Cigars.
First Ave. Joe Anicich, Prop.

THE TELEGRAPH LINE.

The government telegraph line is in fine working order from Valdez to Eagle and from Eagle to the outside world via the Canadian lines. The line from Eagle to Nome, via the Tanana is completed with the exception of about thirty miles, and this gap will be finished within sixty days. This will place the Yukon and Tanana valleys in instant communication with the States. NOW FOR THE RAILROAD.

WOODWARD THE STENOGRAPHER.
First Avenue. Fairbanks.

SCOTT, BENNETT & DUNBAR.
Freighters to the Mines.
Fairbanks, Alaska.

O'CONNOR & SONS
FREIGHTERS.
Fairbanks, Alaska.

An order has been signed by Judge Wickersham fixing July 27th at Rampart as the time and place for hearing the petition for the incorporation of Fairbanks.

COPELAND & NOYES.
HOTEL.
Good Rooms. Bunks.
Free Bus to and from all Steamers.

GENTS FURNISHING GOODS.
AT BARNETTE'S STORE.
Fairbanks. J. Wada.

15

UP THE KANTISHNA

We are the failures of long ago
and victims of circumstance;
And so, we hit the Alaska trail,
the trail of the One Last Chance!
And Alaska welcomed us to its work,
and asked us for nothing more,
Friend in our need and a friend indeed
for it gives us an open door.

—M. A. Metcalfe

MAY 16, 1903. IT is a cloudless May day, bright and warm. We loaded our packs and Mark and Hannah on the *Isabelle* at Fairbanks at noon, and at one o'clock dropped down the little river bound for Chena. The people of Fairbanks are greatly interested in our expedition, and more than a hundred came with us to the lower town on the *Isabelle*. They escorted us with flags flying and the dance hall band.

Privately I entertain the suspicion that the real purpose of the Fairbanksians is to let Chena know that the river that connects the two towns is navigable by steamers as far as Fairbanks—that it is not is the one Chena argument against the location of the courthouse at Fairbanks—and to let it be known, also, that the Mount McKinley expedition is from Fairbanks and not from the lower village. Anyway, the members of my party were most kindly entertained by both factions and both cheered us on our way.

Our steamer, the *Tanana Chief*, was loaded and waiting for us when the *Isabelle* reached the lower landing but we had yet to get our supplies from the Chena store and transfer our mules from the *Isabelle*. Our supplies consisted of flour, bacon, beans, dried apples, prunes, three hundred feet of good rope, alpenstocks, footwear, and one hundred pounds of rolled oats and a bale of hay for the mules. After stowing our equipment we had a good dinner, cooked on a real stove by a real Yankee woman from Massachusetts, after which we cast off and started down the Tanana River at 9:30 PM, though the sun was yet above the horizon. The *Chief* is pushing a small barge into whose open hold we loaded our packs and the mules.

May 17. We passed the Indian village of Tawtilla, at the mouth of the Nenana or Cantwell River, early this morning. Some years ago a famous prospector and hunter by the name of Frank Dinsmore reached this point on a prospecting trip and explored the Nenana up to the gorge. He reported the existence of large coal seams in that neighborhood and told his friends at Circle of a high mountain to the southwest, which was called Dinsmore's Mountain until Dickey gave it the name of Mount McKinley.

We overtook a small flat-bottomed steamer called the *Jennie M.* belonging also to Hendricks and Belt. That enterprising firm put their freight from Weare or Tanana a few miles up the Tanana River early in the spring while the Yukon winter ice was solid, and now hope to make quick return to Chena and enjoy big profits before other freight can reach camp. Ducks and geese are resting on every sandbar, and clouds of these summer visitors are winging their way to their northern nesting places. Heavy ice is piled high on the bars and riverbanks.

WE REACHED THE MOUTH of the Kantishna at noon and much to our surprise and disappointment, found it running full of heavy winter ice, probably coming from some big lake. The Kantishna break-up is a week later than that in the Chena; our steamer cannot enter the river and we are tied to the bank just below the terrific outflow of heavy Kantishna ice. Captain Hendricks at first declined to wait for it to clear but finally agreed to remain until evening, and says if it clears by that time, he will put us up a few miles.

Just as we landed Webb discovered a boat in the drift on a bar, and he and McLeod crossed in the *Chief*'s canoe, pulled it out of the drift, and brought it over to us. To our great delight it proved to be a well-constructed clinker-built boat, sixteen feet long, and show-

Steamer Tanana Chief *with the Mount McKinley party on board.*
(Charles Sheldon Collection, Box 5, Folder 3, Archives,
Alaska and Polar Regions, University of Alaska Fairbanks)

The steamboat Jennie M.
(Alaska State Library, Alaska Historical Society Photograph Collection, ASL-P9-081)

ing but little damage from its experience in the Tanana ice. Who its former owners were we had no means of knowing or how it came to be in the drift—but it is a welcome bit of flotsam.

While waiting for the Kantishna ice to run out we are cleaning and caulking the boat, and find it a good craft. We have borrowed oars from Captain Hendricks and now find ourselves in possession of watercraft as well as land transportation. We have named it *Mudlark.* The crew unanimously elected me Admiral of the Fleet, and even if the *Tanana Chief* fails us, we will use the *Mudlark* in conjunction with the mules for transporting our load across the rivers, which are very high at this season.

By six o'clock the heavy run of winter ice had passed out of the Kantishna, and Captain Hendricks will run us one day's steamer journey up the river. Owing to the swift current at the mouth of the Kantishna, we had much trouble and delay in getting into the side stream, but finally after much puffing and smoking our craft worked up to the point where the Kantishna current was more confined and regular, the river deeper and navigation easier. The stream is larger and more sluggish in consequence and we were making better time as we turned into the bunks at midnight.

May 18. Our craft chugged along all night, and when we turned out this morning at six o'clock we were delighted to find we were in a lake-like expanse of quiet water, five or six hundred feet wide, and apparently quite deep. We are making good speed. We have remained in these beautiful lakes all day. They are connected by short, rapid, narrow streams, and the river stretches out in the general direction of Mount McKinley.

The Kantishna is as large as the Wabash, the Sacramento, or the Illinois, and our boat is the first to enter its waters. It is a glorious spring day; far across the evergreen valley ahead of us the distant summits of the snowy range sparkle in the sunshine. The landscape bears no resemblance to an Arctic land; it more nearly resembles a scene in the lower valley of the Mississippi.

Sail ho! The *Tanana Chief* cast anchor in midstream as a canoe came alongside. The solitary occupant greeted us with surprise but with evident pleasure. His name is Butte Aitken and he tells us he has hunted and trapped along the river near the Toclat* all winter. His boat is filled with bales of furs gathered on his lonely expedition, which has now lasted for nearly a year. He quit his hunting and trapping camp and started downstream toward civilization after the ice went out three days ago. He intends to follow it down to Tanana and thence to St. Michael, where he will take the steamer for the States to dispose of his catch. He says there are no other white men in the valley, though there is an Indian camp about fifteen miles up stream, and informed us it is about forty miles to the Toclat. He asked a few questions, gave us some general information about the river, and floated downstream for the great outside.

ABOUT TEN O'CLOCK TONIGHT we reached the vicinity of the Indian camp on the right bank of the river. Our boat is now out of fuel and tied to the bank near a good bunch of dry timber burned over last summer by forest fires. All hands turned out with axes and for an hour we felled dry trees, cut cordwood, and carried enough aboard to run the ship back to Baker Creek. The Indians gathered around in evident astonishment at the sight of a steamer on the Kantishna in the midst of their hunting grounds.

When we had "coaled ship" the *Tanana Chief* pushed up to the Indian camp and we unloaded our mules and supplies. We thanked Captain Hendricks for his assistance and courtesy, gave him some letters to mail, and bade him and the crew goodbye. He turned the nose of his craft downstream and went round the nearest bend at full speed, while his boat's shrill whistle filled the midnight stillness with strange wild echoes never before heard in this valley. We are now cast loose in the wilderness with our supplies in our packs. We hastily put up a cache in some trees near our camp, hoisted our supplies, above the reach of marauding malamutes, and turned in.

May 19. We awoke this morning in the camp of Nachereah, the moose hunter. Fifty Athabascans and a hundred malamute dogs gazed at us inquiringly. When our mules were put off the boat at midnight the natives gathered in open-mouthed wonder. As Jumbo, the gigantic elephant, or the elongated giraffe is to the country crowd, so are Mark and Hannah to the Kantishna natives. "White man's moose" they were dubbed at once, and when too closely examined Mark's heels hit the skyline. There was scurrying to safer distance and loud commands from Olyman, the wise. Every malamute strained at his leash eager for

* Toklat River, a branch of the Kantishna.

the chase. After a solemn midnight treaty we had employed a guard to watch our animals while we slept. Neither the natives nor the dogs had ever before seen a mule. A loosened malamute might have run them into the swamp or crippled them beyond further use.

THE CAMP IS NOW at breakfast. While some of the squaws are gathering wood and others are cooking, the men are snoring or yawning and waiting for the repast. Two hunters came in from an early visit to the duck swamp with a brace of teal. A quarter of a moose was lowered from the limb of a tree and every needy squaw cut meat for the meal. Frowsy and unkempt children ran from beds of boughs in the tents to the breakfasts in the skillets, and back again with hands full of food. Dirt and disorder; color and squalor; barbarism and waste; it is a typical scene in a Tena camp of northern Apaches.

Their hasty meal finished, they gathered round us to learn whence, whither, and why. McLeod informed us they were from the mouth of the Tanana, and brought forward Kudan and Rayede, two young men who had had some schooling with the missioners. At my request he tells them of our journey to the big mountain and our wish to reach its summit. Kudan told us in broken English, "Mountain sheep fall off that mountain—guess white man no stick 'um." Incredulity appeared on every unwashed face at the statement of our purpose. "What for you go top—gold?"

No, we go merely to see the top, to be the first men to reach the summit. This information imparted by the interpreter caused Olyman to remark in brief Indian phrases, which McLeod translated after the rude laughter had subsided as "He says you are a fool."*

Having learned our business in the wilderness and given us their opinion of it, they turned away to attend to their own. A few interested squaws watched Webb make bread in the flour sack and cook our breakfast over the coals. But plenty is in the Tena cache; bellies are round and children and dogs are fat, so we ate our breakfast without annoyance.

* "Abram & Simon, two young Indians, who speak English came aboard & made us maps of trails &c. to McKinley. . . . I asked him 'Abram, your name, what name mountain?' He answered promptly 'McKeenly.' 'No,' I said, 'What is Indian name' & he said 'Dē̄ē-na-thy' (*a* as in father)" (May 18, 1903).

The Indian camp of Nachereah on the Kantishna River.
(UAF-1975-0146-00001, Archives, Alaska and Polar Regions, University of Alaska Fairbanks)

THIS BAND OF TENA had left their winter camp on the lower Tanana in the latter days of February for their annual early spring hunt. A dozen toboggan sleds, ten feet long, constructed of split spruce boards, with high curved bow, corded on each side with moose thongs, carried their supplies and babies. To each toboggan bow half a dozen or more lean and wolfish Indian dogs were hitched, each dog tied by a single cord to a central thong or rope knotted to the sled. A brutal driver had flogged the poor starved beasts along the trail, while the squaws and Olyman siwash had followed on foot.

Nachereah, the moose hunter, shod with heavy snowshoes, had broken trail, and had led the band along the river, across the well-known cut-off, through the forest, and over the hills. Day after day this sorry cavalcade had struggled towards the headwaters of the Kantishna, to the old Toclat camp, which their ancestors had thus visited time out of Tena mind. Hunters scouted the side lines and one lucky day Cheah had killed a moose. The caravan had turned aside to the carcass and remained in camp till they had eaten it. Again they had struggled along the snowy trail, but with renewed strength and happier hearts. Finally they had reached the old site at the mouth of the Toclat where they had camped and prepared for the hunting season.

Now, after a good spring hunt, they were on their way back to the fish camps at the junction of the Tanana and the Yukon. Everyone is well fed and a pack of sleek and round-bellied malamutes are tied to nearby trees, howling in joy at the abundant camp fare.

These Apaches of the Yukon have learned the art of securing their dogs so they cannot chew off their leashings. They cut a hole in the flattened end of a small pole; tied a heavy thong of moose hide around the dog's neck and slipped it through this hole so as to bring the pole close up to the neck; the other end of the pole, which is five feet or more in length, is securely tied to a tree. Thus tied, the dog cannot cut the thong at his neck or at the tree, nor can he chew the pole itself. The Indian hunter is now assured he may not be abandoned in a distant forest camp with a heavily loaded sled and no cur to furnish motive power, a matter of life or death in Tenaland.

THE INDIAN DOG IS a vagabond and thief. He is utterly shameless and entirely devoid of even business honor. He has been starved for countless generations in famishing winter camps of unfed Tena. Every bone was cracked and every spot of rancid grease was licked clean before his turn came. He lives to steal and necessarily steals to live; it is his only joy and his greatest accomplishment. He will climb a ladder, stand on the highest rung, gnaw a hole in the cache door, then crawl in and eat or carry away the food contents; climb the corner logs of a cabin and rob the miner of his last bite placed on the roof for safe keeping; crawl under the tent and abstract from underneath the owner's pillow his only can of beans; carry it off, open the tin with his fangs, and devour the contents without cutting his lips.

An attorney friend who struck it rich on a stampede where he had passed all others by the speed of his dogs afterward built them good warm kennels and fed them to bursting. This kind treatment, however, did not change their age-old habits or nature. He had to carry home to careless neighbors hams and sides of bacon, cans of lard, moose quarters, and canned butter that his dogs had stolen and for whom he could find an owner, and then had enough unidentified property left to feed a family of four! It is not surprising, therefore, that the Edisonian ingenuity of the Tena nation was devoted to constructing the nongnawable leashing, attached to nonreachable pole, tied to a nonapproachable tree to prevent the nonappearance of a Tena dog at work time.

HE WHO GIVES TIME to the study of the history of Alaska learns that the dog, next to man, has been the most important factor in its past and present development. The Eskimo tribes along ten thousand miles of Arctic shoreline have long used the dog as a beast of burden, and out of the survival of the fittest they have developed a type particularly adapted to the rigors and hardships of Arctic life. Russian discoverers found this dog drawing native sleds along the Arctic ice pack. This faithful animal carried the earliest Hudson Bay Company traders into the remotest recesses of the great fur land and carried out a fortune in furs.

When the discovery of the Klondike and Alaskan goldfields attracted American miners into this region, the dog was found to be their most useful and faithful assistant. He has ever since been the constant companion and servant of the prospector, miner, and freighter, and without his aid the efforts to develop the goldfields must have languished. He carried the United States mail from Dawson to Nome and return, to the Koyukuk and the Tanana. As an aid to the administration of justice he has overtaken many a fugitive criminal, transported the officers of the law and the mandates of the court. In the performance of my own official duties I have traveled more than one thousand miles during a winter along the frozen Yukon with my team of native dogs, my blankets, food, and the court's files and documents.

In the winter of 1903 a whole population of American citizens invaded the wilderness of the Tanana Valley, along a sled-marked trail, and founded permanent settlements in the Fairbanks goldfields, using the dog as the principal means of transportation. Irreplaceable as a beast of burden and a domestic animal in central and northern Alaska, the dog has been to this far northland what the horse has been to the great plains west of the Mississippi.

Congress was not ignorant of the dog's value to the people of Alaska when it passed the Penal Code. In this territory the dog is officially recognized as a treasured possession—and stealing a dog is a crime of larceny.

THIS FORENOON WE SPENT in sorting and arranging packs, loading the *Mudlark*, and consulting with native geographers about trails to the mountain and a guide. The old hunters who are acquainted with the caribou hills near Denali have drawn us a map with charcoal on birch bark, showing the rivers falling away from the high one, and giving us distances from point to point in that direction. Our party must divide for a time; Webb, McLeod, and I will go with the boat, while Jeffery and Stevens will go overland with the mules and meet us at old Koonah's camp, a day's journey above the Toclat.

Seated on the bank of the river, we negotiated a treaty with Olyman and the elders for a guide to Koonah's camp at Tuktawgana, two, possibly three sleeps away. The guide must go overland with muleteers and mules and arrange to gather navy and cavalry at the upper camp. McLeod suggests the employment of Kudan, since he can talk enough English to make himself understood, but Kudan is coy and unwilling. The elders are diplomatic. Olyman suggests that Kudan's absence from camp would cause great anguish to his friends—that he might be drowned in the river, or killed by one of the mules. After every possible objection had been suggested to his absence from the camp for three days, with an appreciation of his services for each, we engaged him. Fifteen dollars and a coat, which must be discarded, were to be paid to him at Tuktawgana after service performed. The mules are now loaded with packs, the photographer strapped to his back a mysterious black box, which the natives look upon with awe, and, guided by Kudan, the cavalry filed off through the forest in a southerly direction just before noon.

THERE ARE MANY THINGS in a camp of Athabascans on the banks of an unmapped river in sub-Arctic Alaska to engage the attention. Since I am to be the steersman of the recently acquired transport, the *Mudlark*, other boats are of special interest, and one now on the Tena ways on the sandy bank of the Kantishna is particularly so. Olyman Cheah is building a birch bark canoe. The ribs of stout birch wood have been carefully shaped with his knife and tied with long tough spruce roots to longitudinal strips of split spruce, thus preparing the framework for the birch bark covering. The sheets of birch bark are stripped from the living tree as the sap is rising in the spring, and Olyman cuts them to fit the frame, allowing overlaps for sewing.

When the birch bark plates are cut and fitted, the old women and their young assistants gather alongside the craft, and squatting on the ground sew the sheets together and to the ribs with spruce root threads, using a bone awl. Meanwhile, Olyman is carving and shaping the bow and the stern posts. A piece of bark is cut and fitted over the bow, the upper parts of the main skin are trimmed and supported by an inner and outer gunwale, and the squaws complete their work by cording the whole length of the gunwale with long flexible spruce rootlets of many colors, thus binding the outer skin of the boat to the ribs and framework.

In this way they are able to put the swanlike and serviceable boat together as quickly as a shoemaker can shape and sew a shoe. Olyman then runs some spruce pitch into the cracks and small holes, paints the framework red, and launches the craft upon the waters of the Kantishna for his trip to the summer fish camps. It is a beautiful and graceful boat, and Olyman rides it fearlessly, but it is an accomplishment to be safely indulged in by the white man only after long practice and many wettings.

HAVING STARTED THE LAND party on its way through the forest we now bid our Indian friends adieu, cast off the lines, and head the *Mudlark* upstream. The river is high from the swollen waters held back by the late ice flow.

Large blocks of heavy winter ice glisten in the sun, yet lie on the bars and riverbanks. Webb and McLeod use the oars while I steer the boat into eddies and still waters easiest to ascend. We are favored with two passengers who express a wish to go two miles up the river with us on their way to hunt moose. At that point we went ashore to repack a bundle and while there had some luncheon. Our passengers waited patiently until the lunch was spread and then graciously accepted their share. The eldest of our visitors is none other than old Cheah, whose name just happened to mean in the Tena language, "to eat." After the exhibition we know the Tena has a pronounced sense of the eternal fitness of names.

After a heavy meal Cheah and his deep-mawed companion disappeared into the forest in the direction of the camp which they had so recently left, and with lighter commissary we went on our way up the river. Rowing round the long circular bends soon became real work, so we put out a rope and pulled the craft along, guiding it off snags and out of the shallows with steering oar. About five-thirty in the afternoon the sky became overcast and it began to rain. We went ashore at a high dry bank, put up our tent, filled it with spruce boughs, minus fleas, flies, and the aroma of a Tena camp, and prepared for a good night's rest.

While we were frying bacon, brewing coffee, and setting our evening meal, our old friend of the morning, Nachereah, came to pay his respects—and remained to dine. While he can never hope to equal Cheah, his capacity for browned biscuits and sweetened coffee excited our chef to express the hope that we might soon get so far away from the Indian camp that no more of our friends could cross the bend and have another meal with us. Nachereah tells us his name means "sunset," that the name of the main [Kantishna] river is "Huntethna"; and that the southern branch at the junction is "Totlot," which means "headwaters."

Father Julius Jetté, S. J., who is an authority on the Tena language of the Tanana, tells me in a personal letter; "The genuine Indian name for the east fork of the Kantishna is Totlot, and means 'water source' or 'headwaters.' It is formed of 'to' water, and 'tlot,' source. . . . The Coskakat Indians still have their hunting grounds on this stream, and formerly used to live there for the greater part of the year, and hence were called 'Totlorotana,' i.e., 'dwellers on the Totlot.'"

May 20. For breakfast we had fried caribou steaks, purchased from a Tena hunter, garnished with crisp bacon browned on the open fire, and Webb's best coffee and biscuits. The perfumes of Araby may be more agreeable to the olfactory nerves of the poet, but for good homey flavor to a woodsman's nose the odor of frying bacon on an early morning campfire in the wilderness cannot be excelled.

The high water, long bends, and the strength of the rising current have made it a day of labor. With all our efforts we have advanced but a short distance. On account of the high water cutting off all open ground for walking near the river we have been obliged to propel the *Mudlark* by oars and the pole.

Fine camp tonight on the west bank of the river in good timber. River rising. Webb and McLeod are good river men and handle the boat skillfully and without fear. We passed the intake of the Toclat an hour before we stopped for the night. The great spring camp of Nachereah's moose hunters is on the south bank of the Kantishna, opposite the inlet of the Toclat, which comes down from the hills to the south. At this wilderness encampment they were in a fine game country. Moose signs are everywhere, caribou are on the hills, now plainly seen toward the southeast, and bands of sheep are higher on the same slopes. Snowshoe rabbits, mink, marten, and fox are abundant. Trails lead in all directions. It is a happy home-spot in a hunter's paradise.

May 21. We made but ten or twelve miles today, even though we did not stop for lunch. The rain poured down on us constantly, and we needed to bail the boat frequently. We are wet, bedraggled, and hungry.

Tonight we have a good camp on the north bank of the river. Our oarsmen are almost discouraged by the tortuous river channel, although we maintain a general southerly course. McLeod persistently declared we passed the same spruce tree three times in the course of the afternoon, and certainly the three trees and the three points bore many signs of kinship.

Moose signs abundant; there must be droves of them or else the few have engaged in a St. Vitus dance! The river is still rising.

May 22. While we were preparing an early breakfast a canoe carrying two white men floated round the bend and landed at our camp.

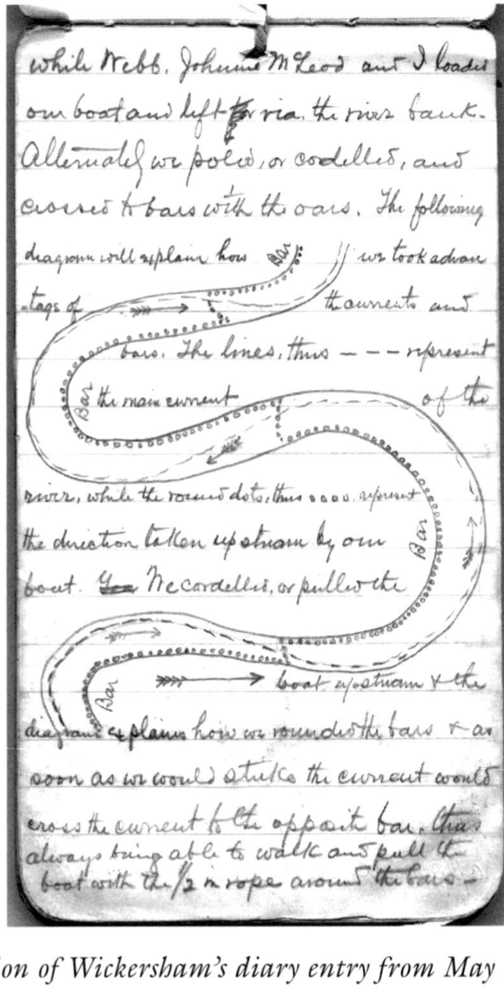

while Webb, Johnnie McLeod and I loaded our boat and left via the river bank. Alternately we poled, or cordelled, and crossed to bars with the oars. The following diagram will explain how we took advantages of the currents and bars. The lines, thus - - - represent the main current of the river, while the round dots, thus . . . . represent the direction taken upstream by our boat. We cordelled, or pulled the boat upstream & the diagram explains how we rounded the bars & as soon as we would strike the current would cross the current to the opposite bar, thus always being able to walk and pull the boat with the 1/2 in rope around the bars.—

A portion of Wickersham's diary entry from May 19, 1903.

(Alaska State Library, Wickersham State Historic Site Collection, m107_001_diary06_1903_may19b)

They are trappers from the headwaters of the Kuskokwim River and are following the ice down to Tanana to dispose of their winter's catch of furs. They have been away from civilization for more than a year. Their names are Frank Peterson and Charlie Lundeen.

They tell us that the Indian camp, Tuktawgana, is yet fifteen miles above us, and that it is about two hundred miles round the bends to the big lake near the Kuskokwim portage. They made a rude map of the upper branches of the river for us, and located the course towards McKinley; gave us some much-needed baking powder and soda which our commissary did not contain, and accepted an order on the store at Tanana for an equal amount. They asked eagerly for news from the outside world and talked while we ate. Both boats left camp at the same time, ours towards the great mountain, theirs downstream towards the great Outside. It is thus wilderness trappers and mountaineers visit.

THE RIVER FELL TWO inches last night but it is yet too high to permit us to line along the banks, except in short stretches, so we are compelled to use the oars like galley slaves, to cross and recross the stream to escape the strength of the current and to obtain the upward force of eddy and backwater. Ducks and geese are coming in great flocks. Moose signs are abundant. Today as we swept noiselessly along underneath a high bushy shore we saw a monster bull about fifty yards ahead. He stood on a protruding point of the bank stretching his great brown neck after a choice morsel of browse that extended forward and overhung the stream. His ungainly head, Roman-nosed and prehensile-lipped, surmounted by new growing horns, was towards us, and he continued in active pursuit of the waving branch, though we were in plain sight.

At the first glimpse of his gigantic form our rowers were silent and motionless; the backwater of the stream and the momentum of the boat drove us towards him, so near that his massive shoulders, seven feet high, seemed to tower over us, before a current of air brought the foul smell of man to his nostrils. Instantly, but as silently as a moving shadow, he drew his magnificent brown body back into the bushes that lined the shore and we neither saw nor heard him again.

IT IS A BEAUTIFUL spring day in the wilderness. The river dances merrily over the shallows and eddies lazily round the bends.

Though the current is steadily downward, our course is upward and we sweated freely as we worked hard at the oars and the tow-line. We think we are nearing the Indian camp marked on Lundeen's map and hope in the course of the afternoon to join our mule drivers, our Indian guide, and the mules. At noon we went ashore on a sunny bank to rest and to eat lunch.

While the crew was thus engaged, I, like Zaccheus of old, climbed a tree. About a mile upstream I saw a small flag, which I knew to be Stevens', fluttering in the breeze. As I shouted this news from my crow's-nest perch my jackies waved their head-gear, cheered like schoolboys, hurriedly threw our grub box aboard the boat, and embarked. In a moment we were off for the Indian camp, where Jeffery, Stevens, Kudan, and old Koonah's dogs welcomed us at the landing. The cavalry had arrived a day ahead of us, though on account of the Indian dogs, they had not yet swum the mules over to the Indian camp, which is on the east side of the river.

16

THE APPROACH

O'er evergreen valley and low Tena home,
the crest of Denali towers massive and lone;
By wintry clouds hidden from mortal sight,
it stands resplendent in summer light;
Its sunlit walls bared to azure sky
promise lowland Tena their God is nigh.

WE ARE GATHERED AT Tuktawgana, in the land of Koonah, the blind sage of Kantishna. Here is wood and water and hunting. It is the spring-and-summer camp of Koonah's band. Our boat was hauled into the harbor of the shallow slough fronting the camp and our outfit quickly unloaded, our tent raised, and we began housekeeping near our Tena friends. We paid fifteen dollars and the old coat to Kudan, the guide, who quickly disappeared into the wilderness on his homeward journey.

May 23, 1903. From Koonah's camp there is a beautiful view of the snowy mountains to the south and east. The land rises by gentle gradations from our valley to the rounded foothills thence ascending to an elevated tableland upon which rests the mountain-mass, from which it leaps skyward to the massive dome of Denali. The rising summer heat has not yet dissolved the greater snow banks, which last winter's storms deposited on the slopes of the lower mountains, though windswept areas are bare and brown. These extensive snow banks give a pleasing parti-colored aspect to the mountain view adding freshness and beauty to the landscape. Above the range, which divides the Toclat watershed from the Kantishna, is a prominent mountain, which the Indians call Chitsia, or Heart Mountain, because its peak resembles the point of a moose heart.

Far beyond Chitsia rise half-a-dozen snowy peaks, some of them reaching a height of ten or twelve thousand feet (judging by Mount McKinley), and covered with perpetual snow. But these great peaks are mere hills by the side of the towering summit of Mount McKinley, which rises almost two miles above their tops, and more than nineteen thousand feet—nearly four miles—above our camp.

KOONAH'S CAMP IS A moving panorama of Indian life, color—and sound, thanks to the happy children and the scampering dogs. The camp is situated on the lower end of an island formed by the Kantishna on the west and a wide marshy slough on the east. Its view opens eastward and south, across the still waters of the lake-like slough; the dark spruce forest in the background provides shelter from the wind and an abundance of fuel. On this high, dry ground, stand the summer tents and bark houses of his people, and the high drying racks for jerking caribou and moose steaks, and smoking salmon, beyond reach of the hungry curs. Next to the slough is the Tena shipyard, a sloping sand bar where they frame, sew and caulk birch-bark canoes. A fleet of canoes and boats, including our transport, the *Mudlark*, are anchored in the quiet harbor abreast the village.*

One ancient gray-haired dame, bent with the work of many years, is laboriously scraping a wet moose hide strung across a horizontal pole, shoulder high. Her scraping implement is a thin stone. She skillfully removes the hair and fat from the skin so it may be rubbed soft and dry for tanning. Another squaw cleaned both sides of a great hide, tied the ends to a post and inserted a round stick in the loop of skin, twisting it with all her strength to squeeze out the water. After drying it will be stretched on a pole frame above a smudge to give it a beautiful brown color on one side, leaving the other side white. Thus cleaned, tanned, and smoke-colored the finished product is made up by the squaws into moccasins, leggings, and other articles.

* "This is the ideal Indian Camp. It faces the waters of a slough—and far away—25 to 50 miles is a range of magnificent snow capped mountains.... It is the most beautiful mountain view I have ever seen and over shadows all the beauties of the Rockies & Cascades. The Indian camp, itself, is full of beauty—as a barbaric and rapidly passing phase of American life...all the life and color [of] a Sioux or Comanche camp. It is the most spirited Athapascan camp to be seen in the north—in a splendid game and fish country—and on a river visited only by the few hardy & daring spirits that have camped along its shore over winter for its fine trapping" (May 22, 1903).

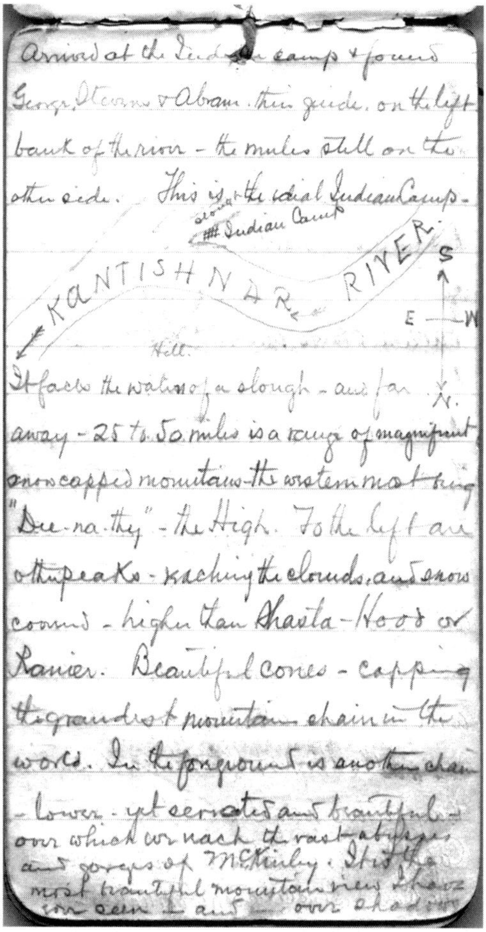

Portion of Wickersham's diary entry from May 22, 1903, with his map of the Indian camp at Tuktawgana.

(Alaska State Library, Wickersham State Historic Site Collection, m107_001_diary06_1903_may22c.)

SOON AFTER WE ARRIVED at this camp yesterday afternoon we called at old Koonah's wigwam to pay our respects to the sachem of Tuktawgana. When we entered he rose and received us with a native modesty and simplicity that adorns and ennobles the primitive man. He is blind, slender, and rather tall, though well-proportioned, and about fifty years of age.

He enjoys the blessings and labor of two wives; the youngest is an active bright-eyed Tena Hebe, who keeps the chieftain's home cheerful and neat and his moccasins dry; the elder tans mephitic moose hides, and prepares salmon for the drying rack, smoking them dry and brittle for the well-worn teeth of her master. She keeps away the malamute dogs with a club and a raucous voice. In civilized lands, or in a Circle City court, the old lady would have had the law on the co-respondent long ago, and possibly alimony of at least two of Koonah's best dogs and one moose hide per annum, but in Tenaland she snares rabbits for the household and sleeps by the blaze under the fish rack.

Today we put Mark and Hannah across the Kantishna,* which is threateningly at high water, much against their will. A mule loves the water as a cat does, but like that animal can swim if thrown into the stream. We first led Hannah gently to the high bank above the wide and rolling torrent and kindly invited her to enter and swim, as if it were an ordinary everyday matter, but she backed away, shaking her big ears in violent negation. Again and again we courteously led her to the jumping-off place, begging and pleading with her to "be nice, old girl, it's all right," only to be denied in the most positive manner. Finally Webb gave her a most unsportsmanlike kick, took a rough-mouth hitch over her head with a long, heavy rope, the other end of which lay coiled in the stern of the *Mudlark*. With all hands on the hoisting rope we gave her a sudden rush over the bank and landed her broadside on the river current. The crew of the *Mudlark* hastily pushed off as they saw her strike the water and drawing her head rope taut, towed her ashore. We made short work of Mark and thus brought

* In addition to the difficult river crossing with the mules, May 23 was marked by the first major sign of dissension on the expedition, when McLeod threatened for the first time to quit.

"The first disappointment today: Johnnie McLeod has cold feet and is going to desert us. He has been intensely scared out by the Indian stories about the inaccessibility of the mountain." With Wickersham's urging McLeod pledged to keep going, but he had resolved that he would remain with the mules and not attempt to climb the mountain itself (May 23–24, 1903).

our quadrupedal companions into the village, whose inhabitants, biped and canine, lined the home bank and howled in happy unison at the first circus performance ever exhibited in Tenaland.

THE TENA IS A modest and peaceful gentleman. Born in the solitudes of the birch and spruce forests he has never known the necessity for war, offensive or defensive. If he cannot retire when war or personal encounter threatens, he meekly turns the other cheek. Retaining the ancient hunting grounds of their forefathers, occupying their earliest camping places, living the simple life their common ancestors lived before the southern bands migrated to the Columbia basin, to Oregon, Arizona, and Mexico, the Gens de Butte, the men of the mountains, the Tanana Tena, still exhibit the peaceful disposition of Yako, the gentle magician, the Athabascan Adam.

The Tena is a story teller—a transmitter of oral tales. Having no written annals to assist his memory or hamper his imagination he passes tribal legends along by oral communication from father to son. His quiet and gentle nature is clearly disclosed in his timidity while thus engaged, for any exhibition of unusual interest, such as inquiry and preparations to write down his statements, will cause him to retire behind a barrier of silence from which he cannot be coaxed. He loves to relate them at the twilight hour, beside a low campfire in the great forest, or, still better, under the darkness of night to his young native friends resting beneath adjoining sleeping robes or in the spruce bough beds. He shrinks from exposing his tribal traditions to those who claim superiority of education, of position, or race, or to those who smile as they are related.

It is always the midnight hour to old Koonah, but the loss of his sight has sharpened his other senses, and he will not relate the ancient tales until there is restful peace among his listeners, be they Tena or alien. Thus, in silence, we rested round the campfire while he talked to us softly and slowly about the divinities and demons of Tenaland; of those wicked men of former days whom Yako, the ancient shaman, changed into animals, birds, or bees, to be forever the servants of their Tena brothers; of other animals given immortality that they might have eternal life and happiness in the land of their fathers; of the supernal divinities of Denali, whose everlasting snows he can no longer see, but whose majestic heights and stupendous outlines are imprinted on his memory with photographic accuracy.

Anotoktilon, the Indian hunting camp at the junction of Moose Creek, or Chitsiana, and the Kantishna River.

(Alaska State Library, Wickersham State Historic Sites Photograph Collection, ASL-PCA-277-4-106)

The campfire had long since burned out; Koonah's voice grew low and sleepy, and that of the interpreter finally ceased. We stole away to our tents and our midnight slumbers for the tales of Koonah, the sage of Kantishna, were ended.

May 24. Our expedition marched again this morning; the cavalry with Jeffery and Stevens, assisted by an Indian guide, went south along the edge of the birch bluffs east of the river, and the three jolly tars on the *Mudlark* laboriously poled her round never-ending bends against the increasing current. We are to meet at the Indian camp at the mouth of Moose Creek, or Chitsiana, as the Tena call it. After making twenty miles along the river highway we are glad to rest tonight at a camp on the east bank of the river.

May 25. We reached the Indian camp of Anotoktilon this afternoon at the junction of Moose Creek, or Chitsiana, and the Kantishna, and found the other members of the party already in camp and our mules in good condition. We now note that present-day maps of this region are incorrect in extending the headwaters of the Kuskokwim to the Chitsia Range, for that river rises in a low range of hills to the westward of the Kantishna. The Indians at this camp are from the big lake at the head of the right fork of the Kantishna River. They tell us its name is Minchumina.* They call the great mountain Denathy or Denali, the small peak Chitsia and the river Huntalhno. Their summer home is at Lake Minchumina in the midst of their hunting grounds, and Chief Shesoie is their leader. They are engaged in building birch-bark canoes and tanning moose hides.

May 26. We remained in camp this morning for it is raining hard and blowing a gale. In the afternoon we climbed the bluffs to study the country in company with the chief and old Ivan, who have for many years hunted round the heads of the streams approaching Denali. These hunters traced the location of the streams in that direction and the gaps in the hills through which we must go to reach the glacier they tell us comes down from its summit. They also traced the course of the Kuskokwim to its source in the Nuchusala, or Bull Moose Mountains.

---

* According to the *Koyukon Athabaskan Dictionary* (Alaska Native Language Center, 2000), p. 96, Lake Minchumina literally means "Big-lake Lake."

May 27. After consultation with the Indian chief and his aged hunters we have determined to cache our boat up the slough a mile or two, and go overland across the Chitsia hills towards the base of Denali. We accept their judgment and are rearranging and repacking our outfit for the overland journey. On that account we were late in getting away from Anotoktilon this morning. The Indians instructed us to follow the slough south for about two miles, where a stream comes in and to cache our boat. From that point we will go eastward, thus avoiding streams hard to ford. By mistake, however, our muleteers got off on another stream and we had to send out a searching party, which finally found and brought them to our camp.

Here we met with one of those minor accidents, which too frequently assume great importance in the wilderness—Webb dropped our only axe into the waters of the creek, and we spent hours in its recovery. The stream is sluggish, filled with trees and brush, and diving into its cold brown waters chilled even the ardor of us mountaineers. After Webb and McLeod had each dived a dozen times into these dangerous depths, the latter finally brought up the axe.* We camped here for the night after we had pulled the *Mudlark* into the big timber, and cached a sack of flour above it in a tree.

May 28. Our united party afoot and each carrying a heavy pack on his back, swung eastward from the river today, away from our boat and the last Indian camp. Our base of supplies from this time forward is in our packs, those on our backs, and on the broader backs of Mark and Hannah, and in our rifles. We will not see any more Indians or Indian camps before we return to the Kantishna. Our trail ran between two small lakes and we were obliged to wade the connecting stream, whose cold waters reached nearly to our arms, and to lead the mules across with the packs so as not to wet our supplies.

About three o'clock we reached a beautiful, round birch hill sloping to a lake on the south, two miles or more in length, in whose clear waters McKinley was reflected like a great white cloud. Throw Mount Hood, Mount St. Helens, Mount Tacoma [Rainier], and Mount Adams together for mass, then pile Mount Baker on their summits for height, and you will have a fair view of Denali from the upper

---

* Wickersham referred to the loss in his diary as a "serious 'axe-cident'" (May 27, 1903).

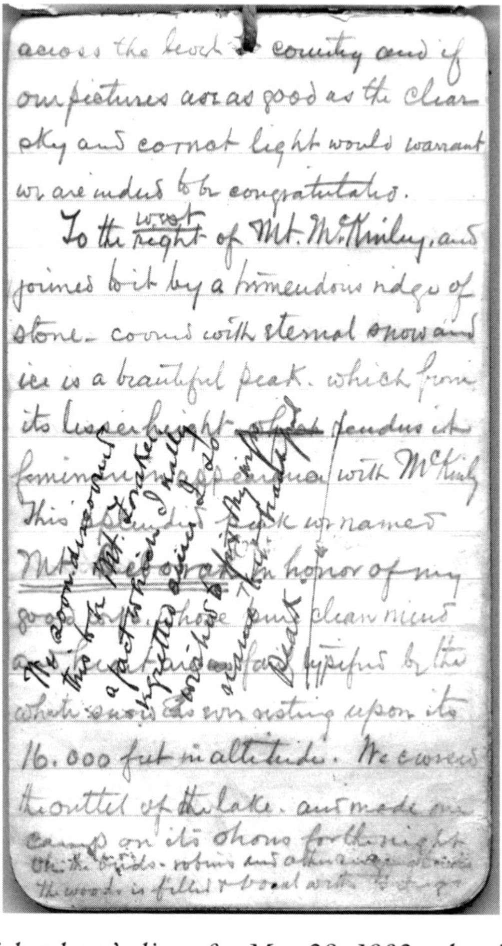

across the broken country and if
our pictures are as good as the clear
sky and correct light would warrant
we are indeed to be congratulated.
To the ~~right~~ west of Mt. McKinley, and
joined to it by a tremendous ridge of
stone- covered with eternal snow and
ice is a beautiful peak. which from
its lesser height lends its
feminine appearance with McKinley
This splendid peak we named
Mt. Deborah in honor of my
good wife, whose pure clean mind
and beautiful face typified by the
white snows ever resting upon its
16.000 feet in altitude. We crossed
the outlet of the lake. and made our
camp on its shore for the night

A portion of Wickersham's diary for May 28, 1903, when he first saw what he thought was an unnamed giant peak next to McKinley, which he named Deborah after his wife. "We soon discovered this to be Mt. Foraker," he later wrote across the page.

(Alaska State Library, Wickersham State Historic Site Collection, m107_001_diary06_1903_may28c) valley of the Kantishna. We exposed several photographic plates of the glacier-capped dome, shining crimson and gold in the setting sun.*

Here, too, we had our first sight of a symmetrical high peak to the west of Mount McKinley to which it is joined by a tremendous ridge. We supposed for a time we had discovered a new giant, but it proved to be Mount Foraker, as we subsequently ascertained, which Lieutenant Herron, USA, saw and named in 1899.†

HERRON'S MILITARY EXPEDITION IN the summer of 1899 from Cook Inlet to the Kuskokwim via Rainy Pass was seeking an All-American route across the Alaska Range to the Yukon River, where the government was building a military post at the mouth of the Tanana called Fort Gibbon. His command comprised some twenty soldiers with a pack train of horses. Reaching the great flat on the Kuskokwim side where the glacier streams spread their milky summer floods, the party became lost in the swamps. Their animals mired and could go no farther. In their bewilderment the soldiers piled the packs of supplies, turned their horses loose to shift for themselves, and started northerly on foot trying to find their way out of the swampy country and somehow make it to Fort Gibbon. It began to snow; the supplies carried on their backs gave out; they lost their way and were about to perish.

The soldiers were saved thanks to a greedy bear and a kindly Tena Indian chief. Sensor, the chief of the Elide (Tena) village,** had tracked and killed a bear. Upon butchering the bear he ascertained it had been eating bacon, and being interested in learning where it had obtained this white man's food he followed on its back track, which finally led him to one of Lieutenant Herron's abandoned caches. Until that moment the Indian had not known there were white men, or bacon, in his country. He immediately set out to follow the white man's trail and so found Lieutenant Herron and his soldiers afoot, lost and starving, in the maze of the Kuskokwim marshes. He took

---

* Wickersham said it was "the most imposing scene I ever witnessed. We cleared some trees and with the lake and more distant hills as a foreground we made two exposures with each of our cameras. No better view will ever be had of this immense mountain . . . and if our pictures are as good as the clear sky and correct light would warrant we are indeed to be congratulated" (May 28, 1903).

† Mount Foraker was the peak that Wickersham originally hoped to name Mount Deborah in honor of his wife. See page xii.

** Telida Village on Swift Fork of the Kuskokwim River.

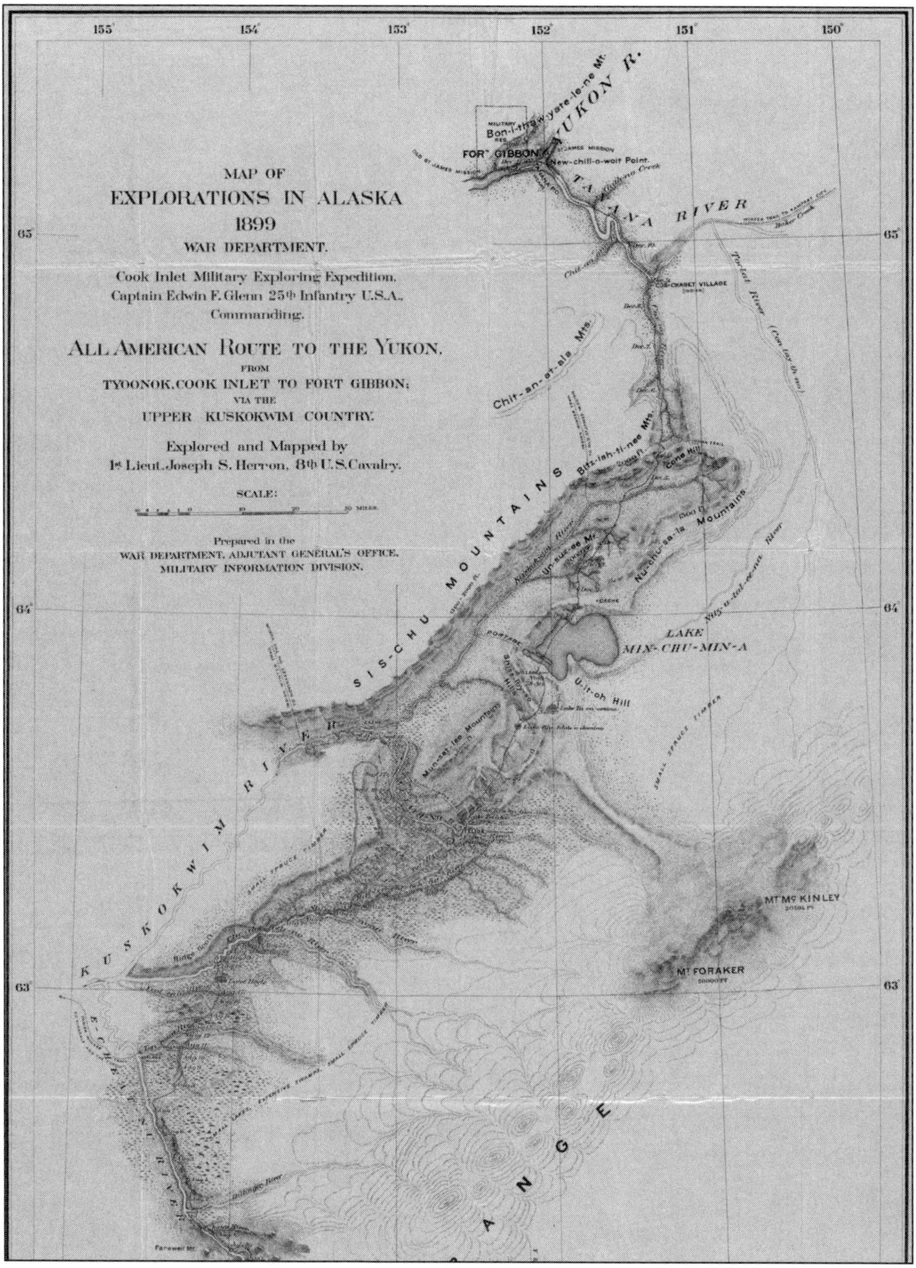

The map of the Herron Expedition's route across the Alaska Range to the Tanana and Yukon Rivers, showing no accurate knowledge of the Kantishna River.

(Rare Maps Collection G4370 1899 W3, Archives, Alaska and Polar Regions, University of Alaska Fairbanks) them safely to his village where he sheltered and fed them for two months, and then guided them over his Costa trail* to the Tanana River and the route to Fort Gibbon.

TONIGHT WE HAVE A beautiful camping place in a birch grove on high ground, from which we can see far and wide across the Kantishna valley. I sat long hours on the hillside listening to the cries of the waterfowl and the grand chorus of the robins. The balmy air of spring in this vast wilderness landscape highlights the joy of life that primitive man has in his surroundings. Whether man is happier as a wanderer in the wilds, or as a cog in the complicated machinery of civilization, is a question.

May 29. Dirty, delighted, and dog-tired! Today we crossed three forks of a creek, each falling from the highlands into the valley, as we went south towards the lode star—the great white summit of Denali. Tonight we are encamped on the south bank of the third fork, quite abreast of Chitsia. We saw a monster bull moose spring from a willow thicket near us and run far across an old burn; he resembled a long-legged Kentucky mule with a big rocking chair set on his head.

May 30. Beautiful spring day. Had much trouble this morning in getting the mules across the creek owing to its running deep between perpendicular banks. Tonight we are high enough on the hill to have a view across the valley and over the Bull Moose Mountains to the westward.

May 31. Generally we are traveling through a light forest of birch and Christmas-tree spruce where the trail is not difficult, but when we are obliged to ford the small streams, which come down from the high ground, we have to use the axe to cut trail.

At noon we camped by a beautiful small lake behind a beaver dam. Masses of winter ice floated in the lake, and here McLeod's wilderness experience came into practical use. Walking quietly along the shore, gazing into the depths of the water, he suddenly sighted his rifle and fired. He immediately waded into the lake about knee deep, reached down, and grabbed an eighteen-inch pickerel that his shot had stunned and threw it on the shore. In half-an-hour we had thus taken a dozen large pickerel, each flashing with color and crystal

* Cosna River trail.

drops of ice water. We cooked a meal of juicy fish steaks, and stowed the remainder for supper and breakfast. It was the first time I had ever witnessed fishing for pickerel with a 30-40 rifle. The method might have surprised and shocked good old Isaac Walton.*

AFTER OUR PICKEREL LUNCH we sat silent and watched for the beaver. Soon an old brown-coated mason appeared on the surface of the pond, but at our slightest movement his big tail hit the water with a loud "flop," and he disappeared. Beyond the bend a faint ripple showed that another was curious, but again the warning signal stroke gave notice of the presence of enemies. At its resounding thwack, every member of the colony, old or young, instantly dives and scurries away to safety in the water lane approach to the underground home.

The dam is constructed of beaver-cut logs and poles carefully laid down and interwoven, leveled, supported, buttressed, reinforced, filled, and plastered, and is altogether as practically perfect a specimen of scientific engineering and mechanics as if an engineer had done the surveying, drawn the plans, made the blue prints, and erected the superstructure. It stands as securely as a concrete dam, anchored to a bedrock base, between mountain walls.

June 1. We left our camp in the valley at ten o'clock and three hours later we had reached the high flank of Chitsia. Stevens had gone ahead to the top of the ridge and had located two caribou across the gorge on the next ridge. Webb and McLeod went after them while we made camp in the highest bunch of small spruce on the ridge side. With our glasses we could see the hunters approach the caribou and saw them kill both animals. Jeffery took the mules round the gulch head and they soon brought them into camp. This afternoon McLeod instructed us in the art of cutting poles and building a drying rack, and we began jerking or drying caribou cutlets for use on the journey.

June 2. Our camping place on the high ridge affords a superb view across the Kantishna valley and the Nuchusala Mountains, but

* The original diary entry reads: "What would Izaak [*sic*] Walton say to that? Well, he never hunted pickerel with a 30-40 so he don't count" (May 31, 1903).

we have determined to go to the summit of Chitsia. We know from Koonah's description that it affords a rare view of the lowlands.

In three hours from camp we reached the summit of Chitsia. Far to the east we can see the bluffs at Chena, and beyond, Fairbanks; the Tanana and Tolovana hills are in view across the northern horizon, while the Nuchusala hills in the west rise hardly to our level. Minchumina Lake lies to the westward and glistens like silver in the sunlight. The view continues far south of Minchumina to the massive McKinley range.

June 3. Three of our party went over to prospect Chitsia Creek for gold, while McLeod and I remained in camp and jerked caribou cutlets. They returned late in the evening reporting prospects of placer gold and ruby sand. We will remain here tomorrow and locate mining claims.

June 4. We staked placer claims on Chitsiana today for each member of our party and for Captain Hendricks of the *Tanana Chief*; discovery claim was located for me opposite the intake of Two-Moose gulch, and the other claims were staked along the creek above and below discovery. These are the first mining claims located in this region, and we will be obliged to record our notices at Rampart when we return there in July. We found colors but have no time to prospect or sink bedrock shaft.

When we filed our notices of location of these claims in the recorder's office at Rampart in the following July, we also filed a map as a part of our description, showing the general locations and direction of descent of the creeks from Chitsia and the Kantishna highlands. It was immediately copied by numerous prospectors and the next year a horde of these hardy men explored every creek in this land for gold, and actually located rich placer diggings on our Webb (Moose) Creek, across which we had carelessly passed with our eyes fixed on the crest of Denali. It became the center of the rich Kantishna mining district.

June 5. We left Chitsia camp at noon following the high summit direct toward Denali. A mile or two after leaving we crossed a lower flat, and here we startled a great bull moose, which almost ran over us in surprise. We continued on the high ridge beyond, from which we could overlook the western valleys. On a spur of this ridge, beside

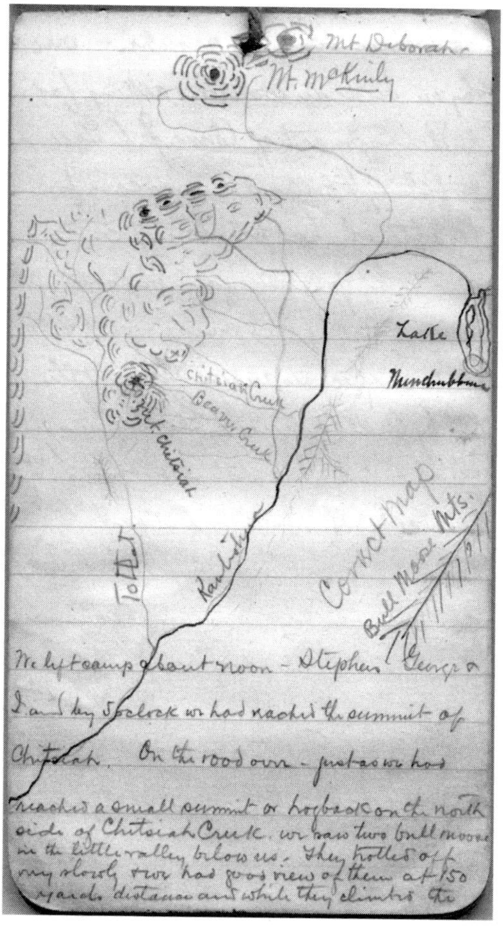

A portion of Wickersham's diary entry for June 2, 1903, with a sketch map of the terrain leading up to Mt. McKinley, including "Mt. Deborah," which he subsequently realized was Mount Foraker.

(Alaska State Library, Wickersham State Historic Site Collection, m107_001_diary06_1903_june02b) a long snow bank, we saw a herd of caribou cows and calves. The mothers were lying at rest on a dry spot in the sun, and the calves on the nearby snow banks were running and kicking up their heels and playing like a flock of lambs. When Mark and Hannah appeared in sight along the ridge, the bank of graceful creatures scampered off down the gulch side, waded the stream at the bottom, and the last we saw of them they were trotting around a butte on the opposite mountainside, each calf running with its mother. We called the creek they crossed Ten Caribou Creek.

June 6. A great bear fight. Being ahead of the train half-a-mile scouting, I saw two big black bears across the gulch on the opposite mountain meadow. Jeffery and Stevens are photographic cranks, inseparable companions. They asked to be allowed to slip down a draw into the gulch and up the other side to a point nearest to the great feeding brutes, hoping while the engagement was on, to be able to get a good photograph of one or both of the animals. We agreed to remain hidden on our side until they were in position.

They passed down into the gorge and climbed the opposite hillside to a point just below where the bears were still digging roots. They signaled us to wait until they could get closer, but McLeod mistaking the signal for one inviting action, raised his old Hudson Bay gun and fired at the bear. The big male raised his head at the report and began to walk slowly toward the gulch rim just above the photographers. At this we all fired, and one of us (each made oath he did it) hit the big fellow on the ham with a bullet, and then the fun began. The female ran off in the opposite direction, but the old male tumbled over the edge of the hill and slid down the snow bank towards Stevens and Jeffery, roaring with fright and pain. As he came floundering down the snow incline Stevens shouted, "Run, George, run, here comes a grizzly!" Both started at full speed along the gulch side. Owing to his better position when the bear first appeared, George was ahead, Stevens next, and the wounded bear just behind him snorting and growling.

When George and the bear rounded the point of rocks and stretched out in the hillside race, the positions of the two men had changed; Stevens was ahead, with George second and the bear a close third, growling and roaring at every jump. In the meantime our three guns were pumping bullets at the bruin as fast as we could from the opposite bluff top, but each shot sent the bear forward at renewed speed. Just as the raging beast reached Jeffery's heels, it turned down the hill into the gorge and disappeared in the brush.

THIS EVENING AROUND THE campfire Stevens told the rest of the story:

> When I saw the bear come over the bluff on us I shouted to George to run, which he did ahead of me, and the bear at my heels. I shouted to him to stop and help me, but he only ran the faster. I could feel the bear's fangs tearing at my back, but George was leaving me to die alone. Just then we came to that point of rock; George started around it, while I jumped over the short cut, the bear following around after George, and when we came out on the other side I was ahead. God!—what a feeling of relief I had—and, do you know, I—I really felt sorry about George. I ran as fast as I could and did not look back, for I did not want to see George killed. I knew how he must feel—just like I did a moment before—how he would be crushed and chewed—but I was so frightened that I ran to keep ahead for I felt that one of us would be killed. I climbed that high wall and looked back and saw George was not killed—my, but I was relieved!

Webb slowly closed his right eye, but no one so much as smiled.

June 7. A beautiful, warm Sunday morning—but a bad, cold, and rainy afternoon in snow fields and high rough mountain trail. The mules bolted off to the right and we came down into a narrow gorge filled with great boulders and high water. It was midnight before we located a comfortable camp. The mules are tired and worn and Mark is suffering from a bad pack-saddle sore.*

June 8. Today we remained in camp to cure up Mark's saddle galls, to mend shoes, shirts, packsaddles, and do general laundry work, in addition to which we took a dip in the creek.

AND THEN FOLLOWED DAYS of crossing the southern end of the Chitsia Range to the high glacial plain at the north toe of Denali, where the silt-laden waters from the great glacier find their way into

* Wickersham could not resist a political quip in his diary. Alluding to the indefatigable support that Marcus A. Hanna always gave President William McKinley, he wrote, "the mules have run away. Think of 'Mark' 'Hannah' failing to support [abandoning] a McKinley proposition [expedition]" (June 7, 1903).

the main stream, which we called the McKinley Fork. Our course was up a beautiful, clear, and unspoiled stream which the next year's prospectors named Moose Creek. We entered its narrow valley down a short draw in the mountainside where the prospectors who followed us found gold and from which they took small fortunes.

On the upper reaches of Webb Creek we located a small lake, which we named Lake Alma (now Wonder Lake) in honor of Stevens' sister, and there camped several days while prospecting and hunting.*

* Wickersham's party camped on the shore of "Lake Alma"—which fortunately has preserved the more apt name of Wonder Lake—on June 11–12, 1903. The Judge thought a "more beautiful game country does not exist" than the plain between Wonder Lake and Denali, and stunned by the beauty of the lake and the majesty of the mountains ten miles to the south, he said the scene reminded him of "Spokane with a back ground of Switzerland magnified 100 times."

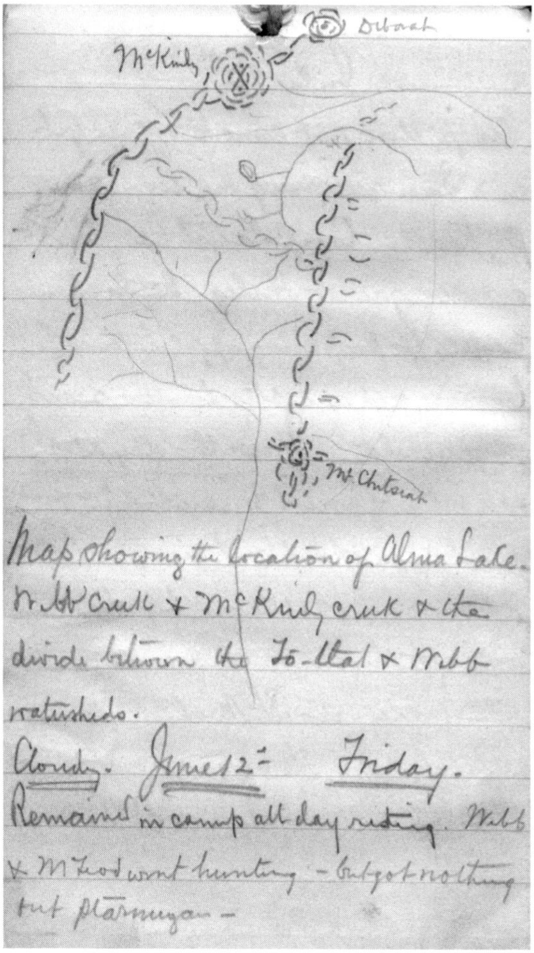

A portion of Wickersham's diary for June 11 and 12, 1903, showing the location of Wonder Lake (which he called "Alma Lake").

(Alaska State Library, Wickersham State Historic Site Collection, m107_001_diary06_1903_june11dand12)

17

ON THE SLOPES OF DENALI

Last night when the city slumbered,
far up in the star-lit sky
I heard the honk of the wild goose,
and in the discordant cry
Came to me the Call of the Northland
that rings in the ears of men
Who have known its joys and sorrows,
and who long to get back again.

—Spencer Gaylord

June 13, 1903. Our trail today lay over the high meadows of the caribou country immediately north of Denali, which the Minchumina chief told us was the hunting ground of his band. These meadows are on a high table-land surrounded by mountains. We kill ptarmigan on the hills and ducks in the lakes—it is a hunter's paradise. An old Indian lodge on the hillside with its skeleton pole rack for drying jerked caribou, stands where the Munkhotena camped on their last annual hunt. Caribou antlers, dry and white with age, yet attached to the skull, show where herds of that hardy animal have been slaughtered by the Indians in years gone by. We saw several caribou off on the hills, but made no effort to hunt them.

Bull caribou shed their horns annually like the Alaska bull moose. By midsummer, and the beginning of the mating season, the horns have reached maturity; are hard, sharp, and strong; and are ready for use in the battles which the bulls wage for the favor of young females. After the mating season in November is over, the horns begin to dry and grow weaker at the base and about midwinter they drop off, leaving scar-like spots from which next year's pair will sprout and grow.

In the late fall, when the horns were ready to shed, one of my friends, for whose ability as a hunter the whole Eagle City camp could vouch, climbed to the high moss fields on the divide between the Seventy Mile and the Tanana, to get a good caribou for the camp table. On reaching the comb of the ridge he was delighted to find a large herd just below him on the grassy flat.

A fine bull stood in the midst of the herd, watching for enemies, while the rest slept. Taking aim at a vital spot on the body of the guard, the hunter fired. The sharp crack of the rifle startled the deer as if a galvanic shock had struck each animal at the same moment. With a wild leap every caribou sprang to his feet, running for life. The guard, untouched by the bullet, led the frightened animals away across the mountain meadow. The hunter gazed in astonishment upon the scene following his shot—not a skillet of meat was left, but 581 pair of great horns, dropped by frightened bulls as they sprang to their feet, were left on the ground!*

THIS AFTERNOON WE REACHED the high bank of McKinley forks, the glacial stream that comes down from the great northeast glacier,† whose course we can trace far towards the summit of Denali. When we had camped we removed the packs from Mark and Hannah and turned them loose to graze, and the caribou evidently mistaking them for moose came trotting across the plain to inspect them. Their friendly curiosity cost one his life for Webb shot it to replenish our larder with fresh steaks.

We made camp on the south side; Mount McKinley now seems to hang over us, its great white dome rose-tinted with the rays of the setting sun.

---

* This is one of those stories that must have improved every time the Judge told it. His original diary entry was less detailed and far more skeptical.

"A miner told me this story about caribou hunting, which is not quite as correct [as it] possibly [might be]. Finding a herd of cariboo he crept carefully near and fired. The report of the gun caused the animals to start suddenly, leap away and jump quickly; it was at the season when they were shedding their horns, and the only result secured by his shot was an acre of cariboo horns which they shed in the shock. Both moose and cariboo are known sometimes to shed their horns upon such a start, hence the story" (January 20, 1901).

† McKinley Fork, now called McKinley River, originates at the foot of Muldrow Glacier, which the Judge refers to as "the great northeast glacier."

WE HAD ASSUMED THAT one of our main difficulties in approaching the mountain would be the scarcity of fuel—that the mountain would stand on a base so high as to be treeless. We were relieved to find that a large spruce forest skirts the east side of the main McKinley fork. This forest ought to be withdrawn from disposal and preserved for the use of those who shall come after us to explore the highest and most royal of American mountains. It extends to within four miles of the perpendicular inner walls of McKinley which rise from the top of the glacier.

On this wide plain where future photographers will follow our example, our photographer made several exposures of plates hoping there might be sufficient strength and cunning in the chemicals to mark the perfectly white edge of the mountain summit line from the deep blue of the sky above. It is too much, however, to expect more than a flattened outline of the great dome now glowing with the blending colors of the sun, the snow, the clear sky, and the deep blue of glacial ice.

June 15. We moved our camp nearer the creek bank to escape the mosquitoes. Webb and McLeod went back with the mules to bring in a caribou killed yesterday. We have seen caribou on the nearby mountain sides all day. This afternoon we saw two grizzlies on what initially seemed to be a moraine, a mile or two upstream. Instead of a moraine, however, we found the lower, dirt-covered end of a great glacier, over which the grizzlies had climbed. It appears they were frightened away by our presence and the smoke of our campfire and had crossed the glacier to escape from our neighborhood.

We now had our first view of the moving mass of ice that comes from Mount McKinley between high mountain ridges.* It is a mile or more wide and about five miles long from the inner mountain wall to the outer point where it plows deep into a hill that has checked its forward movement. McKinley Creek pours out of a cavern in the side of the ice sheet.†

June 16. Sunshine and showers here; snowslides above. For many days we have inspected the high slopes and summit of Denali with our glasses, under the most favorable weather conditions, seeking the line

* Peters Glacier.

† McKinley Creek is the stream now known as Muddy River.

Mark and Hannah avoiding mosquitoes.
(Charles Sheldon Collection, Box 5, Folder 3, Archives, Alaska and Polar Regions, University of Alaska Fairbanks)

of easiest ascent. From every vantage point en route it has seemed to us that the western slope affords the easier grades, but now that we are here we are not so sure. The western side is one vast snow slide from the highest points in sight to the glacier at the base, but a prominent ridge runs far towards the summit, and our glacier may put us on that highway. We also carefully examined the conditions over a sharp escarpment of the north ridge where the abrupt drop discloses that a glacier descends from the summit, and we seriously discussed returning to the northeastern [Muldrow] glacier, if the one we are on [Peters Glacier] does not lead us towards the top. All the tales the Indians told us about snowslides at this season seem to be true, for the whole western face of the mountain, above the glacier, glistens with ice sheets streaked with mineral discolorations from recent slides.

June 17. Today we are cutting wood for the mules to pack to the highest point we can reach with Mark and Hannah, and repacking a necessary outfit for the mountain. Other parts of our equipment will be left at the base camp. We will go forward in the morning, all hands and the mules, but we will send the latter back from our upper camp with McLeod who will watch them on the lower pastures until we return.* Pasturage is good here and McLeod has put a staging

---

* Tension in the expedition party exploded on June 17, as Webb finally had enough of Morton Stevens and Wickersham barely managed to keep his crew together:

"Hells to pay & no pitch hot! Webb got mad at Stevens this morning, packed up and left us. Though I begged him not to go. After going a mile or two and cooling off he saw how bad it would look for him to come in without us, so he put his pack down & came back and asked me for a statement which I gave him in this form:

Mt. McKinley, June 17 1903

To whom it may concern:
Very much to my regret Mr. Charles Webb has this day voluntarily left my party to go home.

Respectfully, James Wickersham

I then begged him to take flour &c but he didn't. He remained in camp awhile & I then approached him to take the mules, & with McLeod go down on a raft & thus make it appear that he [is] returning for me. This mollified him & this evening he has finally agreed to remain with me. Have had a bad time with both he & McLeod who has been a dozen times on the point of desertion on account of his fear 1st of grizzly bear & 2nd of the mules. He is a Mackenzie River lad & the mules are as dangerous in his eyes as grizzlies & then the boys have told him such yarns about mules that he is really afraid to stay at camp with them" (June 17, 1903).

in the trees so he can sleep above danger from either grizzlies or mules, which are about equally alarming to him. Jeffery and Stevens went over to photograph the glacial stream where it emerges with a deafening roar, as a full-fledged river from underneath Denali's great western glacier.

June 18. A glorious summer day without a cloud. We loaded one mule with wood and the other with our packs, and set out for the upper end of the glacier underneath Denali's walls. An old game trail led us easily to the top of the high lateral moraine on the north side of the glacier, whose summit roadway we followed with little trouble to the very base of Mount McKinley—where its precipitous walls covered with ice and snow rise almost fifteen thousand feet above our heads.

While we rested for lunch on the big boulders Stevens examined those on the lower side with the field glasses and suddenly cried out, "A bear!" I snatched up the rifle and ran to the edge of the higher moraine upon which we stood, but could not see the bear. "There," he exclaimed, "by the big rock. Don't you see his big flat head by that rock?" I could not, but looking carefully I saw a wolverine. He excitedly called to me to shoot the bear and while I was looking for it the wolverine ran under the rocks. "There," he said, "it's gone under the rocks." We went down where he saw the bear and finally killed the wolverine. The field glasses had magnified ten diameters—and made a bear out of a wolverine.

WE UNLOADED OUR WOOD and packs and sent the mules back down the moraine to our lower camp under charge of McLeod. We are at least four thousand feet high in this camp (we afterward ascertained we were really about five thousand feet high), and the glacier continues to rise as it turns an acute angle to the southwest. Its long fingertips climb the ridge some miles ahead, and we hope now for an easy approach up that ridge to the summit. We will make permanent camp here and carry our packs forward from this point. Tomorrow evening we will start on the upward climb, when the sun gets so far down in the north as to permit the snow to set and stop the snowslides. It was midnight before we finished cleaning two caribou we had shot, washing our clothes, and choosing a soft place on the rocks to sleep.

June 19. When the sun is always shining, one loses one's sense of time. Webb's digestion and slumbers remain normal under all circumstances, and when I punched him in the ribs and roused him from deep sleep with the shout "It's nine o'clock," he sat up, rubbed his eyes, looked at the sky, and inquired, "Day or night?" On being advised that it was day, he made his toilet at the rushing, icy stream, and joined us in roasting caribou ribs and cooking breakfast.

In making camp we were careful to get far enough away from the mountain to avoid possible slides, which frequently plunge down its slopes. During the night, although the sun was shining, we were alarmed by the thundering noises of an avalanche that came down some distance ahead of us. Great masses of snow and ice broke loose far up the mountain and accelerating at great speed shot straight down thousands of feet, spreading millions of tons of rock and ice on the surface of the glacier below.

June 20. We left camp last night at ten o'clock, Webb, Jeffery, Stevens, and I, each with a knapsack filled with provisions—bread and meat, dried and jerked caribou, chocolate, and an assortment of good substantial grub—enough to last us three or four days. Each man carried a hundred feet of small but strong rope and an alpenstock, armed at one end with a sharp point of iron, and with pick and cutting edge on the other. I carried the glasses, and Jeffery the small camera, but otherwise we were limited to necessities.

The road on the medial moraine led us far out from the mountain wall, and offered us safe and solid, but exceedingly rough, traveling on a most remarkable causeway. What compels this glacier to build a medial moraine of great angular boulders on its back, and carry it forward in an unbroken line for miles we cannot fathom. The causeway, like a high railway grade, rises from ten to forty feet above the surface of the glacier exactly in the center of its swiftest current of ice. We blessed the power or principle that created this rocky road, as there were neither crevasses nor other dangers along its course.

THE GREAT MOUNTAIN IS glaciated from summit to base. Snowslides of every size, and every form of glacial movement, are on exhibition in this great natural amphitheater, and we viewed their wonders in safety from our high, dry seats on the great moving, curving causeway along the glacier's backbone. And over all these manifestations of the force of nature, there is a riot of shades, shadows, and colors produced by the rays of the ever-circling, never-setting sun, acting on sky, mountain, ice, and snow; and the rainbow's perfect curve. It is easy, now, to understand how the mind of the gentle Tena lowlander is filled with fears of the supernatural forces that can so easily destroy him on Denali, for here Nature is ever ready—to destroy.*

ABOUT FIVE MILES UP the main glacier we came to the confluence of a parallel branch glacier on the left-hand side, coming down from a high bench on McKinley, which seemed more directly headed for the altitudes which we desired to reach.† This left-hand glacier, which we have chosen to follow, climbs higher and higher towards the much desired ridge, which may lead to the summit, and we toiled upwards during the long sunlit night. We walked fifty feet apart in Indian file. The leader kept sounding for crevasses with the long hickory handle of his alpenstock and when he found one, sought for the safest snow bridge, which he crossed carefully on his hands and knees, those behind holding his life line so as to break the drop and catch his weight should he fall into the depths of ice. The second man, fifty feet from the leader, and the same distance ahead of the third man, would follow in the same careful way, and thus each man was eased safely across several bottomless crevasses.

About seven o'clock this morning, after traveling for nine hours, without rest, we reached an arête or sharp ridge of bare rock at the extreme upper end of the bench glacier. We found, to our intense disappointment, that the glacier did not connect with the high ridge we were seeking to reach. It still seemed as far above us as when we began the ascent. We are now about ten thousand feet above sea level on a sharp ridge of rock, at the face of an impassable precipice. Here our bench glacier roadway ends. Our only line of further ascent

* The Judge's diary reveals he was as fearful of the mountain as any of the "gentle lowlanders." He said the snowslide on the night of June 18 was loud as "the roar of a hundred great guns" and a brutal reminder of the power of nature. "One feels his insignificance in the presence of such a stupendous catastrophe which he cannot control nor from which he could possibly escape if within its path. It sent a shiver of fear down every back & warned us to keep clear of the avalanche's path—& we will."

† Jeffery Glacier, named by Wickersham for George Jeffery, the Judge's assistant on the expedition and his stenographer and secretary.

would be to climb the vertical wall of the mountain at our left, and that is impossible.

Our position on the bare rocks is, happily, safe from snowslides. High above us, resting insecurely on a sloping shelf, are great angular blocks of discolored ancient ice, as large as city blocks. Evidently the noise we had heard at our last camp was caused by one of these falling a thousand feet or more upon the bench glacier near where we are now marooned. Others seem likely to fall at any moment.

We now had an opportunity to study the innumerable surface snowslides, which the constant rays of a June sun bring down in thundering falls. These long, beautiful, cloudless summer days have made the monster mountain sweat. Torrents of water and melting snow are pouring down its ice-enshrouded body. About two o'clock this afternoon a thunderstorm added its downpour to the already perspiring mountain. In this heat the lightest breath of wind may start an avalanche at any moment, and certain death awaits anyone approaching the summit in its path. We recognize we are inviting destruction by staying here and have reluctantly concluded there is no possible chance of further ascent from this side of Denali at this season—or at any other for that matter.

WE HAVE NOW CAREFULLY examined the main glacier, and have mapped its snake-like course upward from its lower end. Over the top of the ridge, circling the distant outer rim of this ice field, appear the tops of Mount Foraker and other lofty glaciated summits toward the south and east whose names, if they have any, we do not know.

We have organized an Alaska Board of Geographic Names to christen a few of the most interesting of the natural phenomena in sight. Of course the officials may reverse our baptismal judgments, but that shall not deter us. My loyal followers insist that since we are the first to view this new glacial world, we may do so, and especially since the Tena were unable to give us any particular names for these geographic points. In their zeal the majority insist that the great glacier be called the "Wickersham Glacier." Vanity is not generally thought to be a virtue, though it has accomplished more in the development of the human race than any half-dozen admitted virtues, but mine shrank from the exhibition, and modestly but firmly the suggestion was vetoed. We then discussed the names of the friends of William

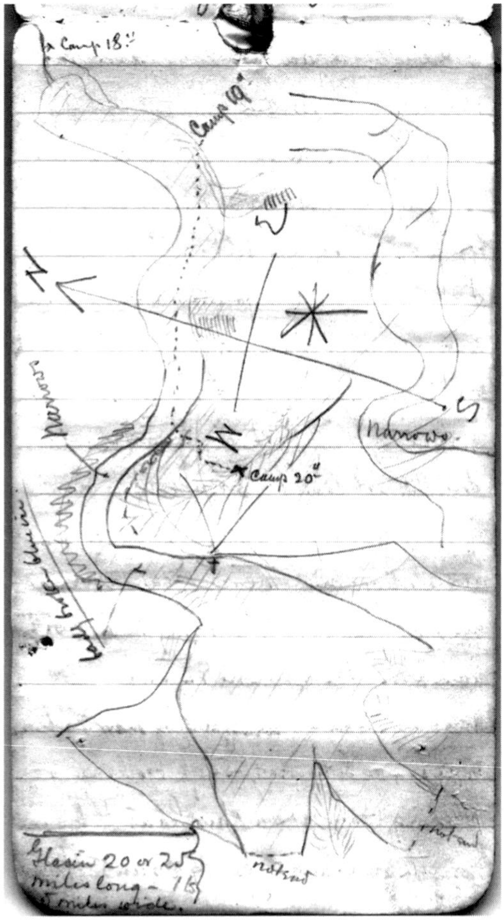

A portion of Wickersham's diary entry for June 20, 1903, showing his route up the Peters Glacier to the Wickersham Wall.

(Alaska State Library, Wickersham State Historic Site Collection, m107_001_diary06_1903_june20c)

McKinley, the martyred President, after whom Dickey had named the mountain. We determined to name the great glacier the Hanna Glacier after Senator Marcus A. Hanna, another famous Ohioan.* We gave the name of our long-legged photographer to the bench glacier, which enabled us to reach the Jumpoff, and called it the Jeffery Glacier.

The marvelous blue depths of the abyss through which the widespread upper névé pushes broken bergs deserves more sentimental consideration, and must not be used to perpetuate the name of any mere man, however famous. The poetical nomenclature of the lowland Tena, who view with awe and deep feeling the mysterious manifestations of Yako's power on this great mountain, must be considered. Their name for an iceberg, anglicised, is TLU, and for a river, NA. We have determined to preserve their general names for the great cleft in the mountain, and its "iceberg river," and so Tluna Gorge it is by unanimous vote. The Jumpoff named itself. After a farewell glance over the great névé and up the vertical walls beneath the séracs and the deep blue bergs in the depths of the narrows, we reluctantly turn our faces towards our lower camp.

June 21. We left our rocky perch at the Jumpoff last night at nine o'clock and reached our previous camping place at the elbow at five o'clock this morning. We floundered down the soft snow field, wet and weary for the want of sleep and proper rest. Down, down to the Hanna glacier, and back along its high medial moraine we trudged, hour after hour, while far overhead the dome of Denali glowed like a great friendly light. When we finally reached our camping place we were all but exhausted from the physical strain of the three days and nights' journey, and from long hours of wakefulness under the glare of incessant sunshine. We threw ourselves upon the grass on a dry spot and slept.

When the noonday sun finally woke us, we boiled a pot of coffee. We arranged our remaining stores into packs, hoisted them on our backs, and followed the old game trail back to McLeod and our mules. We found McLeod and the mules safe enough at the base camp. He had slept on the high platform in the spruce trees, and thereby escaped any possibility of attack.

---

* The name Marcus A. Hanna Glacier did not stick; the large glacier by which they had approached the high ground had already been named the Peters Glacier in 1902 by geologist Alfred H. Brooks.

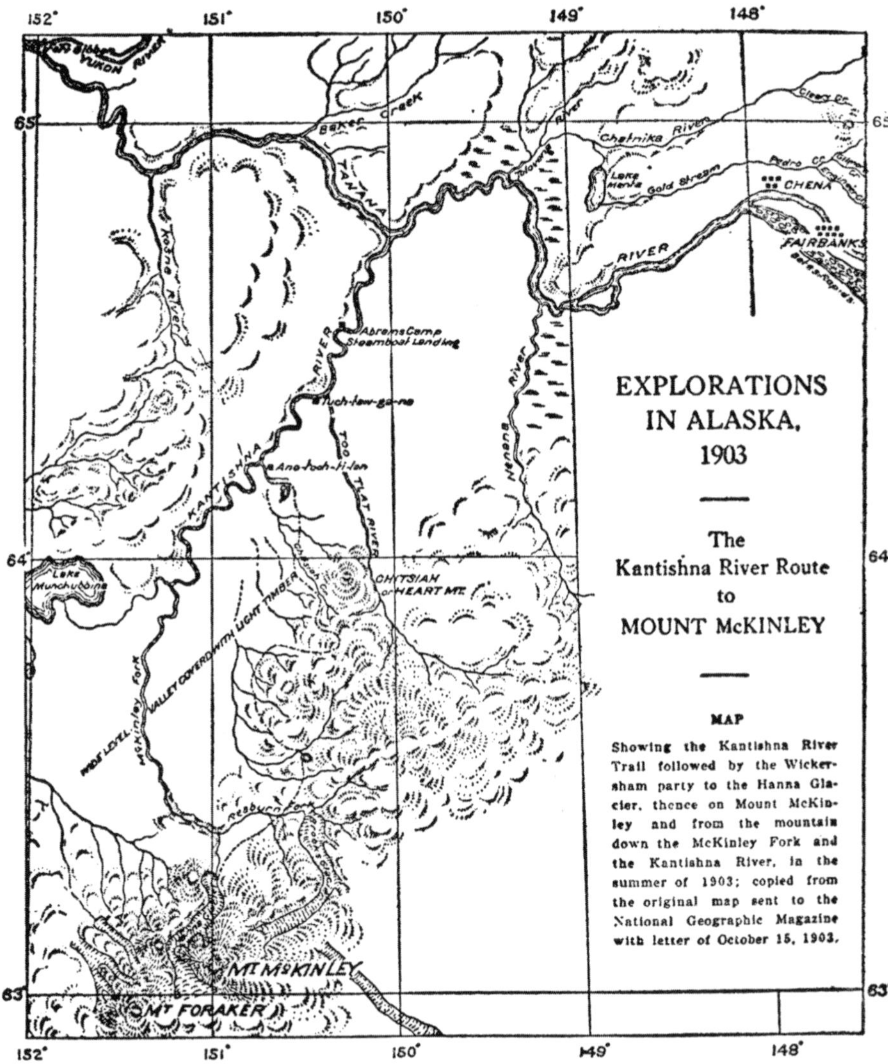

Wickersham's map of the expedition route to and from Mount McKinley that he sent to the National Geographic Society in 1903.

Tonight we held a council to consider what further efforts we should make to ascend the mountain by the [Muldrow] glacier rising from the northeast angle, since it is now apparent to us that that is the glacier the Munkhotena Indians referred to as leading to the summit. We are sure the Hanna [Peters] glacier does not afford any chance to lead one to the top, and from our examination the northeast [Muldrow] glacier seems to afford the road we have been looking for. We are agreed on that. But our food supply is almost exhausted and the time is short before the opening of the term of court at Rampart. The long, hot June and July days are making the snow fields dangerous, and we unanimously decided to defer any further attempt to climb Denali's walls till another season.

We shall start back to civilization tomorrow morning.*

---

* On June 21, 1903, the day they decided to turn back at the face of the 16,500-foot cliff now known as Wickersham Wall, the Judge's stress, exhaustion and disappointment is evident from his diary entry:

"The days are so hot and the temperature so productive of avalanches that we have had to do all our work at night when the heat is less liable to produce slides of snow and glacial ice.... We were climbing on a spur as sharp as a house roof, rapidly rising to where it was nearly perpendicular—solid glare ice.... It was so apparent to me that further effort was futile that I declined to go farther—to the evident relief of Stevens who agreed with me that no man could reach the summit in the present condition of the mountains. It is ice encrusted from summit to base—in most places glaciers exist in every small niche, and they are so undermined now by the constant warm west winds of two or three days past—that hundreds of slides are coming down in every direction—every moment the swish of a snow avalanche, or the thunder of a glacial ice slide is heard. Even the smallest would be fatal to our whole party... and I ordered a retreat to our camp. I offered to remain in camp & let any or all of the others make an effort, if they desired, but each personally declined to take any further risk. In the condition of the mountain an attempt in another quarter would be equally as dangerous so we abandoned the whole effort to reach the summit."

18

RAFTING HOME

If you've lived up in Alaska,
where the Arctic breezes blow,
Till you've seen the Autumn ice come,
and you've seen the Spring ice go,
And survived one long dark winter,
when the mercury ran low
You can drop the name "Chechako,"
and become a "Sourdough."

—Esther B. Darling

June 22, 1903. After a good sleep on spruce boughs we got up this morning refreshed. We had an early breakfast, packed the mules for the homeward journey and the return to the legal disputes over mining claims that awaited me in Rampart.

When we came to the camp a week ago the boys caught a young fox which they brought in and tied to a small tree where he could hide cunningly under a big rock. His beautiful glossy coat and brush, and his bright beady eyes were a source of pleasure to us and he was well fed. When we were ready to go to the mountain we turned him loose and "shoo-ed" him out of camp, but when he gets hungry he comes back, gets under his rock and peers out wistfully until he is fed, then scampers off until his appetite again urges his return to the safety of the rock and a never-failing food supply. When we said good-bye to him today he was large enough to catch mice and gather his own food; but we left enough caribou meat under his rock for ten days after which he can make his own living nicely.

We had little food to leave when we abandoned camp for our supplies were running low but we possessed a full sack of table salt, and in addition a large flat can with a tight top filled with heavier crystals, the latter we concluded to abandon. We placed two large flat rocks near together, put the can of salt between them, and placed a larger flat rock on the other two as a cover to the can, and a protection against wind and rain.*

With a last lingering look at the base of the great mountain we start our well-rested, fat, lazy mules down the natural boulevard amid the beautiful parks on the wide sandy bars of McKinley Fork.

June 23. Camped last night in the gorge on a bar. The near proximity of side walls prevented the winds from scattering the mosquitoes and gave them a chance to attack us en masse which they did.

This morning we saw an eagle's nest on the rocky wall of the gorge, above which the bird o' freedom circled and screamed defiance while we climbed to the nest and examined the two eaglets who blinked unconcernedly while we turned them over for better inspection. The wild cries of the parent birds, their attacks on the armed intruders who fought them with clubs, and that national sentiment which connects these birds so intimately with the political aspirations of our people, suggested the name for this wild and beautiful canyon—Eagle Gorge.

A mile or two farther down the gorge, a moose cow and yearling calf suddenly ran out of the willows across our path, and in spite of my warning shout not to do so, McLeod shot the cow. The rest of

* It was a welcome find three months later for the party of Dr. Frederick Cook, who came upon their campsite in September 1903, as Robert Dunn, a member of Cooks' expedition, explained in his memoir:

"Where we crossed the glacial stream . . . we saw chopped poles there arranged like a big clothes-horse, meaning an old camp. I investigated, first finding a pair of soggy overalls, and said; 'White men,' to Fred, because Siwashes would never discard a whole pair of overalls. Fred, swearing Indians had stopped there, said; 'Don't Siwashes wear pants?' As I came on two mule shoes, and the Professor appeared with a camera-film wrapper, saying, 'Then your Siwashes have begun to take photographs.' The while I spotted a red copper can lying under a bush, opened it, white stuff was inside, looked like, felt like, tasted like—was salt! Last night Fred was pining to trade off our last fifty pounds of sugar for one small, five-pound sack of salt! Food was slimy without it. Fred wouldn't let the stuff out of his sight, and put enough for use on the mountain into his very dirty handkerchief and hung it on his belt. The red can-full we cached there. Whose camp is this? What are white men doing here? Fred suggested that they are 'Railway surveyors,' that Brooks met last year headed hither from Tanana River. But I think the camp is this year's."

us are angry over the unnecessary killing of the animal, for we have enough jerked caribou to last till we can get a raft built, and we cannot carry the moose quarters or keep them from spoiling. The only excuse we can suggest for this unsportsmanlike shot, is that McLeod shoots game he does not need because so frequently he has needed it when there was none to shoot.

June 24. Rained last night and the mosquitoes were as bad as they could be. We are cutting raft logs today, and have some of them in the river tonight. Just hard work and mosquitoes today.

June 25. With mules and lines we finally skidded the logs out of the woods into the river, and built our raft. We laid a flattened pole across each end of the raft and pinned it down with wooden pins driven into auger holes bored through the cross pole deep into each log at the crossing. We then tied it together at each end with our mountain ropes and now have a rough raft capable of carrying the entire party in good water. It is twenty-four feet long, and has a ten-foot beam; the logs are dry, buoyant, and float well out of the water.

LATE THIS AFTERNOON WE broke camp. I refused to permit the mules to go on the raft, or to go on it myself, until we are safely in the valley. Jeffery and I packed the mules with food supplies, the negatives, films, diaries, salt, and other things which water would injure, and started over the low hills. The other supplies were placed on the raft and Webb, Stevens, and McLeod went as the raft crew.

Just before the mouth of the canyon from which the waters of the McKinley Creek emerge is a great boulder, embedded deep in the sands and gravels. The torrent issuing from the gorge strikes this huge rock and is sharply deflected to the right limit, where it spread into a delta of streams, some following the course of the main channel, others running into the forest. As we came near the bank of the torrent at the gorge's mouth, I noticed a bundle of familiar appearance dancing along on the surface of the stream and called Jeffery's attention to it.

"It's our bundle of blankets and robes!" he cried.

We now saw the raft float by—disjointed and wrecked—following the roll of bed clothes. The cross poles, pegged on with so much labor, were gone, and the craft's timbers were held together only by the stout ropes with which we had lashed them. These had loosened and stretched until the logs were criss-crossed and parted, and the dashing waters of the rapids cast the raft upon the rock. Striking this solid rock end-on, the logs rolled, tangled, and swung farther off downstream and out of sight! As the raft swept past us we saw a man's head at the end of a log. It was Webb.

Immediately we started back along the canyon walls on a run looking for Stevens and McLeod, but could see neither of them. As we climbed over the summit of a ridge we were relieved to see both men coming towards us hatless and half-clothed, and crying out that Webb was drowned. We told them of his descent into the valley, and all hurried back there to rescue him and recover the raft and our blankets. About a mile below the big rock we saw the raft on the opposite shore and Webb on a sand bar, wringing the ice water and silt from his garments. We waded half-a-dozen channels until we were opposite, and assisted Webb across the stream. Then we made camp—wet, tired, hungry—at ten o'clock at night in a cold wind, with no tent or bedclothes for shelter. We built a big fire at a drift pile, warmed ourselves, dried our clothing, and about midnight, turned into our spruce bed feeling much like Robinson Crusoe must have felt the first night on his lonely island.

THE BOYS TELL ME that they cast off the lines and floated round the first bend in good shape, but there the stream turned suddenly to the right into a narrow canyon. Here the force of the current threw the raft on edge and under a rock ledge that scraped it clean, leaving only Webb holding on to the rear logs.

The other two jumped clear and swam until they reached a place where they climbed out; Webb and the raft went on into the whirlpools and over the cascades.

Everything on the raft was lost except the auger and McLeod's gun, both of which had fortunately been tied on. Our grub box, dishes, pots, pans, and supplies of all kinds were lost; and all our blankets except those on the mules under the saddles, for luckily I had put a half-sack of flour and some supplies on the pack mules in fear of just such an accident.

June 26. Stevens, Jeffery, and McLeod tussled with the reformed raft along the tailraces of the river today, where they had to wade and push the logs round timber obstructions and over bars. A dozen times Webb and I thrashed the mules through river channels, wading the cold waters waist deep, and then over dry and dusty trails, and miles through brush and swamps.

Generally the raft went so slowly that we kept in sight of it and tonight we are all in camp together. Having no meat, and no foodstuff except flour, and no pan to mix dough in, we are living on "bannocks" of flour mixed in the sack with glacial water, and baked on a flat rock set facing the fire. That method of cooking with glacial water carrying about one-eighth silt and sand in solution gives one plenty of "sand in his craw," and a fixed gray color to the bread.

As I opened my bannock at breakfast I noticed it was filled with spots of a darker brown than the silt-laden bread, looking something like those small currants in my wife's favorite cake, and calling Webb's attention to them asked what they were.

"Huh," he answered tartly, "them's mosquitoes."

We ate pounds of these sweet song birds embalmed in our bannocks the next three days, but did not apparently diminish the millions which sang about us at night as we tried to sleep with our heads wrapped in horse blankets, the rest of our bodies being left exposed as bait to keep them off our faces and away from our ears. I've disliked vivisectionists and currant cake ever since.*

June 27. McLeod refuses to ride on or wade with the raft; and since we are trying to float it along to deeper water so we can repair it and load the mules and the party and float in safety, I am obliged to ask Webb, Jeffery, and Stevens to act as river men and McLeod comes with me as cavalryman.

It is a tiresome task to guide the mules through the tangled thickets and to keep the packs balanced on their backs. The riverbars are better today, but we were forced to wade the river channels many times.

Both mules mired to exhaustion today, and we saved them from being engulfed in quicksand only by thrusting small logs into the muck underneath them as they floundered and by assisting them with ropes. Tonight, after a long hard day, we found the campfire of the raftsmen and are all together. This afternoon McLeod killed an old gray gander, that we picked free of most of its feathers, split it down the back, and roasted it a beautiful brown.

---

* "Rained last night & the mesquitoes [*sic*] were simply hell!!" (June 24, 1903).

June 28. Remained in camp until two o'clock assisting the raftsmen in making new sweeps in place of those lost in the canyon; when thus repaired the raft floated on downstream. McLeod and I with the mules continued our weary tramp through the dense forest thickets. McLeod's intimate acquaintance with the habits of game interests me. If he observes a rabbit run into the bushes, he produces a rabbit call by the expulsion of his breath on the back of his hand, which brings bunny out of hiding, wide-eyed, to be shot for his curiosity. Today in that way he called a young rabbit so close that he caught it with his hands.

June 29. We are in the finest moose country in the world. We camped on the bar where we saw a bull moose last night and while we were eating breakfast this morning a moose cow and two calves walked slowly along the bar a few hundred feet. The cow seemed greatly interested in our mules, thrusting her big ears forward in mule-like inquiry. The twins frisked and butted into their morning suckle like lambs in the home pasture.

Yesterday afternoon we followed an Indian trail, evidently cut for winter sledding. While eating our lunch on a bar at noon, we saw smoke a few miles ahead, and an hour or two later, we heard Webb's gun calling us. Before evening we came to their camp, and are now on the main Kantishna River, where all the channels are gathered into one, and we are correspondingly happy—except that we are out of food.

Our flour is gone and we have no other food of any kind, except for what we can hunt, catch, or trap. About noon Webb saw a young bull moose come rapidly but noiselessly into the river a short distance above us, driven into the water by clouds of moose flies. Webb ran along the riverbank, and shot the moose in the swift current. A few moments later we salvaged its fat carcass and dragged it ashore at our camp.

While we were dragging the moose from the river, Hannah also went hunting. Finding the last remaining half-handful of our precious salt, she salvaged that for herself and ate it, sack and all. Now it is moose meat alone without salt, or flour, or anything else, till we float down the river to the sack of flour cached by us at our former camp at Anotoktilon.

June 30. Today we rolled our raft logs out on the bar, replaced some which had become water-soaked, and rebuilt the craft. We have pegged three heavy flattened poles across the raft, one at each end and one across the center; reset good sweeps for steering, and put up a pole barricade for the mules, so that we can take our entire party aboard and float with the current downstream at about three miles an hour.

McLeod, however, has been frightened both by wreck and mules, and is preparing his own private yacht made entirely of spruce. He stripped the bark from a large, green spruce tree; sewed the ends wedge-shaped with spruce roots; caulked them with spruce gum; and carved a paddle out of a split portion of the tree. He will henceforth paddle his own canoe down the river.

We now eat nothing but roast moose at every meal, toasted brown at the end of a long stick—not even bannocks are to be had.

July 1. Left camp about noon, McLeod leading in his spruce bark canoe, which floats as light as a cork. The raft also rides buoyantly and the mules act like old sailors. We see moose on almost every sand bar where they rest in the shade and the breeze, thus escaping the mosquitoes. A grand, glorious, lazy day as we float gently along on a beautiful river. How different it is from the raging torrent that wrecked and tore our raft to pieces a few miles back!

July 2. Still floating gently on the river. There are no rapids, no rocks, no drifts, and we manage the raft quite easily with the bow and stern sweeps. Moose are everywhere along the river bars, but we do not allow shooting, for we have plenty of meat to last us to flour and beans—too much in fact. The river is running northeast, and late this evening Chitsia, or Heart Mountain, bears due southeast.

July 3. We reached the mouth of Chitsiana late this afternoon, to find that McLeod had left a sign on the bank saying he had gone up to the Anotoktilon cache for our boat, beans, and flour. He soon returned with the boat and bags. He had rummaged the abandoned Indian camp where he found an old bucket so dirty and old and crushed that even an Indian in the wilderness had cast it away, but it is our only cooking utensil. We scoured it with sand and scalded it as clean as we could, then boiled the bag of beans in it.

Our moose meat is now spoiled so we threw it overboard, and changed our diet. Our menu now consists of sandy bannocks and boiled beans, without salt. The change is momentarily grateful, and after the feast we pushed off anxious to go as fast as the current would carry us.

The mules behave well, they jump off the raft when we stop to cook, and fill their stomachs with grass while we rest; then march down like great mastiffs, and jump on the raft where they stand patiently beside the pole as if they had always traveled this way. Now that we know the river is safe below us, we stop only once a day when we land for mule feed and water.

We have divided the time into two-hour watches. George takes the bow oar and I the stem sweep for two hours, then Stevens the bow and Webb the stern for the same time. The off crew go to their berths of boughs and grass at the mules' heels. The mules also sleep long hours, for flies and mosquitoes do not come on the raft. Waterfowl fill the rivers and ponds, and the summer nesting song of the northern robin adds sweet music to a bird paradise.

July 4. The glorious Fourth was ushered in with a volley of firearms which almost caused Hannah to jump overboard. We ran all night passing old Koonah's deserted camp at midnight and the mouth of the Toclat this morning. The morning's sunrise was gorgeous on the distant Chitsia hills.

This afternoon we floated past old Nachereah's campsite, where the *Tanana Chief* had landed us in May. This too was deserted, for all the Indians have descended the Kantishna to take salmon at their fish camp on the lower Tanana and the Yukon.

July 5. We reached the mouth of the Kantishna, passed out into the Tanana, and floated on down the "Ohio of the North" to the Hendricks & Belt post at the mouth of Baker Creek, where we landed at midnight to find McLeod and his little spruce-skin boat waiting for us at the landing. McLeod had lost what little money he possessed, and sat stolidly on the bank waiting for us to come, that he might eat.

We quickly unloaded Mark and Hannah and turned them loose to graze. They had ridden for twenty-four hours without going ashore, and now lumbered fatly off the raft into a wild meadow of rich mule feed.

For four days we had existed on moose meat cooked at the end of a stick without salt; and for another four days on a few bannocks. We were hungry.

The loaded raft with the men and mules aboard, ready to head for home.

(Charles Sheldon Collection, Box 5, Folder 3, Archives, Alaska and Polar Regions, University of Alaska Fairbanks)

This is believed to be a portrait of Wickersham wearing a mosquito headnet on his return from the McKinley expedition.
(Alaska State Library, Wickersham State Historic Sites Photograph Collection, ASL-PCA-277-018-043)

We kicked at the entrance to the log store till we woke the sleepy clerk, who grumblingly opened his door. We quickly spent every cent we had for provisions and turned into a nearby cabin, whose owner was off on a stampede, where we cooked our makeshift feast.

Along Baker Creek, Webb had found a net set in the creek, and commandeered a great struggling twenty-pound pike, which we added to canned peaches, bread, and coffee. Think of it, coffee with canned cream! Whew, that's great, and peaches and fried fish! If you were never a week behind in eating you don't know how good such food can be!

July 6. After the big feed, and "smudging" the cabin to drive out the mosquitoes, we turned in to sleep, but within an hour the steamer *North Star*, bound for Fairbanks, blew her whistle at the landing. We loaded Mark and Hannah on her little bow in charge of McLeod, and sent them up the river to Fairbanks in better condition than when they started to Denali with us nearly two months ago. We gave the grouching store keeper the *Mudlark*, which had borne us so staunchly on the Kantishna; also our raft for stove wood, in exchange for breakfast. Then we started afoot northward along the overland trail for Rampart, fifty miles away.

We arrived at Glen Gulch mining camp this evening and accepted an invitation to eat with our friends Belsea and Beardsley, and their miners, whom we astonished with our mountain appetites. We bunked with Frank Stevens in his miner's cabin and slept in a real bed!

July 7. We started early on the thirty-mile walk to Rampart. Dinner at 106 Minook Road House, a good hour's rest at "72" and I started on ahead for the fifteen-mile walk down the muddy trail to Rampart which I reached at nine o'clock. I passed a brightly-lighted cabin, where a lovely woman, my wife, Debbie, sat at the window waiting for the return of her wandering husband.*

Soon Julius was cutting my two-months' old beard and introducing me again to bathtub and soap. After these ministrations were concluded he stepped gingerly to the bank of the Yukon and threw my cast-off clothing, with my hundred-dollar gold watch strongly

* Wickersham complained that the fifteen miles into Rampart were "over the worst roads in the world" but he covered the distance in only five hours. "Debbie sat at the window waiting for me," he wrote, but "she did not recognize [me with] my whiskers" (July 7, 1903).

attached thereto by a moosehide string, into the river, where they took up their journey seaward!

THUS HAPPILY ENDED THE first attempt to scale the mighty walls of Denali. The members of our party returned to civilization in perfect health, the mules rolling fat. Not a moment's sickness nor a crippling accident to man or beast had afflicted us. We returned to our normal labors with a glow of satisfaction that we had done so much with so little.

In spite of our unpreparedness, inexperience, and want of equipment, we had blazed the trail to the great mountain's northern base, mapped its approaches, the trails and rivers, and bore back to waiting prospectors the hint of gold in Chitsia gravel bars. No lover of nature, of mountains, glaciers, and high places, can have any sense of defeat after such a journey.*

---

* In reality the conclusion of the expedition was hardly as happy as Wickersham paints here. Though the Judge was certainly proud of what the five men had accomplished with such meager resources, by the end of his two-month-long trek he was hardly on speaking terms with any of his companions. He was most displeased with Morton Stevens, the attorney whom he came to feel was insufferably arrogant and presumptuous, and George Jeffery, the Judge's stenographer and secretary, who seemed to have fallen under Stevens' spell. During their final days on the river, Wickersham insisted on keeping both his gun and ammunition with him personally, because he feared Stevens and Jeffery might otherwise take the raft and leave him stranded in the wilderness.

"Stevens' arrogance has [received] somewhat of a setback—but is so supreme that nothing can quite dampen it," Wickersham wrote after the raft wreck. "George has entirely abandoned all idea of loyalty to me and has become his most sycophantic waiter &c. It is all owing to a 'bull con' story idea that Stevens has suggested to George that in a year they start on a journey around the world (on bicycles)for a newspaper at a big salary, and that during the circum-perambulation they take photos of all remarkable places, and upon their return they start a studio in N.Y. and live happily ever afterward! George is thoroughly infatuated with Stevens & his scheme, and it is amusing, though disappointing to me to watch his abject slavery to Stevens" (June 25, 1903).

The final insult for the Judge came in July, when Stevens asked to have a copy of one of the photographs of Denali, apparently with a view to publication, which Wickersham feared would preempt his own plans. "Stevens was just in very politely requesting a single copy of Mt. McKinley picture which I politely but positively refused. He recognizes that a publication of his magazine article with such a picture would spoil my use of it and not withstanding he went at my expense, and at his own request, & that I paid everything & furnished everything he has the 'nerve' to seek to destroy all my values" (July 14, 1903).

19

THREE THOUSAND MILES OF JUSTICE

Full speed ahead! Crowd on all sail,
Home Bering Sea Patrol!
Until May suns shall shine again,
The Ice King hath control.

—T. R. Shepherd

A TERM OF COURT convened at Rampart on July 20, 1903, in a large warehouse with barroom chairs and benches. Early that morning the military transport Jeff C. Davis landed at Rampart from Fort Gibbon, having on board a United States Senate Committee studying Alaska conditions: Senators W. P. Dillingham of Vermont, Knute Nelson of Minnesota, Thomas Patterson of Colorado, and Henry Burnham of New Hampshire. All four senators were lawyers who wished to be admitted to the Alaska bar. Charles Claypool, the Commissioner from Circle City, moved their admission in open court, and it gave me great pleasure to make the orders admitting them to practice law in the Territory in our makeshift courthouse on the Yukon River.*

* "Four great lawyers and leaders of the nation—probably no territorial [judge] has ever had so pleasant a duty to perform in which so many distinguished men became members of a territorial court at the same moment." Right after the induction ceremony, as the senators were watching, Wickersham nervously lectured the grand jury that they must weigh the truth of corruption charges that had been brought against a U.S. Commissioner. "I instructed [the jurors] to go into the examination at once, and protect their community from a corrupt official, or their local court from the false and malicious attacks of a slanderer. It was a dramatic scene—quiet—and impressive with four U.S. Senators listening at every word to determine if I myself was fair to both parties. They commented very favorably afterward... and I am satisfied" (July 22, 1903). Minnesota Senator Knute

Members of the U.S. Senatorial party in Alaska, 1903.
(Alaska State Library, Perry Moore Photograph Collection, ASL-P487-57)

We made arrangements for the senators to use some of the space in our courthouse for a public hearing at which they heard testimony from the local residents. I testified before the committee on the need for Congress to approve the election of two or three territorial delegates for Alaska—one for southeast Alaska and others for northern and western Alaska—and to build roads.

While the senators attended strictly to their official hearings and the study of Alaska conditions, Dr. Wilcox, their physician, wandered about the camp studying natural history, mining, and health conditions among the Indians. One day he came hurrying down from the old cabins on the hillside back of Rampart, and told Senator Dillingham, "Senator, I have just seen one of the largest specimens of *bos primigenius* known to science out on that hill." Dillingham was just then talking to a notable local character, hunter, trapper, and guide, known as "Windy Jim" Dodson, who became quite as excited at this statement as the worthy and learned doctor.

"Wait, Doc, till I go to my cabin and get my two 30-40 rifles, and we will go and get him. They are dangerous, though, and we must be careful. I killed one over on the Tanana two years ago and they fight like hell!"

When an hour later the large skull and horns of an extinct Alaska bison found in a Minook Creek mining excavation was brought down from an old cabin for shipment to the Smithsonian Institution, Jim sheepishly declared he had thought *bos primigenius* was the doctor's college name for the grizzly bear!

THE STEAMER *SARAH* CAME down from Dawson with Judge Alfred Moore, who had followed me on the Nome district court bench. He told me about his trip to Washington where he had lodged

---

Nelson would later be one of Wickersham's fiercest critics, but at this time he was still friendly:

"I am personally pleased with remarks made to me by Senators Dillingham and Nelson about my official life in Alaska. Dillingham spoke to me about the kind things that people have said since he entered Alaska in support of my administration and expressed himself as highly pleased. Senator Nelson also said to me that he had tried to keep me at Nome, and complimented me on my work there, and said that I ought to have been allowed to remain. Dillingham also spoke of the same matter and expressed regret that I had not been left there" (July 20, 1903).

additional charges against Marshal Richards, but had not yet been successful in having him removed from office.*

The *Sarah* remained tied to the riverbank until late at night. The first mate, a Mississippi-steamboat man by the name of Willett, was rather old and large of body, but active as a youth and as jovial as a friar. After a long night of drinking in the saloons along the waterfront, he slipped and fell into the river. Luckily a deckhand saw him go down and threw him a rope; other deckhands came running to the rescue, and with much exertion they raised the burly mate to the steamer's deck. The captain in his cabin heard the noise but not being able to see what was going on called down, "What's the matter down there, Mr. Willett?" With the water running down his body, oozing out of his clothing and filling his great shoes, the old mate steadied himself by a stanchion and answered, "Oh, nothing, Sir, just a drunk sailor overboard, Sir, but we have him up all right now."†

AFTER THE SENATORIAL COMMITTEE had gone down the Yukon we held a busy term of court. The population of the district was increasing rapidly on account of the Fairbanks gold strike, which was showing better every day as prospecting opened up new extensions of the pay streak, and Rampart, Chena, and Fairbanks were taking on the appearance of permanent towns. Petitions presented to the court asking for their incorporation as municipalities were granted, and local organizations of civil government began to appear in the district. The towns took over a good part of the burden of enforcing law and order.

BEGINNING AUGUST 31ST I had been instructed by the Department of Justice to hold a special "floating court" on board

* "[Judge Moore] was in Washington but met with rather a cold reception and his report seems to indicate that neither Richards nor [U.S. District Attorney Melville] Grigsby will be removed. I learned from him that the last Nome grand jury indicted... Richard's chief deputy & the smoothest and most brutal scoundrel of the lot. But with Grigsby to prosecute [he is safe]. Well, it's a bad lot & the President is playing politics and dare not remove them! He must have North Dakota & McKenzie & the Dakota senators are holding him up hard" (July 29, 1903).

† According to the Judge's diary Willett was not actually on the *Sarah* at Rampart; this story apparently happened to the perpetually drunken sailor sometime when he was the first mate on a ship called the *Puebla* under a Captain Dabney (August 13, 1903).

the U.S. Revenue Cutter *Rush* to patrol the coast of my district from Bristol Bay to Yakutat. Many complaints had come from that region about lawlessness and especially about the sale of intoxicating liquor to the natives. The *Rush* would take us to all the settlements and camps along that coast to make the necessary inspection and provide needed official organization to suppress crime in those distant places. When the Rampart term closed on August 12th we left for St. Michael, where the *Rush* had been ordered to meet our party, which included the marshal, the district attorney, and Capt. D.H. Jarvis, collector of customs for Alaska.*

Captain Jarvis was obliged to make an official inspection of the customs office at Nome, where the *Rush* anchored for a day.† We then

---

* Captain David H. Jarvis was a distinguished officer of the U.S. Revenue Marine Service (now called the Coast Guard) and veteran of the Bering Sea Patrol since 1888. For his heroism in the course of a celebrated rescue of stranded whalers he had received a congressional gold medal, the nation's highest civilian award, an honor that Jarvis shares with the likes of George Washington, the Wright Brothers, Charles Lindbergh, Thomas Edison, etc. During Wickersham's years on the bench, Captain Jarvis would be one of the Judge's closest friends and most trusted advisors. "I am very fond of Capt. Jarvis; he is a loveable, honest and competent man—I think those three words cover about all that is necessary in a man" (September 25, 1901). When Jarvis resigned from government service in 1905 he took over as manager of a major fish packing company and eventually would become the head of the Morgan-Guggenheim interests in Alaska, but he and the Judge still remained close. It was only when Wickersham decided to run for delegate in 1908, and build his political career by fighting the "Guggs," that he had an irreparable break with his old friend, accusing him of a long litany of crimes, including corruption, collusion, jury tampering, bribery, and perjury. For Wickersham, Jarvis became a symbol of Guggenheim greed and the Taft administration's incompetence, and the Judge rhetorically whipped him at every opportunity. But Jarvis did not have Delegate Wickersham's thick hide. On June 22, 1911, Wickersham demanded a new investigation of Jarvis for allegedly defrauding the government on coal contracts. The following day Jarvis committed suicide in Seattle, leaving a scribbled note that said: "tired and worn out." Many of Wickersham's critics accused him of hounding an American hero to death. The Judge's angry response in his diary was: "Poor Jarvis. Until he became the employee of the Guggenheim bunch of Jew thieves he was a man of honor and courage" (June 24, 1911). For a scathing account of the Judge's feud with Jarvis see Elizabeth A. Tower, "Captain David Henry Jarvis: Alaska's Tragic Hero—Wickersham's Victim," *Alaska History* 5(1) (Spring 1990):1–21.

† Jarvis convinced Wickersham not to go ashore with him at Nome, because the political climate there arising out of the Marshal Richards case, and other matters, was decidedly hostile to the Judge. "The nasty mess of Nome factional fight is at a fever heat, and so I am not going to even land on the beach" (August 17, 1903).

On board the U.S. Revenue Cutter Rush *in 1903, Wickersham held a "floating court" to patrol his district from Bristol Bay to Yakutat.*
(U.S. Coast Guard Historian's Office)

sailed for Bristol Bay, where we remained for a week. We held a short term of court at Mittendorf's house at Nushagak, heard applications for licenses, for citizenship, and investigated matters of crime, insanity, and public health in the nearby settlements and at the canneries.

Commissioner Clegg had been appointed by me from Nome and stationed here the year before to organize the minor courts. He had held several persons to appear before the grand jury at Valdez and had both prisoners and two or three insane persons in confinement. The marshal brought them on board the *Rush* to be taken to Valdez for hearing. We looked over the country for a proper location for a site for the commissioner's court and jail and reserved a small tract of public land for that purpose on the north shore of Nushagak Bay, which I suggested be called Dillingham, in honor of the chairman of the senatorial committee.*

Having visited the settlements and organized the law-enforcing machinery on Bristol Bay, we sailed for Unalaska, where like inquiries and organization were completed, a site reserved, and provision made for the construction of a jail. We then sailed eastward along the south coast of the Alaska Peninsula, visiting the settlements at Belkofsky, Unga, Karluk, Sand Point, Kodiak, Seldovia, and Nuchek, appointing officials necessary for the enforcement of law and the protection of the natives from criminals who infested these localities. We also collected all those persons officially charged with crime or insanity to be brought to Valdez.

It was clear weather while we skirted along the coasts from Bristol Bay to Kodiak and we had glorious views of the line of volcanoes rising from the islands and upon the Alaska Peninsula. The symmetrical high cone of Shishaldin glowed at night. By day we had a beautiful view of the rain of black scoria which fell back from the fiery blasts.

---

* "The public business on Bristol Bay is quite important and will deserve attention. There are several canneries here—about 8,000 men are employed here during the summer, but go to S. F. & below in the fall after the season is over. It is a very short season & everybody is now gone except a few who are here to put the outfit away & load the remaining cargo. Clegg has visited every cannery & has statistics & proofs—$25,000 yet due for former years for licenses unpaid, and none paid for this year. There are also several persons in jail for crime—two for murder. Those for felonies will be taken, with witnesses, to Valdez for trial.... Our appearance here, and the formal holding of court... the carrying away of accused persons by the cutter, & all, has strengthened the officers here & [done much for] future good" (August 27, 1903).

Pavlof was also in eruption, and its intermittent puffs of black smoke rose high in the summer sky. Not even Japan has a finer display of volcanic activities, past and present, than Alaska.

While at breakfast on the morning we crossed from Kodiak to Seldovia we were startled by the cry of "man overboard!" When we reached the deck the crew—just out of bed and dressed only in their drawers—was launching the lifeboat, and in the wake of the ship we could see the man struggling in the waves. He was a Chinaman, a prisoner from Bristol Bay, who had jumped overboard. A native of the Flowery Kingdom, accused of crime by "foreign devils," he imagined that as soon as we should land at Valdez his head would be cut off as it might be in China, and frightened to the verge of insanity he concluded to end his life in the sea. As soon as the sailors pulled him aboard the lifeboat we could see them rolling him across the boat seat and using other active measures, as we supposed, to drain the water out of his lungs. We learned later that the sailors having been routed out of their warm beds, and taking to the boat in a cold and drenching sea, had given him a rather violent "third degree" as a punishment. He was kept confined for the rest of the voyage, and suffered no ill effect from his morning bath—nor was he beheaded at Valdez, where our "floating court" docked on September 17, 1903, three thousand miles and thirty-seven days from Rampart.*

THE FIRST REGULAR TERM of the district court ever held in Valdez was called to meet on October 25, 1903. We rented the second

---

* Upon arriving in Valdez, the Judge followed his normal inclination to explore the area and reach the highest peak he could climb, but the steep hike up the hazardous terrain would prove more of an adventure than he expected.

"In company with L. C. Larson, photographer, climbed the mountain [to the] north of Valdez. He gave out and came back but, like a fool, I went on to the top. Brush very bad for 2,000 feet, and also great glacial furrows parallel to the general course of Valdez basin. These are extremely interesting & conclusively prove that Valdez glacier once extended to Prince Williams Sound & was at least half a mile deep. Was late in coming back & my boots were slick & I fell—many times & was so exhausted that I got into the brush again & could not find my way down—always on the edge of a precipice & having to travel along the glacial furrows. Finally I saw the fire Larson had built on the flats and heard him shout & guided through the darkness by his voice & fire at 9 o'clock I reached the flats & thence home in the boat. It was the meanest climb I have had—only 5,000 feet, but the glacial furrows, brush, ferns, grass, & perpendicular walls made it both rough & dangerous" (September 20, 1903).

story of the Hemple building for use as a courtroom, and the marshal rented a cabin for a jail.* After some negotiations we procured the abandonment of a small tract of land and reserved a lot 80 by 100 feet square for a site for court buildings. Telegrams were forwarded to the Attorney General at Washington asking for his approval of an expenditure of $8,000, out of the court funds obtained from licenses and fees for the construction of a courthouse and jail.

The most important case tried at Valdez at that term of court was the contest over the title of the Bonanza or Kennecott copper mines. The complicated background of the case stemmed from the 1898 gold rush, when a half-dozen laboring men in a Minnesota town agreed to join in an expedition to the Copper River region in search of copper mines supposed to exist along that river. This became known as the McClellan party, after R.F. McClellan, the intrepid prospector who organized the first expedition and led it to Prince William Sound in 1898. Though they failed to locate any mines, the group reorganized and returned again the following summer when one member of the McClellan party, and two other independent prospectors, struck it rich by finding the Nicolai Copper Mine on the Chitina River. The McClellan party and the others sold the Nicolai to a group of California capitalists and took stock in the Chittyna Exploration Company (renamed later the Copper River Mining Company). During the 1900 mining season McClellan and several of his men did work on the Nicolai mines for the new company, but at the same time other members of the McClellan group—who were not working on the Nicolai Mine—were out prospecting independently in the Wrangell

* Wickersham had been in Valdez for most of January and February 1903, and had actually opened the first regular jury term of the district court there on February 2, 1903. At that time he had been particularly impressed by the character and good nature of S.A. "Oklahoma Bill" Hemple, the prosperous merchant—sometimes called "O.K. Bill"—from whom they had rented space for the court.

"S.A. Hemple, the banker and merchant, locally known as 'Oklahoma Bill' called to see me this evening. The courthouse & our offices are in his building & he is 'well fixed' for Alaska. He is paralyzed on the left side and is rather spare, drawn & unprepossessing—until you look at his eyes which are clear, bright and intelligent. He is from Missouri, went to Oklahoma & there, he told me, though an invalid and hardly able to walk, he resolved to go to Alaska and make money enough in mines to start a bank and store, and [though] so badly crippled that he could never go to the mines himself, by a careful system of 'grubstaking' other men he has succeeded & is a worthy man—a 'rara avis' by the way, as a banker. He is a good citizen" (January 6, 1903).

Mountains, including Jack Smith and Clarence Warner. One day while Smith and Warner had stopped to eat lunch, Jack Smith spotted a large green spot on the side of a distant mountain; on a high slope, surrounded by glaciers and snowfields, it was an unlikely place for a field of grass. They became so much interested in the strange-looking green spot that out of curiosity they climbed up to it the next day, and discovered an outcrop of an enormous copper vein, one of the richest ever found in history. In the next few days they located twelve mining claims covering this green spot and the area around it in their own names and in those of the others in the McClellan party.

That same year in the same vicinity, the War Department was surveying an "All-American" route from Valdez to the Yukon River. One of the employees in that military expedition was Stephen Birch, a young New York engineer who had made a special study of copper, and when he heard about the location of the Bonanza claims by the McClellan party and saw some of the ore, his trained eyes could see it was the surface outcrop of a great copper lode, and he got an option to purchase the claims from the McClellan party at a very reasonable price.

The issue that faced me in the court was to determine the rightful owner of the Bonanza prospect. The Chittyna Company claimed that the men of the McClellan party who discovered the Bonanza copper lode were employees of the company, and therefore the company was the actual owner of the mines. "This suit is brought upon the theory," as I explained in my decision, "that the defendants who located the Bonanza group of copper mines were at that time the agents of the plaintiff, and that their locations became, were, and now are, the property of the plaintiff." If the plaintiff's claims were correct, then Stephen Birch's options were invalid, and Birch had meanwhile formed a company and had set about to develop the property.

The Bonanza property involved was the most valuable group of mining claims in Alaska, and consequently a great array of eminent lawyers appeared at Valdez to argue the case. Among the plaintiff's attorneys were Senator Weldon Heyburn of Idaho, Congressman Francis Cushman of Washington (in whose honor I had named the main street of Fairbanks), and Andrew F. Burleigh of New York, while the defendants—the McClellan party—were represented by Frank D. Arthur of New York, John A. Carson of Oregon, Fred M. Brown of

Stephen Birch inscribed this portrait "For my friend James Wickersham," although later they would become the most bitter of enemies.
(Alaska State Library, Wickersham State Historic Sites Photograph Collection, ASL-PCA-277-19-145)

Andrew Burleigh (1), Senator Weldon Heyburn (2), and Congressmen Francis Cushman (4), were the lead attorneys for the plaintiffs in the celebrated Bonanza lawsuit in Judge Wickersham's Valdez courtroom in 1903.

(Alaska State Library, Wickersham State Historic Sites Photograph Collection, ASL-PCA-277-007-108)

Valdez, and others. It was a most stubbornly contested case, and the arguments made by these mining lawyers were worthy of their high reputations. When they were concluded, I took the case under advisement, for I had to study the entire record of some two thousand pages of testimony which had been taken by previous depositions, much in Alaska, some in the States and some even in the Philippine Islands.

After three weeks I issued my decision in favor of the defendants. "Warner and Smith were neither agents nor employees of the plaintiff," I wrote in my decision. "They were neither employed, supported, transported, nor paid by it, nor by any one for it. They were independent prospectors in the Copper River country." Immediately after the case was decided in favor of the locators the plaintiffs appealed to the United States Circuit Court of Appeals where the decision was affirmed. The U.S. Supreme Court denied to hear the case, and so the ruling was ratified.*

After the appellate courts sustained my decision, the McClellan party prospectors completed their sale of the Bonanza lines to Stephen Birch and his associates. This in turn enabled Birch to secure financial backing from the Morgan-Guggenheim money powers in New York, and build the Copper and Northwestern Railroad from Cordova to the copper deposit, 196 miles in length at a cost of about twenty million dollars, to open one of the richest copper mines in America. The Alaska Steamship company was established by the mining company, a line of first-class passenger and freight steamers put on between Cordova and Seattle and the Tacoma smelter, and to the date when this line is written, the Bonanza (Kennecott) mines have mined and shipped to the United States from Jack Smith's green spot on the Bonanza Mountain, two hundred million dollars worth of copper.

---

* One of the many ironies of the Judge's career was that his 1903 decision in *Copper River Mining Co. v. McClellan* cleared Stephen Birch's title to the Bonanza mine and therefore opened the door to the creation of the Morgan-Guggenheim "Alaska Syndicate," the financial and commercial conglomerate with which Wickersham would battle constantly during his years in Congress. The decision also earned the Judge the undying enmity of the losers in the case, who helped to stymie his judicial reconfirmation in the U.S. Senate from 1904–1907, particularly the lead attorney, Senator Weldon Heyburn of Idaho. The Judge claimed he was "maliciously assailed" by the Idaho senator (May 16, 1905). "Heyburn's fees depended upon his success in that case & were very large. He has been against me since that time" (February 8, 1905).

Shortly after rendering the decision in the copper case on November 28, 1903, we left Valdez by steamship for Seattle to spend the remainder of the winter in the States. During that time we took a long trip to the east coast by train, visiting both New York City and Washington, D.C.* While making the rounds in the capital I testified before a House committee on the needs of Alaska, conferred with my colleagues in the Department of Justice, and in February had my first opportunity to meet President Roosevelt at the White House.†

BY THE TIME I departed Washington and managed to return to Alaska it was mid-March 1904.** We left Whitehorse in the middle

---

* Probably as a result of his dealings with Stephen Birch, who was clearly impressed by Wickersham and grateful to him, during this trip to the east Wickersham certainly played with the idea more than ever before of quitting the Judgeship and going into business, perhaps with Stephen Birch and his New York associates, or some other investors. "If I can make arrangements for money will abandon the judgeship. Have not made $1,500 per year out of it—nothing but honor & worry!!" (January 28, 1904).

† "Went with Senator [Addison] Foster to call on the President. He received calls in a cheap addition to the west of the White House, and connected thereto by a long low one-story hallway.... After waiting a short time we were ushered into a large plainly furnished room occupied by a large table (around which the cabinet gathers) and many inquiring constituents. The president was busy making the rounds from one to another trying to make the last one believe that he was just a little more pleased to see him than the former. We were near the last, and as Senator [Joseph V.] Quarles [of Wisconsin] and Senator Foster stood together, just before he reached us the President motioned them to go into his private office, where I accompanied them. Soon the President came in and we gave way to Senator Quarles who had his say and went out. I was introduced and we all sat down. The President is a strenuous and rapid talker, and began at once to ask questions and answer them. He was much interested in the big Kodiak bear. I finally told him that I had a picture of Mt. McKinley which I offered to give him. He very kindly accepted it and said he would hang it on his office wall. He volunteered to remark that every Alaskan official had been accused of every crime imaginable, to murder. But laughingly referred to his experience on the Little Missouri in an early day, and said that notwithstanding these charges he thought Alaskan officials came up to the average. He was really good natured but talked of everything else than conditions in Alaska. He is not as ugly as the pictorial papers and his photographs make him appear" (February 10, 1904).

** As the Judge returned north, he was cautiously optimistic—more so than he should have been—about his standing with Congress and the Justice Department. "Am well satisfied with the sum total of my trip to Washington. It seems to me as if I will be reappointed judge now—and that all that is left to my enemies is to scandalize and blackmail me with false affidavits after I am in Alaska and not able to answer" (February 24, 1904).

of March on the overland stage drawn by four horses, and six days later we arrived at Dawson. The next morning we left Dawson on one of Ben Downing's mail stages for Eagle, a two-day trip on the Yukon River ice with the thermometer forty degrees below zero and a cold north wind blowing. When we reached Eagle City we held a week's term of court.*

Captain Barnette, the Fairbanks merchant and miner, and Frank Manley, prospector, came into Eagle with two or three heavy horse teams hauling mining supplies into the Tanana. Barnette asked me to go along with him to Fairbanks on his sleds, which I did, and Manley put my trunk on his load. The trail to Circle was soft and bad, full of drifted snow and the journey was one of hardship.†

April 4. Arriving at Circle, Barnette purchased a one-horse "double-ender" sled, loaded it with supplies, tied his cutter on behind, and we two started over the mountain trail to Fairbanks. We had a hard, cold trip but went along well enough until we crossed the Twelve Mile divide and started down the Chatanika Valley to Faith Creek roadhouse. Here we met Martin Sickinger, a merchant from Dawson going to Fairbanks with a single horse and double-ender

---

* Wickersham had been absent from Eagle exactly one year to the day—March 21, 1903 to March 21, 1904—and even though it was nominally still the headquarters for the Third Judicial District, he was desperate to leave two days after his arrival. For one thing there was virtually nothing for him to do. Despite having been gone for a year, it took less than one week to clear the docket, and with no pressing tasks at hand, it was too easy to be haunted by the memories of his deceased son Howard, whom he had last seen alive when they were together in Eagle. At the first opportunity he would go to Fairbanks and stay there. "Eagle City is no longer attractive to me. It seems as if I must see Howard in his accustomed places and it makes me sad and lonesome. I will be glad to get away for Fairbanks" (March 23, 1904). He would never live in Eagle again, and every visit would rekindle the same sad memories of Howard. When he briefly stopped in Eagle the following year on his way outside to Seattle he wrote: "Eagle looks the same & my heart goes out in memory of the town & Howard. I can hardly realize that my life with him is dead. Our old home looks shabby & is going slowly to decay" (September 27, 1905).

† It was a hard trail to Circle City; the Judge walked halfway, plowing through deep snow in warm weather, and his feet were swollen and sore. He was pleased to reach Circle City and enjoy a night of singing and drinking with a handful of friends, though he remained mindful as always not to overindulge. "Spent evening at Fred Bates cabin—Claypool, Geoghegan, McInroy, Buckley.... 'Give us a drink bar tender' &c. 'Bates old Guitar' and [other] songs—a bottle & good cheer. Bohemianism buys whisky—but nothing else" (April 1, 1904).

The court officials on Ben Downing's horse-drawn sled about to leave Dawson for the trip to Eagle on March 20, 1904. Wickersham is seated on the far right.

(Alaska State Library, Wickersham State Historic Sites Photograph Collection, ASL-PCA-277-001-060)

sled, loaded with merchandise. They told us at the roadhouse that the water was all over the flats below, extending all the way to Cleary Creek, dammed back by deep snow. The next morning soon after we left the roadhouse we ran into these bad overflows on the flats. There was about an inch of ice on the overflow, then a foot of water underneath, and below that the solid winter ice. When the horses stepped on the upper inch of ice their feet would break through, and coming down upon the solid winter ice underneath they would slip and frequently fall. We feared they might break their legs so Sickinger and I joined hands and walking side by side broke the thin ice by stepping on the edge. For miles in this way we broke trail through the thin ice. The horses followed behind us in this broken trail all day. Too often we slipped and sat down in the cold water, we were wet all over, but kept at it for it was the only way we could get the horses and the sleds along.

At dark we were still three miles away from the Cassiar roadhouse where we had intended to remain overnight. At midnight we gave up the struggle, turned into the side-hill woods, and made camp. We shoveled out two feet of snow, set up the tent, made a fire, fed the horses, cut spruce boughs for beds, dried our clothes before the blaze, made some coffee, and turned in for some sleep and a much-needed rest.

The next morning Sickinger and I continued to break ice, the water grew deeper, but at noon we reached the roadhouse where we had a big feed. Here we were met by two of Barnette's men who had come out to find us, but had been stopped by the deep water above the snow dam through which we had waded. They helped us over the lower trails where the traveling was not so bad, though we were wet to our waists all day as we crossed and re-crossed the streams flowing over the winter ice. The third day, while we were still in overflow, it was a better trail, and before night we came into the Cleary Creek valley and from there we had a dry road to Fairbanks.

CLEARY CREEK HAS A different appearance from what it had a year ago when I first saw it. Then there was but a single cabin in the valley, and not a working mine. Now there were hundreds of miners along its pay streak sinking shafts, and many taking out winter dumps of gravel, for the spring cleanup; houses, stores, roadhouses, and better roads gave evidence of prosperity.

But while there was much hope and anticipation on Cleary Creek that year, it was also the site that summer of a sad and mournful ceremony. One day while examining the boundaries of a mining claim, a miner from the opposite side of the valley informed me that a young woman, the wife of another miner, had died suddenly that morning and he asked me to go over to their tent. Three or four other miners had gathered there by this time, and we discussed what to do about her burial. There was not a coffin to be had in the Tanana country, and no lumber with which to make one closer than Fairbanks, twenty-five miles away, and no road by which to get it out to the creek. There was no cemetery or burial ground nearer than Fairbanks, and the trails were so boggy and impossible that her funeral and burial could not possibly take place there. Her husband asked permission to have her interred on the southern slope of the mining claim where their tent was located, which was agreed upon.

There were a few whip-sawed spruce boards used for sluice boxes on one of the nearby mining claims, and the owner willingly gave us enough of these rough, gravel-scarred boards to make a coffin. We then ascertained that there was not a carpenter on the creek, and no person in the little camp capable of constructing a coffin. Having had some experience with saw and hammer in my early days on Puget Sound, it fell to me, assisted by the blacksmith, to do the work. We carried the boards to the blacksmith's shop, cut them the proper length and washed the sand out of them as well as we could, shaped the bottom, and nailed the sides and ends on the bottom boards. We made a flat top to suit the shape and covered the rough structure with black cloth from the skirts brought to us by the wives of other miners. It was a difficult job of carpentry for a blacksmith and a judge, but was accomplished in time for the funeral the next day.

Wildflowers gathered by the six pioneer women living along Cleary Creek were placed on the coffin, the most beautiful moss of many varieties, more beautiful than hot-house plants, enabled the women to line the inside of the box with a bed of soft fronds of exquisite colors. Two homemade buckets from nearby mining shafts, covered with moss, served as a resting place for the coffin during the funeral ceremony. The women sang "Rock of Ages" and they kindly asked me to conduct the service and make a few remarks. Thus, under a bright midday sun in the new mining camp, in the almost unbroken wilderness, we buried the first white woman to cross the last divide and be borne to her grave in the great Tanana watershed.*

More than a decade later Fred Crewe, the historian of the Pioneers of the Tanana, wrote the following lines for publication in the *Fairbanks Times*:

There's a picket fence around her,
but no sign of slab or stone,
To tell the name of the sleeper
or explain why she's alone,
Alone out here on the hillside
in a little fenced-off plot,
Slumbering on in silence,
by every one forgot.
With none to plant a flower

---

* "After breakfast went over & was running my line between discovery on Cleary & my bench on left limit—when Mr. Hastings came over & informed me that Mrs. Crawford was dead. She has been sick for some time & he told me yesterday that she had seemed bad but was much better & when the neighbor women went to see her yesterday evening she said she was so much better that she thought she would get up. She rested comfortably all night but this morning took worse suddenly & died in a few minutes. Dr. King was called at my suggestion & says it was blood poisoning. She swallowed a pin a week ago & it has evidently caused the trouble. Have been with Crawford. He wants her buried—temporarily—on my claim—1st bench off Discovery on Wolf & I am looking after the details for him. Have worked all afternoon planning [*sic*] lumber for a coffin—raining & dismal weather" (August 12,1904).

"Yesterday was a cold rainy day, black in disposition & circumstances. I worked till late in the afternoon—wet, muddy and cold & then went off & left the carpenter to complete the work. He made the coffin too short after I left & when I returned I had to cut out the head & foot boards & lengthen it two inches. We did not get it lined & finished until after 10 a.m. This morning the skies are brighter & the rain has ceased, but the tundras of Cleary Creek are knee deep in mud & water. There is no road on the creek & you just make up your mind where the mud & water is shallowest & wade!

"At 11 o'clock I conducted the funeral of Mrs. Crawford.... The pall bearers were six stalwart miners. The coffin at the grave rested on two upturned mining buckets covered around with soft moss. The box in the grave was banked with same soft and beautiful moss—6 women present—Mrs. Hastings, Mrs. Boone Sr. & Jr., Mrs. Esterly, Mrs. Copes & Mrs. Brown. They sang 'Rock of Ages' and 'Nearer my God to thee.' I spoke as best I could—on the loss of the husband & community—briefly, & upon the fact that it was a miner's funeral and the first funeral of a white woman in the Tanana region! Her grave was banked high with the most beautiful moss I ever saw—25 or 30 miners present" (August 13, 1904).

or shed a single tear,
In honor of the grit and nerve
of the Cleary pioneer,
Who went through all that you did—
camped on the same old trail—
And fought for her life like you did
in the blizzard and the gale.

June 13, 1904. Court convened in the new courthouse though it was without windows or doors which were coming on the up-river boat soon to arrive.* It was the first session of the district court ever held in the Tanana country. Now that the mines were seen to have great value, much litigation had arisen over locations, discoveries, overlaps, and grubstake agreements, and the court was busy.†

* "Instructed grand jury about their duties & sent them out to work. Nothing else possible—as carpenters must finish building" (June 13, 1904).

† The most memorable decision that Judge Wickersham rendered in the summer of 1904—and probably the most famous of his entire career—is his oft-quoted opinion in *McGinley v. Cleary*, 1904, a witty, biting, and outrageously sarcastic legal decision that has sometimes been inaccurately credited to the Judge's eccentric stenographer and clerk, the brilliant linguist Richard Geoghegan. Wickersham said that in the McGinley decision he "roasted" both McGinley and Cleary "to a finish." McGinley, a bartender and proprietor of the Fairbanks Hotel, sued Frank Cleary because in the course of a wild drunken night of illegal gambling, McGinley got so intoxicated that he lost $1,800 in his own—likely loaded—dice game to the almost equally intoxicated Cleary, and signed over a one-quarter interest in the hotel. McGinley sued to recover the property in part because he claimed he "was so drunk at the time he signed the deed as to be unable to comprehend the nature of the contract." Cleary's defense was that it was an honest debt, even if it arose from a crooked game. Incensed at both men, Wickersham dismissed the case, but did so with a light touch never seen before or since in Alaska legal history. For example:

"The opening scene discovers [McGinley] drunk, but engaged on his regular night shift as barkeeper in dispensing whiskey... to those of his customers who had not been able, through undesire or the benumbing influence of the liquor, to retire to their cabins. The defendant was his present customer.

"...At about 3 o'clock in the morning of the 30th [November 1903] they were mutually enjoying the hardships of Alaska by pouring into their respective interiors unnumbered four-bit drinks, recklessly expending undug pokes, and blowing in the next spring cleanup. While... catching their breath for the next glass, they began to tempt the fickle goddess of fortune by shaking plaintiff's dicebox. The defendant testifies that he had a $5 bill, that he laid it on the bar.... That defendant had a $5 bill so late in the evening may excite remark among his acquaintances." According to Wickersham, McGinley's testimony indicated

The Fairbanks Hotel (right) on Front Street in Fairbanks was the establishment in question in McGinley v. Cleary, *Wickersham's famed decision about drunken gamblers and crooked games of chance.*
(Alaska State Library, Wickersham State Historic Sites Photograph Collection, ASL-PCA-277-011-001)

The first bridge across the Chena River, from the foot of Cushman Street had been finished and gave better highway facilities between the mining camps and the town. The spring rush of population was larger and increased with the arrival of every boat.* Business houses and cabins were being constructed on every side, and the sound of the saw and hammer was heard both night and day. The Northern Commercial Company, the successor of the pioneer A.C. Co., had erected a great store building and was filling it with all the supplies needed in a mining camp. A good camp newspaper, the *Fairbanks*

---

that the barman's "brains were . . . benumbed by the fumes or the force of his own whiskey." Another denizen of the bar sleeping behind the stove testified that when he woke up the plaintiff was throwing dice and "so drunk that he hung limply and vine-like to the bar," while the defendant was in contrast relatively sober as "he could stand without holding to the bar."

The Judge summarized the imponderable legal questions that came out of this drunken evidence. "Who shall guide the court in determining how drunk [McGinley] was at 3 o'clock in the morning . . . ? How much credence must the court give to the testimony of one drunken man who testified that another was also drunk? Is the court bound by the admission of the plaintiff that he was so paralyzed by his own whiskey that he cannot remember the events of nearly 24 hours . . . ? Upon what fact in this evidence can the court plant the scales of justice that they may not stagger?"

In conclusion, the Judge soberly ruled the court could not be a drunken-gambler's "insurance company" that would pay off whenever "the drunken, unsuspecting, or weak-minded" mark accidentally beat the odds, but neither would it help the equally undeserving—but-not-quite-so-drunk—defendant fortunate enough to profit from an illegal game of chance. Case dismissed (McGinley v. Cleary, 2, *Alaska Reports*, 1904).

* The greatest fear in Fairbanks in the spring of 1904 was that perhaps the Chena Slough would be simply too shallow in the summer months for the boats to come in at all. Low water in the last few days of May 1904 threatened to leave Fairbanks high, dry, and empty, but as dedicated a booster of Fairbanks as Wickersham was, he remained optimistic: "A very blue day, yesterday and today . . . as the river is so low that the boats cannot get up to Fairbanks and our Chena friends are knocking this town effectively on account of it. In spite of the low water the *Isabelle* is plugging away—carrying freight & passengers from the Tanana to Fairbanks—Capt. Barnette is working night & day—200 or 300 people are now here, & to my surprise they are coming to this town!! I really expected that the low water would frighten many of them into settling at Chena—but they are not. Several heavy firms from Dawson—machinery men—grocers & storekeepers are here and all others coming. Tents are going up—houses ditto, & every place is overflowing. The *Tanana Chief* came up today loaded, and every poling boat on the river is at work. Several teams & wagons came & at last a farm wagon & good team of mules is to be seen in the Tanana Valley" (May 31, 1904). Twelve days later the steamer *Lavelle Young* unloaded twenty head of cattle and a cow, the first in the Tanana Valley (June 11, 1904).

Wickersham addressing the crowd at the July 4, 1904, celebration at the new Fairbanks Courthouse.

(R. C. Force Papers UAF-2003-0174-00512, Archives, Alaska and Polar Regions, University of Alaska Fairbanks)

News, was established in the previous September by George M. Hill, Frank Mason, and Bob McChesney, managers and printers.* The streets were being cleared and graded and the town was taking on municipal airs.†

July 4, 1904, was a beautiful summer day and an enjoyable celebration by pioneer patriots in the Tanana wilderness was held for the first time. Every person present seemed proud and happy, the new town made a gallant appearance, with clean streets, new buildings, flags flying, the band playing, fine floats filled with gaily dressed children, drawn by four big horses, all covered with bunting. Florence Heilig read the Declaration of Independence from the courthouse porch; Mrs. Napoleon Dupras sang the "Star Spangled Banner"; Bessie Stone was the Goddess of Liberty, and I delivered the oration. It was a happy crowd of patriotic pioneers, gathered in the wilderness to renew their allegiance to the flag and the Constitution of the Nation to which they belonged.

As stirring as the July Fourth ceremonies and the dedication of the new courthouse had been, the real event that marked the coming of age of Fairbanks was the transfer of the headquarters of the Third Judicial Division from Eagle to Fairbanks. The location of a real bonanza mining camp at Fairbanks had finally attracted the

* Privately the Judge thought the *Fairbanks News* not much of a newspaper and along with other leading citizens urged a Dawson City publisher to "send newspaper plant at once. The 'News' man here is a 'dead one' & I hope to see his plant absorbed & a good daily paper going in a week or two" (June 1, 1904).

† No home probably had more "municipal air" about it than Wickersham's new house itself on the east side of town. In April 1904 he had purchased a lot for $175 at the corner of First and Noble. It was to be his "summer home," since technically the seat for his court was still in Eagle. He was determined to have a real house—not a miner's shack—with all the flourishes, including a picket fence and a grassy lawn, and with the handsome rental income he anticipated earning from his commercial property at the corner of First and Cushman, he and his wife Debbie would no longer have to live in "Poverty Flat" and could instead look forward to a life of financial security for the first time since he became judge.

"Have worked last three days on building fence &c at my proposed summer residence at corner of First Ave & Noble Street. . . . Am building the first picket fence in the Tanana Valley—real planed pickets & will paint them. Have put on my old clothes & worked hard, digging postholes, sawing & driving nails. We'll begin on the house tomorrow" (May 22, 1904). He spent $313.81 on lumber and within a week the framework of the house was done, and the lawn was ready for seeding by the beginning of June. "No doors or windows for my house yet—but *sowed timothy, bluegrass* & *clover seed* in my yard *today*" (June 2, 1904).

attention of the government at Washington for on October 26, 1904, I received a letter from the Attorney General asking me whether it would not be for the good of the service to move the headquarters of the district court from Eagle to Fairbanks.*

The change was immediately approved by our whole official family, and orders came back instructing us to make the change from Eagle to Fairbanks as of December 1, 1904. Our dream of finding a Klondike camp and establishing a Dawson on the Alaska side of the boundary line had come true. This change made Fairbanks the principal metropolis in the Yukon-Tanana country—the Dawson of the central Yukon basin.

Judge Wickersham and his wife Deborah at frame home in Fairbanks, complete with a grass lawn, flower beds, and a picket fence.

(Albert Johnson Photograph Collection UAF-1989-166-242-Print, Archives, Alaska and Polar Regions, University of Alaska Fairbanks)

* "Today I received a telegram from the Attorney General saying...'Want your opinion as to whether it is desirable to remove official residence from Eagle to Fairbanks.' I answered this peremptory demand by saying that in my opinion it was desirable to make the transfer!!" (October 25, 1904). Approval of the transfer came the following day: "Your residence and that of Attorney and Marshal changed to Fairbanks commencing December first" (October 26, 1904).

Mail and freight on the Valdez summit.

(Albert Johnson Photograph Collection UAF-1989-166-1177-Postcard, Archives, Alaska and Polar Regions, University of Alaska Fairbanks)

20

THE VALDEZ–FAIRBANKS TRAIL IN 1905

Oh, tough as a steak was Yukon Jake—
Hardboiled as a picnic egg,
He washed his shirt in the Klondike dirt,
And drank his rum by the keg.
In fear of their lives (or because of their wives)
He was shunned by the best of his pals,
An outcast he, from the comraderie
Of all but wild animals.

—Edward E. Paramore, Jr.

ON FEBRUARY 21, 1905, after a long and laborious term of court at Valdez, I left with a dog team to head north over the mountains to Fairbanks, where my next court session was soon to convene. Bob Coles, a young Valdez prospector, went with me to handle the team of six dogs.* Heavy snowstorms had covered the Valdez flats and Lowe River Valley several feet in depth and filled the Keystone Canyon with dangerous slides. At the Wortman roadhouse, at the foot of Thompson Pass, our highest divide, we found many other inbound dog teams waiting for good weather. The following morning was clear and bright; the trail was well marked up the Dutch flat approach and we reached the summit at about noon.

At all the roadhouses along the trail we met many men and dog teams transporting mining supplies into the Copper River country and to Fairbanks. One clear and cold morning—perfect weather for traveling by dog team—we got away at six o'clock so as to reach Copper Center on the

* Wickersham paid Bob Coles $250 to accompany him to Fairbanks (March 10, 1905).

Copper River, fifty miles away, for a night's lodging. At about noon the weather grew warmer and it began to snow, but we pushed on as rapidly as our dogs could travel. Unfortunately darkness overtook us while still on the trail, and as the snowfall grew thicker, going down the long and narrow bluff-side trail we met with our first accident.

WE HAD CONFIDENCE IN the keen sight and sagacity of our lead dog, and let him follow the trail at his own speed. But as the team realized we were nearing the roadhouse, they had increased their speed and carried us along the side hill at too rapid a gait. As we were rounding a very steep point the sled struck a pole that lay across the road; the sled flew off the trail and down the hill into a mass of snow-covered brush and logs. I was thrown from the handlebars of the sled and rolled down the hillside like a small boy at the end of a string of school boys playing "pop the whip." I flew through the air and made a none-too-soft landing on a log.

The force of the overturned sled dragged Bob and the dogs backwards down the hill until the sled was stopped by an accumulation of logs and brush. Our supplies were scattered along the hillside. With much shouting, pushing and pulling, and cutting through the brush, we finally righted the sled, found and repacked our supplies by lantern light, and got both the team and the sled back on the trail. We had no serious injuries, though my hands and face were bleeding and my hip felt as if it had been cracked from landing on the log.

We rough-locked the sled, proceeded more cautiously to the valley below, and reached the Copper Center roadhouse at midnight. Here a hot bath and a roll of sticking plaster made me new again. The next morning, however, my ankle was so badly sprained and swollen that we concluded to lay off a day for rest and hospital treatment, though the sourdough hot cakes we had for breakfast may really have been the strongest inducement.

ON FEBRUARY 27TH WE arrived at a roadhouse that stood in a forest of small black spruce on the Gakona (Rabbit) River. It consisted of a small open-front cabin with a tent lean-to in which the owner's mule team was lodged. A rough board sign announced that the "Chippewa Roadhouse" furnished meals for two dollars, and a place to spread your blankets for the night for an additional dollar.

Several frail sisters en route to Fairbanks had been stalled there for two days due to a long stretch of overflow on the Gakona. They hailed the advent of one "Belle" and her prize-fighting friends from New York (whom we had passed on the road) and prepared to make a night of it.* From their packs they brought out several bottles of liquor and for the greater part of the night their joy was unconfined and noisy. Not wishing to be a death's head at the feast, and needing sleep, for we had traveled twenty-six miles uphill to reach this hoped-for haven of rest, I betook myself to the mule tent, where there were half-a-dozen bales of hay safely stowed away from the mules. I spread my blankets on these hard but level bales of hay and passed the night more agreeably than those who remained in the shelter of the cabin.

Early on the following morning we left the "Chippy-wa-wa" roadhouse, as one of the participants in last night's gay party called it, and waded the icy overflow all day up the wide flat valley. Luckily the sun shone warmly and the north wind abated. Also, luckily, I had provided a pair of high rubber boots in fear of just such overflows and thereby escaped much discomfort. The trail of those who had preceded us, and here and there a blazed tree, guided us safely to the upper Gulkana in the last small body of evergreen timber on that stream above the big lake. Here we found another tent roadhouse (afterward known as Paxson) where we passed a cold (forty degrees below) and cheerless night. Distance traveled twenty miles.

From the top of the ridge over which we crossed from the Gakona to the Gulkana watershed, we had a glorious view of the high mountain summits of Drum, Sanford, and the Wrangell volcano standing far south of our position. Masses of heavy black smoke poured out of the great round crater on the Wrangell tableland, and rolled before the strong north wind across the mountain ice plain, without rising from its surface.

On March 1 we saw rising in front of us, towards the north, great rounded ridges of gravel that had been left by an ancient glacier. Climbing over this loose footing we came up to beautiful Summit Lake, then covered with ice and snow. About noon we entered Isabelle Pass, and soon the gravel bars began to slope downward towards the Tanana—we had crossed the Alaska Range at an altitude of 3,300 feet

* These included "Ed de Mug," "Billy de Pug," "John the Trashman," and "Belle de Bitch" (February 28, 1905).

Makeshift accommodations for the horses
on the Valdez–Fairbanks trail.
(Anchorage Museum at Rasmuson Center, Crary-Henderson Collection, AMRC-b62-1-1-302)

above sea level. That night we made camp at a place called Casey's Cache, where we found several other tents occupied by those who had preceded us thus far towards Fairbanks.

DOWN THE BIG DELTA we came to a roadhouse that night at a late hour, a rough log cabin constructed two years before by some prospectors led by a Negro by the name of Bill. Since we had left the Gakona roadhouse on the Copper River, every roadhouse had been housed in a tent, so this log structure was a notable improvement.* During our visit the manager was "Butch," who supplied mountain sheep and caribou for the table, while an English remittance man, who read the classics and wrote for foreign magazines, did the cooking. Belle and her two prizefighters caught up with us here, and the rough pole bunks and the gravel floor in the hostelry's single room were crowded.

The head of my pole bunk was against the log wall opposite from the rough board table upon which our meals were served. At five AM the chef lighted the fire in the Yukon stove just across the small table from my head. With half-closed eyes I watched the Englishman mix the dough for biscuits. Balancing it in his hands and mixing and kneading, he accidentally dropped the whole mass upon the gravel floor, carpeted with evergreen needles and dirt. Hastily recovering the ball of uncooked dough he brushed off as much of the dirt as he could without too much labor, picked out most of the evergreen needles, and then quickly turned it inward to conceal the soiled parts. He placed the dough on the table, after first wiping off the tobacco leavings, and rolled it out with a bottle. He then cut it into squares for the pan.

Though I am particularly fond of biscuits for breakfast, my meal that morning consisted of fried lamb chops and coffee. Belle and the prizefighters ate biscuits and fried meat gravy—none the worse for the experience!

Two days later at Joe Henry's "Big Kid" roadhouse, midway in the Tanana Valley, we first heard of the new strike of gold placers at Tenderfoot Creek about four miles east. My companion and excellent dog-driver, Bob Coles, determined to take a chance on the new camp,

* Wickersham called this the "worst" roadhouse on the trail. "It is a good warm house & I slept well, but dirt and laziness riots" (March 4, 1905).

so early next morning he started on a stampede to Tenderfoot; with one dog to my sled I started towards Fairbanks. Bob located a claim on Tenderfoot for each of us, but they panned out heavy in gravel as too often happens. Reached the Salcha roadhouse for the night—twenty-eight miles.

The next morning I started on the last forty-mile span of my trip to Fairbanks, accompanied by a tall Missourian, one of the locators of Tenderfoot Creek. Ten miles out of Fairbanks my brother Edgar met me to inform me that it was the tenth anniversary of his marriage, that the neighbors were preparing to celebrate it, and would I please hurry in to the party.*

I did, and came into the brightly lighted streets of Fairbanks at seven o'clock, having traveled 371 miles in 14 days—all of which I walked except an occasional ride of a mile or two downhill.†

BEFORE LEAVING VALDEZ I had purchased a large phonograph of the latest model with large horn amplifier and a hundred tubular records. They were packed in excelsior in a long watertight wooden box, covered with waterproof tarpaulin and securely tied upon our sled. Our cooking outfit, bags, and other parcels were piled on top of the box and covered with our tent. When we waded the deep overflow on the Gakona River, our sled, buoyed up by the box, floated like a cork and we brought the box and its contents into Fairbanks without injury.

When our friends learned of the presence of the new musical instrument from the outside world which few of them had ever heard, they asked permission to open the box, set up the strange machine, and satisfy their curiosity and love of music. Later the great red horn was thrust out of an open window between pillows to keep out the cold, and until an early hour the still wintry air was vibrant with the strains of grand opera, Sousa's marches, etc. While the people of the town seemed delighted with the unaccustomed

* "Edgar met us 14 miles out—*on a damned bicycle*—and urged me to get in early as it was the 10th anniversary of his marriage. . . . Fairbanks has grown wonderfully and the long lines of electric lights give it the appearance of a real city" (March 7, 1905).

† On his first day back in the office he noted: "Everything in good shape so far as I can see, but I am sore and tired" (March 8, 1905). His feet were "badly blistered."

music, the greatest applause came back to us from the malamute sled dogs, which answered each tune we played with long howls. A good time was had by all, for it was the first music-box concert in the Tanana Valley.

The steamer Lavelle Young *at Fairbanks, June 1904.*

(Anchorage Museum at Rasmuson Center,
Crary-Henderson Collection, AMRC-b64-1-66)

21

THE JUDGE GOES ON TRIAL

GOLD! We leaped from our benches.
GOLD! We sprang from our stools.
GOLD! We whirled in the furrow,
fired with the faith of fools.
Fearless, unfound, unfitted,
far from the night and the cold.
Heard we the clarion summons
followed the master lure—GOLD!

—Robert Service

LEST THE READER GET the idea that I was honored and respected for enforcing the law as I saw fit, and that I retired from office with the confidence and esteem of all litigants, the story of how my enemies tried to run me out of Alaska must be told. The vindictiveness of human nature readily appears in a frontier mining camp peopled with men from all quarters of the globe intent only on getting a fortune as soon as possible. Scruple and detachment are usually in inverse ratio to the value of the stake. Lust for gold when frustrated by an adverse decision not infrequently turns to malice towards the judge. No slander is too vile, no means of revenge is too base to satisfy the thirst for vengeance. It was my misfortune to be required to decide more cases involving great fortunes than any other judge in Alaska at that time; consequently my enemies were numerous and particularly vindictive.

A district judge in Alaska is appointed by the President of the United States, generally upon the recommendation of the Attorney General and must be confirmed by the United States Senate. A disappointed litigant could appeal a judgment of the Alaska court to the United States Circuit Court of Appeals at San Francisco. If he failed to get satisfaction in that way he frequently filed charges against the trial judge in the Department of Justice, hoping thereby to procure his removal from office, or to prevent his reappointment or his confirmation by the Senate.

In my day too often these charges were "confidential." If the charges were grave, as they usually were, a reappointment might be denied without a hearing or even notice that charges had been filed. There was never a closed season for protection of the district judges in Alaska as there was for brown bear and other varmints. Most of our early Alaska judges were removed from office upon secret charges without notice or a hearing; all of them were maliciously assailed and more or less intimidated in the performance of their judicial duty without an opportunity to defend their judicial acts or character from the malice of disappointed litigants.

WHEN MY FIRST TERM of office expired in June 1904, the Department of Justice had in its files at Washington charges against me for nonfeasance, misfeasance, and malfeasance in office, as well as spurious charges concerning my private life. These charges had been filed by Alexander McKenzie's associates and by some disappointed litigants in lawsuits decided by me at Valdez and Fairbanks.

Late in the summer of 1904 word reached me at Fairbanks that Hon. William A. Day, the first assistant to the Attorney General of the United States, was en route to Alaska to investigate all charges on file against Alaska officials connected with the Department of Justice, including the grave accusations against me.

Coming north from Seattle, Judge Day tarried awhile in Juneau to hear testimony against the judge for the first division. He then came, via Skagway and Dawson, to Eagle City, my official headquarters. Since I was then holding a regular term of court at Fairbanks, Judge Day remained in Eagle only long enough to inspect the courthouse and interview a few prominent citizens, after which he came by riverboat to Fairbanks. Captain D. H. Jarvis, collector of customs for Alaska, traveled with Judge Day and introduced him to local officials, prominent miners, and businessmen.

When they arrived at Fairbanks we were engaged in trying important mining cases. Litigants, lawyers, witnesses, jurymen, and a large number of interested persons from the surrounding mining creeks crowded the courtroom all day long and far into the night. Without even calling upon me Judge Day procured the town hall in which to hold his meetings, inserted a notice in the evening paper inviting the public to appear there "where he would meet any one who had information to impart bearing on the matters under investigation"—which referred to the charges against me.

While I held court at the courthouse, Judge Day and his assistants were engaged in trying me on undisclosed charges at the town hall. I did not attend my own trial, but instead gave my undivided attention to trying other men's cases in the district courtroom.

No notice of the hearing was given to me, except the public announcement in the newspaper; no copy of charges against me was served upon me, either privately or publicly. No effort was made to procure my presence at the hearings.*

Curious crowds alternated between the courthouse where I was presiding, and the public hall where I was put on trial. The presence of the assistant to the Attorney General of the United States at a small mining camp in the Yukon wilderness to hear testimony in support of long-pending secret charges against the district judge, created intense excitement among the miners.

Generally the accusers were unsuccessful litigants in former cases, their attorneys and witnesses, while those who rose to my defense were largely the successful litigants, and their attorneys and witnesses. Unhindered by the strict rules of evidence of a formal court proceeding, these rowdy gatherings served a useful purpose, revealing more fully in their own way the true nature of the attacks on me, and dispelling the poisonous fog of secrecy and malice.

---

* Wickersham initially feared the charges against him would come from the people of Chena, angry that he had backed Barnette's townsite at Fairbanks instead of their location downriver. "I do not know of any open opposition to me here—but from recent attacks made by the Chena *Herald* I am expecting the people down there to make all they can out of their opposition town site fight, and try to place a burden upon me. Amid my numerous administrative duties the appointing of commissioners and the location of their offices gives me the most trouble, but I shall always be proud of the fact that I established & named Fairbanks, Alaska" (July 31, 1904).

AFTER THE MEETING IN the town hall had been in progress for three days Judge Day called at my office and gave me orally an outline of the most important charges against me. He allowed me to make such explanation as I wished of some of them. No copy of the charges, however, was given me, or a list of my accusers or their witnesses. All that I ever learned about these matters came to me from friends who attended the town hall meetings. Judge Day asked me many questions about the difficulty at Nome over the marshal's accounts and fixing of the jury in the embezzlement case against the postmaster, and general conditions during the time of my service there as judge.*

When Day left for Nome to hear the testimony of Marshal Richards and others who were against me, the public interest in the investigation against me called down, but it continued to afford the sporting element a subject of much talk and some betting on the result in the cigar stores, pool halls, and saloons.

After months of waiting, on November 16, 1904, a telegram came from one of my friends, a newspaper correspondent in Washington, saying the President had reappointed me. Governor John Brady, who had also been investigated by Judge Day, also received another term, but Judge Brown, in the first division, fell under the ban and retired. The first dispatches were that Judge Moore of the second division must also retire, but on further consideration the President reversed that order, holding that Moore deserved another chance because he had been "surrounded by the worst kind of officials" at Nome, and among the "worst kind" was my nemesis Marshal Richards, whom the President removed for jury fixing. While none of us ever saw the record of the Nome hearings we were amused at the story that one of the hostile witnesses had declared to Judge Day that "Wickersham

* After meeting with Judge Day and learning the nature of the secret charges, Wickersham was both relieved and disgusted. "The mountain has labored and it's a mouse! I spent part of the day and all evening with Judge Day & his assistants and I hope explained every pitiful charge to the entire satisfaction of the court. The old scandal of 1887–89—Tacoma was the principal charge [the Sadie Brantner case]—the conviction of Richards was another . . . a dozen, small & insignificant matters. But not a single charge of incompetency—dishonesty or wrongdoing in my office! I am simply disgusted at the 'small talk' which disappointed litigants and narrow minded enemies imagine are worthy of consideration by the Dept. of Justice" (August 1, 1904).

"CARPENTER" WICKERSHAM AT WORK.

Wickersham as seen by his enemies, the destroyer of all that is decent, fair and upright.

(Fisher Collection)

is a damn bad man but a good judge, while Moore is a damn good man but a bad judge."

I never had the chance to read Judge Day's final report, but privately a Washington friend sent me a copy of the part that concerned me. After keeping this matter a secret for nearly thirty years, I feel that I am justified in now making it a part of this narrative.

In his report Judge Day stated he had been impressed by the evidence that hosts of friends and citizens had adduced in my behalf. He said Judge Wickersham "is an able, honest, and upright judge; that he administers justice promptly and firmly; that he possesses the confidence of the people of his division; that his long residence in western communities and his familiarity with mining laws and customs peculiarly fit him for the position he holds; that he deserves reappointment, and that the best interests of the people of the third division—and all of Alaska for that matter—would be subserved by his continuance in office."

EVEN THOUGH JUDGE DAY'S 1904 report should have officially cleared my name, it did nothing to stop the smear campaign against me. Following Day's favorable recommedation, President Roosevelt reappointed me and sent my name to the Senate for confirmation. However the same jumpers and speculators, whose schemes for despoiling the country through subservient judges had not been going so well since the ouster of Judge Noyes, still opposed my confirmation for the next three years.

These included Alexander McKenzie, the leader of the Anvil Creek conspiracy, and his henchman R. N. Stevens, the brains of the combination, as well as other Nome partisans; a group of copper speculators from Pennsylvania who interested themselves in the Copper River mining case at Valdez against the original locators of the Kennecott copper mines; and a particularly resentful miner from Fairbanks who had also lost a case before me.*

* The "particularly resentful miner from Fairbanks" was apparently Frank G. Manley, the namesake of the town of Manley Hot Springs. Wickersham had ruled against Manley in a celebrated 1905 mining case (*Boone v. Manley*) brought by Ben Boone and his father D. T. Boone, two Texans who owned a one-quarter interest in four of Manley's richest claims. Even though the Ninth Circuit Court of Appeals would eventually overturn Wickersham's decision, the Judge and Manley would remain sworn enemies. In 1906 Manley actively lobbied against

Though Judge Day had found that their charges against me were false, these were now rehashed and filed with the Senate Judiciary Committee to block my confirmation. Senators McCumber and Hansbrough of North Dakota, who had attempted to persuade President Roosevelt not to reappoint me, led the campaign. McKenzie and Stevens had long been their chief political supporters. It had been on McKenzie's behest that Senator Hansbrough had introduced in the Senate the notorious "Hansbrough Amendment," intended to give a semblance of legal standing to the plan of taking the Anvil Creek gold mines from their rightful owners.

In addition to the two senators from North Dakota, Senator Heyburn of Idaho had been the leading attorney for the Pennsylvania group of claimants in the Kennecott copper case tried by me, and the Pennsylvanians tried to influence their Senator Penrose and others against my confirmation.

My application for leave to come to Washington and present my defense was at first refused, but later a telegram from the Attorney General instructed me to appear. A month after my arrival at the capital the sub-committee heard the new charges, but neither charges, accusers, nor witnesses were made public. Of course the general character of the charges was known to me through friends who had

---

Wickersham's reconfirmation on Capitol Hill in tandem with Senator Nelson of Minnesota, and allegedly had gone so far as to try to bribe Kentucky Senator Joseph C.S. Blackburn—for whom Mount Blackburn in the Alaska Range is named—to vote against him (March 27, 1906).

In retaliation the Judge decided to dig up what dirt he could on Manley and "crucify" him (February 21, 1906). The Boones, who had their own longstanding feud with Manley, told Wickersham that Manley's real name was Hilliard B. Knowles, and he was a wanted man in Texas (February 22, 1906). In addition Wickersham suspected that Manley was having an adulterous affair with the wife of his business partner. "She is a natural born whore, & Manley would be fool enough to divide with her—a fine outfit to be fighting [me]—a fugitive from justice & a prostitute" (February 27, 1906).

Perhaps because of his own skeletons, in the end Wickersham refused to expose Manley's sordid past in Texas. But the story eventually did come out as a result of the ongoing war between the Boones and Manley. In January 1909 Frank Manley/Hilliard B. Knowles was hit with various charges—including perjury—stemming from his sudden disappearance from Texas more than a dozen years earlier. Though Manley would go on to survive the embarrassing revelations, Wickersham's pleased comment at the time was: "if Manley had behaved himself...and been honest for a time he could have been rich, happy and safe—but his innate 'cussedness' gave him the swell head & the Sheriff 'got im'" (January 2, 1909).

heard them discussed in the investigation at Fairbanks, but I knew nothing of the new charges.

Some of the Alaskans then in Washington were permitted to make short statements or to file affidavits in favor of confirmation and the defense was closed.* Then, two months after the beginning of the contest the subcommittee made their report to the full committee, and a vote was taken. The vote was six to four in favor of confirmation. Senators Knox, Bacon, Clarke, Culbertson, Foraker, and Patterson voted to confirm. Senators Nelson, Pettus, Blackburn, and Kittridge voted against confirmation. Senator Foraker was instructed to prepare a favorable report to the Senate.

TWO DAYS AFTER THIS favorable report was ordered, *Appleton's Booklovers Magazine* for May 1906 appeared with Rex Beach's famous article about the gold conspiracy titled "The Looting of Alaska," and concluded with a bitter attack on Senators McCumber and Hansbrough and the McKenzie group.† The North Dakota senators immediately complained that I was responsible for this publication. They also complained that I had urged the editors of the *Washington Times* to attack them for their connection with McKenzie. These personal efforts of the North Dakota senators were dangerous, but the additional false charges proved ineffective. On the last day of May, Senators Nelson, McCumber, Hansbrough, and Pettus held the floor in executive session for four hours supporting and amplifying the charges and their personal objections to my confirmation. Senator Piles, of Washington, who had long known me led the fight for favorable action. No vote, and the matter went over until the next day, again the senators talked.

That night the evening Washington paper reported: "The Senate in executive session yesterday resumed the discussion of the nomination of James Wickersham to be judge of the district court for . . . Alaska. Opposition to confirmation was again led by Senators McCumber

---

* In response to the accusations against him, Wickersham was forced yet once again to explain the details of the Brantner seduction case from Tacoma.

"I brought out my personal 'skeletons'—set them up in the highway and exposed them to the light of day—a humiliating thing to do, but I did not shield myself in any respect—just did what [former President Grover] Cleveland did when they accused him—he said to his friends—'tell the truth about it,' and that's just what I did—at length" (February 9, 1906).

† Beach's fictional account of the conspiracy, *The Spoilers*, would become one of the most famous novels ever written about Alaska.

and Nelson. After two hours' consideration the Senate was adjourned without action."

Senator Foraker, who had charge of the matter for confirmation, declared that he intended to call it up every day and make the opposing senators talk, and that when they quit he would call for a vote, but they never quit. And thus began a filibuster which lasted until it threatened to hold up other matters of greater importance.

The session of Congress was drawing near its close and those opposing confirmation seemed determined to filibuster to the end. After a week of daily contest in executive session the Washington evening paper reported that "thus the big business of the session is jammed in the small end of the funnel.... It is a great opportunity for manipulation and trades. Back of all these features of the greater legislative program lies the Wickersham Federal judgeship case, before the Senate in its executive capacity. Nothing in years has aroused such intensity of feeling in the executive sessions as this case, and trades and influences otherwise unexplainable are accounted for by reference to it."

A large majority of the Senate would vote for confirmation if it could be brought to a vote. But under the rules a vote could not be had as long as the opponents of confirmation continued to talk, and Senator Foraker now became convinced of the determination of the opposing senators to filibuster to the end. He wrote a letter to that effect to the Attorney General, advising that the case be allowed to go over until the next session of Congress and that I be given another recess appointment. Two days later Attorney General Moody replied:

> I have brought to the attention of the President your confidential letter of the 19th instant in regard to the nomination of Judge Wickersham, now pending in the Senate. The President believes strongly that Judge Wickersham has been one of the best of our Territorial Judges and has displayed courage, integrity and high judicial qualities in his office. He earnestly hopes that the nomination, which he conceives to be the best possible, will be confirmed.... It is his purpose until the nomination is acted upon, to continue Judge Wickersham in his present position by recess appointment.

On Monday morning I went to see President Roosevelt at the White House. When I arrived, Mr. Loeb, his secretary, told me: "Wait at this door and I will tell the President you are here; he is busy discussing an important matter with a group of visitors."

As the secretary entered the executive office, the opened door disclosed a number of gentlemen sitting round the President's large desk. In a minute the President appeared at the half-opened door. Hesitating a moment as he concluded a sentence addressed to his visitors in his office, the President quickly stepped out into the hall and confronted me, and without giving me a chance to say a word, smilingly grasped my hand, and said (as well as I can remember):

> Judge Wickersham, I have read everything in or about your case—the evidence on the investigation, Judge Day's report, all the charges against you, your testimony before the judiciary committee, your printed defense, and I understand the whole case fully. I am satisfied with you and will reappoint you. Go back to Alaska and continue your work as judge—don't talk to newspaper men or to anyone else about these matters—don't let Senators hear anything from you—facts and conversations are often distorted. I will be President yet for two years and eight months and I will support you that long. You shall be judge in Alaska as long as I am President.

And he quickly backed through the door into his office. Before the door closed he addressed the gentlemen inside, saying, "Now with respect to that English note, etc."—and that ended the interview!*

Naturally I was "deelighted" at the friendly reception the President had given me, and the positive assurance of his future support. I chuckled when I recalled that my friends in the Attorney General's office had suggested a short statement I should make to the President, as if I could have uttered a single word! When I returned to the office and related the story of my one-sided interview, they rolled in their

* "This is only the substance of a much longer monologue which [President Roosevelt] delivered while his strong eagle eye looked into mine. I feel sure, now, of my position with him, & of his fighting support. I am now ready to believe that he . . . would keep me in office for the balance of his term without regard to what the Senate said. He is certainly my friend & supporter, & it will take more positive proofs of my defects than my enemies now have to change him. He is, it seems to me, prejudiced in my favor, and against my enemies all of whom, thanks to my lucky star, are now fighting the administration. . . . I must go home & it is the greatest relief imaginable. If the Senate does not reject my confirmation this session, but passes it over, and he reappoints me, my case then becomes a strictly Roosevelt administration fight, and I can view it with quite a different feeling from what I have heretofore had" (June 25, 1906).

chairs with laughter, but expressed their relief that the President had assumed personal responsibility for action on the appointment.

LATE IN MAY 1906, in the midst of the struggle for confirmation, the great fire in Fairbanks occurred which destroyed both the courthouse and the jail. My own business house in the next block to the courthouse was burned along with the greater part of the business houses in the central part of town.*

The labor of procuring funds from Congress with which to rebuild the courthouse and jail naturally fell upon my shoulders, though the officials of the Department of Justice gave active assistance. The committees in Congress acted promptly and an appropriation of $25,000 was carried in the sundry civil appropriation bill, which was passed and approved on June 30, the last day of the session. Although Congress approved the funds for the new Fairbanks courthouse, the Senate refused to confirm me for a new term as the judge to be seated in that new facility, and on that same day President Roosevelt gave me another recess appointment.†

EARLY IN SEPTEMBER 1906, Nome District Attorney Henry M. Hoyt arrived in Fairbanks. He called at my office in the courthouse, and informed me that he had been instructed by the Department of Justice to investigate a new charge that had been filed against me by Senator McCumber. He informed me that he had in his possession a certain letter written by Senator McCumber to President Roosevelt

* Due to the protracted battle for his reconfirmation, Wickersham stayed in Washington, D.C., from January to July 1906. He returned to Fairbanks on July 22, two months to the day after the devastating 1906 fire that destroyed the center of the business district and his own business property, and he believed the fire had been a blessing in disguise.

"The town looks fine—as usual a big fire hurts individuals, but helped the town very much. The old log cabins—unsightly spots—the different sorts & styles of buildings have gone—and whole blocks of well built buildings occupy the places. The streets have been widened—in the fire swept division—the banks, stores & business houses all rebuilt & the town looks better than ever" (July 22, 1906).

† Though he never would be reconfirmed by the U.S. Senate, Wickersham took solace in the unwavering support he received from President Theodore Roosevelt:

"Am greatly pleased to know that the President has again—for the fifth [actually the seventh] time—reappointed me as judge of the Dist. Court. It is especially satisfactory to have the President stay by me so strongly. It will give me courage to do my duty without fear or favor" (July 5, 1906).

The start of the great fire in Fairbanks, May 22, 1906.

(Albert Johnson Photograph Collection UAF-1989-166-255-Print, Archives, Alaska and Polar Regions, University of Alaska Fairbanks) about the new charge, and upon my request he gave me a copy of the letter. In this letter Senator McCumber declared that he then had in his possession evidence against me "that neither Judge Day nor any other person on earth can meet, or has attempted to meet—record evidence that is conclusive and unassailable."

Neither the charge nor the evidence in its support were stated in the letter, nor did Hoyt, then examining me officially as a representative of the Department of Justice, give me a copy of the accusation or the names of the witnesses against me. He seemed to think this most serious charge should be kept secret until evidence could be obtained to insure conviction!

However, it did not take long for me to discover from his questions that the charge was substantially that I owned, directly or indirectly, some interest in the Dome Creek placer mining claims, the titles to which were then on trial in court before me. I said there was no truth in it, a denial which he clearly did not believe.

I could not imagine upon what evidence the charge could be based, for I had never had any mining claim or claims of any kind on that creek, nor anywhere near it. After our conference, I sent for one of my discreet friends, told him of Hoyt's insinuations and asked him to investigate. He came back the next day and told me that some months ago a location notice for an associated placer mining claim of 160 acres on Dome had been filed and recorded in the recorder's office at Fairbanks, in which my name appeared as one of eight locators.

The alleged evidence was patently false. If I or any other person had located a claim that included these immensely rich gold claims on Dome Creek, then in litigation before me, there would have been instant and vigorous objection by those whose claims had been "jumped." If the location notice had included the name of the district judge before whom these men were then appearing in court, there would have been instant objection.

At my request some of my friends undertook to find out how the location notice came to be in the official records. They discovered the man who had signed and recorded the notice of location had been employed to make a trip up the Tanana River about eighty or a hundred miles south of Fairbanks; while there he had gone out upon an unknown wild creek which he named "Dome Creek." He had set a few stakes and marked some of them with the same names as those on the true Dome Creek, located twenty-five miles north of Fairbanks. The "Dome Creek" he used for these false and unauthorized locations was more than one hundred miles south of the rich mining claims on the true Dome Creek subject to litigation in my court. It had been a copy of this fraudulent location on the fictitious "Dome Creek" that had been sent to Washington to smear me.

These were the "facts" which Senator McCumber had called "conclusive and unassailable." I forwarded a full report to the Department of Justice and that was the end of the Hoyt investigation and the fabricated "Dome Creek" charges.

When Congress adjourned on March 4, 1907, still refusing to confirm my appointment, President Roosevelt gave me yet another recess appointment. A further rehash of the charges was made to hold off my confirmation, but President Roosevelt had had enough. In May 1907 it was reported that "the Department of Justice today announced that further investigation of the charges against the Alaskan Judge Wickersham is to be stopped by order of President Roosevelt. The President has notified the department that he will stand by the judge on his record up to date, including, as it does, the former strong report in his favor filed by Judge Day."

AS THE DISTRICT JUDGE for the third division of Alaska, I was the last on the long roster of United States judges. In the judicial hierarchy my office was unimportant, and I was the lowest judge on the bottom rung of the American court system. Yet for three years and more a combination of about half-a-dozen powerful United States senators, influenced by the McKenzie-Dakota group of the worst gang of lawbreakers ever known in Alaska, had viciously opposed my confirmation.

They were motivated by malice and a desire to punish me for thwarting their conspiracy. But for the support of many friends and the determination of President Roosevelt to protect even the least of the judges in the performance of sworn duty, the backwoods judge would have been irreparably broken.

I sent my resignation to President Roosevelt in September, 1907. I closed the records of my court on December 31st and immediately thereafter opened an office in Fairbanks as an attorney—but more particularly as a candidate for delegate from Alaska to Congress. On the second Tuesday in August 1908, the people of Alaska elected

The NEWSPAPER of ALASKA

Fairbanks Daily Times

The PAPER THAT STANDS for RIGHT

VOLUME II — FAIRBANKS, ALASKA, THURSDAY, JANUARY 24, 1907. — WHOLE NUMBER 242

WICKERSHAM OUT!

Washington, Jan. 12.--(Received at 2 A. M. today. President Roosevelt has decided not to reappoint Judge Wickersham again. In a few days, it is understood that he will send the name of Harry Ballinger, of Port Townsend, to the senate for confirmation as judge of the third division of Alaska.

In Hoyt's report to the president none of the charges against the integrity of Wickersham were proved, but Mr. Hoyt recommends his discontinuance in office on account of the division of sentiment in the Tanana, and the president has come to realize the uselessness of attempting to force his confirmation.

Time and again Wickersham's enemies gleefully wrote his political obituary, such as this premature announcement in January 1907 that he was on his way out of office. When he left the judgeship one year later, he was the longest serving judge in Alaska up to that time.

me as their representative in Congress, which office I held for twelve years. While the tales and trials of my service in Washington, D.C., deserve to be told in another volume, the last day of 1907 marked the end of my *Old Yukon* trail.*

* Wickersham left the judgeship with a sense of relief, but also bitter disappointment. By 1907, the threat of a third official investigation into his conduct, and three years of defeats in Senate confirmation battles, had worn him down mentally and physically. "I am tired!" he wrote in May 1907. "Tired all the time & sometimes in court I feel as if I must adjourn & go out to the mountains & rest. My friends tell me that I work too hard—too many hours on too many days & months. But I can't stop for a while—not till the Annual Investigator has come & finished" (May 9, 1907). In the summer of 1907 he grudgingly admitted that no matter how long he remained in office he could never be confirmed by the Senate. "The longer I stay in Alaska—the more I feel that I am falling forever away from my home and friends" (August 26, 1907).

At the time he thought his resignation marked the end of his political career—after all, he was a judge who could not be confirmed—and perhaps the end of his life in Alaska. He dreamed of relocating to a milder and less isolated location like Seattle, where he hoped to become general counsel for Stephen Birch's Alaska Syndicate. In an ill-chosen phrase that would come back to haunt him, Wickersham said his prospects as a private attorney in Fairbanks were "satisfactory, still I long for the flesh pots of the 'outside.'" Ultimately, his ticket out of Fairbanks would be to run against the Guggenheim interests as delegate to Congress and move to Washington, D.C., but except in the pages of his diary, that was a story he preferred to leave untold.

INDEX

Italic page numbers indicate caption; "fn" indicates footnote.

Y